NATIVE AND CHRISTIAN

The people of the town have little need. They do not hanker after progress and have never changed their essential way of life. Their invaders were a long time in conquering them; and now, after four centuries of Christianity, they still pray in Tanoan to the old deities of the earth and sky and make their living from the things that are and have always been within their reach; while in the discrimination of pride they acquire from their conquerors only the luxury of example. They have assumed the names and gestures of their enemies, but have held on to their own, secret souls; and in this there is a resistance and an overcoming, a long outwaiting.

—N. Scott Momaday
House Made of Dawn

■ ■ ■

"There are some things I have to tell you," Betonie began softly. "The people nowadays have an idea about the ceremonies. They think the ceremonies must be performed exactly as they have always been done, maybe because one slip-up or mistake and the whole ceremony must be stopped and the sand painting destroyed. That much is true. They think that if a singer tampers with any part of the ritual, great harm can be done, great power unleashed." He was quiet for a while, looking up at the sky through the smoke hole. "That much can be true also. But long ago when the people were given these ceremonies, the changing began, if only in the aging of the yellow gourd rattle or the shrinking of the skin around the eagle's claw, if only in the different voices from generation to generation, singing the chants. You see, in many ways, the ceremonies have always been changing."

—Leslie Marmon Silko
Ceremony

Native and Christian

Indigenous Voices on Religious Identity in the United States and Canada

EDITED BY JAMES TREAT

ROUTLEDGE   NEW YORK AND LONDON

Published in 1996 by

Routledge
29 West 35th Street
New York, NY 10001

Published in Great Britain in 1996 by

Routledge
11 New Fetter Lane
London EC4P 4EE

**Library of Congress Cataloging-in-
Publication Data**

 Native and Christian : indigenous
voices on religious identity in the
United States and Canada / edited by
James Treat.
  p. cm. —
 Includes bibliographical references.
 ISBN 0-415-91373-X. ISBN 0-415-
91374-8 (pbk.)
 1. Indians of North America--United
States--Religion. 2. Indians of North
America--Canada--Religion. 3.
Christianity--United States. 4.
Christianity--Canada. I. Treat, James.
E98.R3N385 1995   95-10863
277.3'0089'97--dc20   CIP

Front cover:
"Baptism on the Trail" (1991) is the work
of Joan Hill, an accomplished painter and
one of the most honored living American
Indian artists. She is a descendent of
prominent Creek and Cherokee families
and is an enrolled citizen of the Muscogee
(Creek) Nation; her studio is located on
her family's original land allotment in
northeastern Oklahoma. Hill has won more
than 260 awards in regional, national, and
international exhibitions, and nearly one
hundred of her works are in the permanent
collections of public museums and
agencies including the National Museum
of the American Indian, the Smithsonian
Institution, and the Bureau of Indian
Affairs. "Baptism on the Trail" depicts
ceremonies conducted by Cherokee Baptist
minister Jesse Bushyhead and his
missionary colleague Evan Jones during
the Cherokees' forced removal from their
ancestral lands to Indian Territory during
the 1830s. The dispossession and exodus
of the Cherokees and other southeastern
Indians is commonly referred to as the
"Trail of Tears"; Hill created this work in
order to subvert the tragic American
mythology that imagines American Indians
as the passive victims of Manifest Destiny.
She intends to demonstrate that her people
have actively and successfully struggled to
survive this and other ordeals, and
"Baptism on the Trail" depicts an act of
religious renewal and commitment as one
of these strategies for survival.

· Contents · ▪ ▪ ▪ ▪ ▪ ▪ ▪ ▪

· PREFACE · · · · · · · · · · ·

This book represents the culmination of a project that has been both a professional interest and a personal journey; it began as a concern over where I am going, it developed as a study of where I came from, and it is slowly resolving into a vision of who I am in this particular place and time. The research for this book began seven years ago, during my first year of graduate school, as a class presentation in a course on Latin American Liberation Theology. This initial effort evolved into a master's thesis, "Native Americans, Theology, and Liberation: Christianity and Traditionalism in the Struggle for Survival," in which I examined the relationship between native Christians and the global liberation theology movement. In the words of my original thesis proposal, it was a search for "a Christian theology of liberation originating within the Native American community, in light of and in response to various aspects of the North American experience." I was fortunate to have Professors C. S. Song, George Cummings, Eldon Ernst, and Jorge Lara-Braud serving on my committee, and they each taught me important lessons in the process. I am also grateful for the many ways in which I have benefited from knowing Paul Schultz, Judy Wellington, and other friends at the Bay Area Native American Ministry, as well as the faculty, staff, and students of the Native American Studies program at the University of California, Berkeley.

I graduated from the Pacific School of Religion in 1989 and matriculated at the Graduate Theological Union that fall; my plans for developing this anthology were delayed while I completed my doctorate and began teaching at the University of California at Santa Cruz. I was able to update my research periodically thanks to Newhall Fellowship funds granted by the Graduate Theological Union, and faculty research funds granted by the University of California at Santa Cruz. Several colleagues have encouraged me in my work, especially Rudy Busto, Ann Braude, and Nancy Ammerman, and in 1994 I received a Summer Stipend grant from the Louisville Institute for the Study of Protestantism and American Culture to complete the manuscript. I am indebted to Joanne Barker, Ann Braude, Sandra Bunn, Rudy Busto, Michael McNally, Jean Molesky, Laura Murray, Barry O'Connell, Forrest Robinson, John Sanbonmatsu, C. S. Song, Judy Wellington, and Judy Yung, each of whom read parts of the manuscript and made critical and constructive comments. I have also enjoyed working with the writers who contributed to this collection and appreciate their cooperation and encouragement. I have used many of these essays in my seminar "Native Americans and Christianity" and have learned a great deal from students at the University of California at Santa Cruz and at the Pacific School of Religion, especially Christine Albany, Steven Danver, Joanne Doi, Vickie Glazier, Michael Heart, Pat St. Onge, Margaret Thomas, and Karen Winkel. It has been a pleasure to work with Marlie Wasserman, Mary Carol DeZutter, Kimberly Herald, Andrew Rubin, and Liz Tracey at Routledge, and I have appreciated the enthusiasm they have shown for this project. Finally, I am grateful to family and friends who have provided the foundation that made this project both possible and meaningful, especially my grandmother Betty Jewel Oklahoma Evans Jones, my aunt Bertha Pickard, and my parents Jimmie and Marcia Treat, who defied the logic of human determinism by giving me life.

James Treat
February 1995

■ ■ ■ ■ ■ ■ ■ ■ ■ ■ ■ ■ ■ ■

JAMES TREAT

INTRODUCTION
NATIVE CHRISTIAN NARRATIVE DISCOURSE

■

This anthology of recent essays by native writers in the United States and Canada documents the emergence of a significant new collective voice on the North American religious landscape. It brings together in one volume articles originally published in a variety of sources (many of them obscure or out-of-print) including religious magazines, scholarly journals, native periodicals, and topical anthologies, along with one unpublished manuscript. These essays represent a new form of literary expression among contemporary native people, and they bring a fresh perspective to the global liberation theology movement. Not all of these essays are "academic" in the institutionally determined, professionally privileged sense of the word, though they all demonstrate the intellectual sophistication suggested by the practice of "scholarship." Tribal footnotes are implied in the writings of native Christians, who silently cite extended families, revered elders, oral traditions, sacred landscapes, visionary messengers, and mythic imagination as points of reference in their communal "bibliography." The native writers who contributed to this collection come from a number of distinct tribal backgrounds and work as academic scholars, church administrators, ordained leaders, and lay activists; they write on the basis of their involvement in a variety of Christian religious traditions including mainline Protestant denominations, the Roman Catholic church, Evangelicalism, the Pentecostal/Charismatic movement, Mormonism, and the

Native American Church (peyotism). These religious leaders are engaged in formulating and articulating their own distinctive religious identities; their experiences and interpretations bear important insights for anyone interested in the intersections of religion, culture, politics, and race in a diverse and conflicted world.

The terms "native" and "Christian" categorize humanity in ways that are both ambiguous and contested. I am using these words as broad, generic signifiers that point to acts of intentional, coherent self-identification. "Native" refers to all indigenous individuals and communities in the United States and Canada; it includes people who are commonly called American Indians, Native Americans, Eskimos, Inuits, Native Hawaiians, and First Nations people, and who are also known by a variety of assumed and imposed tribal designations. This term includes both recognized and unrecognized communities and both full-blood and mixed-blood individuals. "Christian" refers to all religious individuals and communities who are associated with the historic complex of religious traditions (beliefs, ceremonies, ethics, scriptures, institutions) commonly attributed to Jesus Christ or his followers. This term includes both orthodox and unorthodox communities and both affiliated and unaffiliated individuals. I have not relied on any other specific doctrinal, behavioral, legal, or biological criteria in using these terms to signify self-identified native Christians, and I am not prescribing a hierarchy of identity in formulating the compound noun "native Christian."

The essays in this collection were selected on the basis of several specific criteria. I looked for recent articles and manuscripts by native writers that focus on the problem of native Christian identity and that attempt to grapple with this problem in a serious and substantive manner, whether doing so on theological, political, communal, or personal terms. What does it mean to be native? What does it mean to be Christian? Should Christian identity be subordinated to native identity, or vice versa? Is it possible to be both native and Christian in any meaningful way? All of the native authors represented in this collection have faced these questions, though not all of them would today identify themselves as Christian, which is one indication of the gravity of this dilemma. These writers describe a wide range of solutions to the problem of native Christian identity, but they all share certain common assumptions: (1) they take seriously both the native cultural/religious heritage and the Christian cultural/religious heritage, as well as their own relationship to each; (2) they value their own spiritual perceptions and experiences and those of their extended communities; (3) they acknowledge that the idea of a native Christian identity is problematic, both culturally and historically; and (4) they realize the need to work through this problem in order to arrive at a reasonable accommodation that will facilitate personal and communal survival.

I also looked for writers who could represent the widest possible range of native communities and Christian communions in the United States and

Canada, and I especially worked to achieve a balance of women's and men's voices. This anthology approximates, but ultimately falls short of, each of these goals. A variety of complex and interconnected historical, social, and cultural factors have quieted native Christians in many tribal and religious contexts and have made it particularly difficult for native Christian women to publish their spiritual convictions, though I take full responsibility for any unnecessary editorial oversights or omissions. Taken together, these essays document the style and substance of an ongoing debate among native Christians over the nature of religious identity. The powerful vitality of this debate demonstrates that many native Christians will be the agents of their own religious destinies; they have chosen to be theological and literary subjects, not the objects of missiological or anthropological or any other form of colonial or neocolonial domination.

FOREBEARS

"The religion of the Indian," wrote Charles Alexander Eastman, the Santee Sioux physician, "is the last thing about him that the man of another race will ever understand." Dr. Eastman published *The Soul of the Indian* in 1911 in order to remedy the cross-cultural misapprehensions that were afflicting many non-native Americans, a condition he attributed both to simple ignorance and to racial and religious prejudice. His self-conscious "interpretation" of Indian spiritual philosophy was rooted in his own childhood experiences with Dakota beliefs and practices; he readily admitted that his "little book" would not be mistaken for an ethnological monograph, filled with pristine data on exotic tribal cultures. Dr. Eastman examined white America and diagnosed the colonial myopia that envisioned Indians as vanishing Americans, the cultural narcissism that branded them as primitive savages, the religious arrogance that christened them as devil-worshipping pagans, and his book is the prescription for a simple remedy: human empathy and respect. "I have not cared to pile up more dry bones," he averred in the foreword, "but to clothe them with flesh and blood. So much as has been written by strangers of our ancient faith and worship treats it chiefly as matter of curiosity. I should like to emphasize its universal quality, its personal appeal!"[1] That the book is still in print eight decades later is testimony both to the clarity of Eastman's analysis and to the resilience of the social pathology he hoped to cure.

Eastman was born in present-day Minnesota in 1858, and four years later fled to Canada with his paternal relatives as refugees from the 1862 Sioux Uprising. They called him Ohiyesa (the Winner), a name that commemorated his band's victory in an athletic contest, and together they lived a traditional subsistence lifestyle, hunting buffalo, elk, antelope, deer, sheep, and grizzly bears, while also trapping and fishing in the wooded river bottoms of southern Manitoba. At the age of fifteen, Ohiyesa "was about to enter into and realize a man's life, as we Indians understood it," when his father unexpectedly arrived at their camp. Many Lightnings, who had served three years in prison for his role in the uprising, had also assumed a Christian identity and taken the name of Jacob Eastman. Ohiyesa reluctantly returned with Jacob to the newly founded Santee Sioux community of Flandreau, and eventually acceded to his father's wish that Ohiyesa join him in following the Christian way. Ohiyesa was baptized Charles Alexander, names he chose for himself out of a book he borrowed from a local minister.[2]

Eastman enrolled in mission schools at Flandreau and on the Santee Reservation, learned English in the process, and then took college preparatory courses for several years at schools in Wisconsin, Illinois, and New Hampshire. In 1883 he matriculated at Dartmouth College, where he excelled both academically and athletically, and then went on to the Boston University School of Medicine. Eastman attended a Congregational church in Boston; "I continued to study the Christ philosophy and loved it for its essential truths," he later recalled, "though doctrines and dogmas often puzzled and repelled me."[3] He graduated in 1890 and applied for an appointment with the Indian Health Service, and was soon commissioned to the Pine Ridge agency, arriving in early November of that year. Less than two months later, Dr. Eastman was the attending physician for the Lakota victims and survivors of the Wounded Knee massacre; he treated wounded and dying Ghost Dancers as they lay on the floor of the Episcopal mission chapel. Eastman left Pine Ridge in 1892 and practiced medicine sporadically during the next decade, as he increasingly turned his attention to speaking and writing about Indian life and government policy. Eastman soon became one of the leading public figures in Indian affairs and worked with a variety of organizations including the Society of American Indians, the Young Men's Christian Association, the Boy Scouts and the Camp Fire Girls, and the Bureau of Indian Affairs. During his long and noteworthy career, Eastman published eleven books and numerous articles (many of them written in collaboration with his wife, Elaine Goodale Eastman), including two autobiographies.[4] He undoubtedly had his experiences at Pine Ridge in mind when he ended his second autobiography, *From the Deep Woods to Civilization*, by reflecting on the legacy of American Christianity:

> From the time I first accepted the Christ ideal it has grown upon me steadily, but I also see more and more plainly our modern divergence from that ideal. I confess I have wondered much that Christianity is not practiced by the very people who vouch for that wonderful conception of exemplary living. It appears that they are anxious to pass on their religion to all races of men, but keep very little of it themselves. I have not yet seen the meek inherit the earth, or the peacemakers receive high honor.[5]

Eastman struggled throughout his life to reconcile two seemingly contradictory allegiances: native and Christian. This struggle is evident in his writings, in which he labored to represent his paradoxical sense of self before an American public that ever prefers essentialist definitions of religious, ethnic, and racial identities. In the minds of many of Eastman's white admirers and benefactors, his life story was proof positive of the logic of assimilation, a classic example of primitive acculturation and ample testimony to the potential for the civilization of all native people. But Eastman rejected superficial solutions to an existential dilemma that carried both personal meanings and political implications; he refused to resolve colonial conflict through clever cultural terminology. He survived his own life by moving between two religious cultures through space and time, but to label him as "bicultural" and leave it at that is only to mystify the complex internal negotiations he engaged in. For Eastman, there would be no easy accommodation in moving from the deep woods to civilization. "I am an Indian," he concluded, "and while I have learned much from civilization, for which I am grateful, I have never lost my Indian sense of right and justice. I am for development and progress along social and spiritual lines, rather than those of commerce, nationalism, or material efficiency."[6]

Despite his personal affinity for Christian teachings, Eastman remained a sharp critic of the hypocrisies of white religion. In *The Soul of the Indian* he argued that there is much in "primitive Christianity" that would appeal to native people, "and Jesus' hard sayings to the rich and about the rich would have been entirely comprehensible" to them. "Yet the religion that is preached in our churches and practiced by our congregations, with its element of display and self-aggrandizement, its active proselytism, and its open contempt of all religions but its own, was for a long time extremely repellent." Eastman generously pointed out that "the white man's religion" should not be discredited solely on the basis of the poor example set by "the drunkards and licentious among white men," but he argued that it is "not so easy to overlook or to excuse national bad faith."

> When distinguished emissaries from the Father at Washington, some of them ministers of the gospel and even bishops, came to the Indian nations, and pledged to them in solemn treaty the national honor, with prayer and mention of their God; and when such treaties, so made, were promptly and shamelessly broken, is it strange that the action should arouse not only anger, but contempt?[7]

Yet Eastman realized that religious hypocrisy is always an easy target, so he summarized his perceptive critique by moving to a deeper level of reflection. We know that conventional wisdom, both in Eastman's time and today, suggests that "native" and "Christian" are mutually exclusive identities: a native who has become wholeheartedly Christian has lost some measure of native authenticity; a Christian who is still fully native has fallen short of Christian orthodoxy. Like many other native Christians before and after him, Eastman recognized the folly of maladaptive dogmatism in a rapidly changing world. He responded by appropriating the language of religious/ethnic/racial determinism, redefining the criteria for comparative analysis, and offering this startling reversal:

> It is my personal belief, after thirty-five years of experience of it, that there is no such thing as "Christian civilization." I believe that Christianity and modern civilization are opposed and irreconcilable, and that the spirit of Christianity and of our ancient religion is essentially the same.[8]

Many observers would judge a native Christian identity as inauthentic or unorthodox. Eastman's formulation suggests that religious and cultural and racial contradictions are socially constructed rationalizations, not self-evident facts; his life embodied a reconciliation of these oppositions that arises from human freedom and personal choice, not from the predictable conflict of deterministic identity politics. "The Christ ideal," he reasoned, "might be radical, visionary, even impractical, as judged in light of my later experiences; it still seemed to me logical, and in line with most of my Indian training."[9] Eastman was probably right: the religion of the Indian may very well be the last thing about him or her that the person of another race will ever understand—especially if that Indian also happens to be Christian.

Charles Alexander Eastman was not the first native Christian to wrestle with the problem of identity and, as the essays in this volume demonstrate, he was certainly not the last. Liliuokalani, the last reigning monarch of the Hawaiian kingdom, was a contemporary of Eastman's and the author of *Hawaii's Story by Hawaii's Queen*, which she published in 1898, the same year that the United States completed the overthrow of her government by annexing the "Sandwich Islands." Like some other members of the Hawaiian royal family, Liliuokalani was a devout Christian; she directed church choirs and was known for her remarkable musical abilities, composing more than two hundred songs and hymns during her lifetime. Hawaiian independence had been increasingly threatened during the nineteenth century and was actively subverted, beginning in the 1870s, by a small group of wealthy white American merchants composed of Protestant missionaries and their descendants. Queen Liliuokalani assumed the leadership of the Hawaiian constitutional monarchy in 1891 in the midst of an intense power struggle with the "missionary party," which actively opposed her legitimate assertion of Hawaiian sovereignty. The Queen was forcibly deposed by the missionary party in 1893; two years later, after a failed rebellion by Hawaiian loyalists, she was charged with treason, held under house arrest, and compelled to sign a formal abdication of political authority.[10]

Liliuokalani endured deception and betrayal at the hands of white religionists and was publicly condemned, both before and after her coronation from the pulpit of Kawaiahao Church, the leading Protestant mission in Honolulu and her religious home since childhood. Yet she remained a Christian throughout her life, though this was a religious identity she maintained on her own terms. The provisional government attempted to erase her testimony by destroying most of her letters, papers, and diaries, but Liliuokalani would not be completely silenced. *Hawaii's Story by Hawaii's Queen* is her autobiographical account of the overthrow, a four-hundred-page indictment of American imperialism and white religious hypocrisy. Liliuokalani's modern biographer concluded that she was "remarkably tolerant" of religious diversity and believed that "all religions had their 'rights' and were entitled to equal treatment and opportunities."

At various times in her life Liliuokalani identified herself with the Protestant mission church as well as Episcopals, Catholics, Mormons, Eastern mystical traditions, and Hawaiian traditional religion, finally developing "a synthesis of her own, which she felt was the basis of mysticism, hidden in all religions."[11] She defended Hawaiian religious insight and self-determination by asserting that "the habits and prejudices of New England Puritanism were not well adapted to the genius of a tropical people, nor capable of being thoroughly ingrafted upon them. But Christianity in substance they have accepted; . . . " In 1888, leaders of the missionary party had tried to enlist her participation in a conspiracy against her brother, King Kalakaua, but she refused: "Perhaps it was because I had gone hand in hand with them in all *good* works that they thought I would cast in my lot with them now for evil, . . . If so, they found themselves much mistaken." Liliuokalani concluded her written argument for Hawaiian autonomy with a plea to the American public, whose elected leaders were then debating the annexation of Hawaii under the provisional government led by Sanford Dole, the wealthy son of a Yankee missionary:

> I implore the people of this great and good nation, from whom my ancestors learned the Christian religion, to sustain their representatives in such acts of justice and equity as may be in accord with the principles of their fathers, and to the Almighty Ruler of the universe, to him who judgeth righteously, I commit my cause.[12]

The United States Senate responded by ratifying the annexation treaty on August 12, 1898, and in 1900 organized Hawaii as a territory, rewarding Dole's exploits by appointing him as the first territorial governor.

Several generations before Eastman and Liliuokalani published their autobiographical works, another native Christian recounted his own life story and in the process addressed many of the same questions Eastman and Liliuokalani faced. William Apess, a Pequot from New England and an ordained Methodist minister, published *A Son of the Forest* in 1829; it is the earliest autobiography published by a native writer, and the first of five literary works Apess produced during his brief but remarkable career.[13] Born into an impoverished Pequot community lingering on the margins of white society, Apess's childhood was defined by abandonment, abuse, and indentured servitude. In *A Son of the Forest*, Rev. Apess recounted his religious pilgrimage; he described his early confusion over identity, his intense spiritual struggles beginning at the age of eight, and his teenage conversion to Christianity—a conversion not from Pequot religious traditions, but from being "friendless, unpitied, and unknown, . . . surrounded by difficulties and apparent dangers."[14]

Apess, like Eastman and Liliuokalani after him, used his autobiographical narrative as an opportunity to articulate a passionate critique of American society. Like Eastman and Liliuokalani, Apess condemned the hypocrisies of white religionists who preached universal salvation while practicing exclusionary racism, wondering aloud "how much better it would be if the whites would act like a civilized people." Like Eastman and Liliuokalani, Apess found in Christian teachings the rationale for an egalitarian social order, becoming convinced that "age, sect, color, country, or situation made no difference." Like Eastman and Liliuokalani, Apess believed that certain religious ideas and experiences are universal truths; he considered the "internal witness" of the Spirit to be a fundamental religious principle, asserting that "the Spirit of Divine Truth, in the boundless diversity of its operations, visits the mind of every intelligent being born into the world."[15] Barry O'Connell, who edited Apess's collected works, has argued convincingly that Apess "employed his Christian identity so as to assert, more forcibly and coherently, his identity as a Native American," and that, in Apess's understanding, "for a Pequot to convert to Christianity is not . . . to take on white ways but only to claim one of her rights as a human being."[16]

Rev. Apess, Queen Liliuokalani, and Dr. Eastman are three of the few native leaders who experienced a measure of educational opportunity, professional stature, financial stability, and media access, the prerequisites of literary production in the dominant culture. Their lonely but uncompromising voices speak on behalf of countless native Christians who harbored similar convictions but who found themselves silenced by historical circumstances and the culture of domination.

NATIVE AND CHRISTIAN?

Today, native Christians throughout the United States and Canada are continuing their centuries-long struggle for religious self-determination.[17] Denominational missionaries have settled in native communities preaching a gospel of cultural conformity, condemning native religious history on the basis of ignorance, and dictating artificial criteria for institutional acceptability. Academic anthropologists have toured native communities looking for pure, primitive culture, dismissing native religious adaptability as tragic acculturation, and attempting to reduce human experience to ethnographic data. Government agents have dominated native communities in the service of colonial expansion, enforcing laws that restrict native religious freedom, and manipulating political power through bureaucratic patronage. Radical activists have defended native communities against these and other impositions, calling for the outright rejection of "the white man's religion" and the immediate revival of esoteric indigenous traditions. Native Christians have been called heretical, inauthentic, assimilated, and uncommitted; they have long endured intrusive definitions of personal identity and have quietly pursued their own religious visions, often under the very noses of unsuspecting missionaries, anthropologists, agents, and activists.

Despite their determined persistence, many contemporary native Christians have also acknowledged, as did Eastman, Liliuokalani, and Apess before them, that they face a fundamental existential dilemma in attempting to resolve their hybrid identities into an organic unity. The idea of a native Christian identity is both historically and culturally problematic. The blatant opportunism and oppressive dogmatism of the missionization process, the open complicity of white religious leaders in widespread land dispossession, and the growing strength of the native traditionalist revival work together to challenge the legitimacy of the personal religious choices many native Christians have made. An educational resource recently produced by native people in the Episcopal Church for use in their own congregations addresses this challenge as a central problem. *In the Spirit of the Circle* is a series of thirty-two color posters depicting various biblical and cultural traditions, with background stories, discussion questions, and group activities printed on the reverse sides. All of the posters are concerned with formulating and expressing a viable native Christian identity, while one poster deals with the issue of legitimacy explicitly. In a high contrast, black-and-white photograph, it shows a turn-of-the-century Indian family dressed in their Sunday best and bears the caption, "Can I Be Indian and Christian?" The text on the reverse side begins by succinctly restating this question: "The story of Christianity among our Indian people is often a sad, confusing story. . . . Why would any Indian want to belong to a religion that was so much a part of the tragic history of our people?"[18] Why indeed?

Yet this is precisely the choice that many native people have made, and continue to make. Native Christians have constructed and maintained their own enigmatic religious identities with a variety of considerations in mind. Like native traditions, Christian institutions can mediate social power and material resources and provide avenues for the development and recognition of religious leadership. Like native traditions, Christian liturgical forms can facilitate community reconciliation and allow for the fulfillment of ceremonial obligations. Like native traditions, Christian teachings can articulate beliefs and values that provide direction in daily life and in overcoming personal struggles, and that form the basis for prophetic critique and political action. Like native traditions, Christian spiritual practices can cultivate meaning and purpose through religious devotion, offering a viable alternative to secular materialism, and can challenge devotees to a life of responsibility and service. Native people who choose to identify themselves with Christian institutions, liturgical forms, teachings, or spiritual practices do so while bearing in mind the community circumstances, family precedents, and personal experiences that define their lives. Furthermore, many native Christians accomplish this identification without abandoning or rejecting native religious traditions. While it may be true that some native Christians have adopted the theological blindnesses of their missionary trainers in what appear to be textbook examples of internalized oppression, many others have not. To dismiss all native Christians as acculturated, anachronistic traces of religious colonialism, is to miss innumerable demonstrations of their insightful historical and social analysis, their complex and sophisticated religious creativity, and their powerful devotion to personal and communal survival. To disregard Indian Christians, either as Indians or as Christians, is to deny their human agency, their religious independence, and—ultimately—their very lives. The story on the Episcopal poster captioned "Can I Be Indian and Christian?" ends with these words:

> Christianity does not belong to any one group of people. It never has. It never will. . . . Can we be both "Indian" and "Christian" at the same time? Yes. It may take some courage. It will certainly take commitment. It will even take a sense of forgiveness when we think of all that has happened to us along the way. But the answer, the very personal answer . . . is YES.[19]

NATIVE CHRISTIAN THEOLOGY?

Native Christians have become increasingly bold in making their voices heard, especially during the past decade, and many of them have also committed their voices to writing. This anthology documents the emergence of a new form of literary expression among native people in the United States and Canada: the theological essay.

Native people have a long history of adopting and adapting the literary tools and techniques of the dominant culture, and have demonstrated their literary expertise in a variety of genres including poetry, drama, novels, autobiography, literary criticism, journalism, history, and ethnology.[20] Contemporary native Christian leaders have considered the possibilities for developing native Christian theology for some time; Steve Charleston (Choctaw), for example, writes that he has been talking about "a Native People's Christian theology" since the mid-seventies,[21] and the Native American Theological Association was founded in 1977 to promote leadership development among native Christians in mainline Protestant churches through education, research, and advocacy.[22] Native Christian theological expression is one measure of religious self-determination; William Baldridge (Cherokee) declares that "a unique Native American expression of Christianity, a Native American theology, is a worthy, a good, and a just goal, and we will continue to develop it."[23] As Robert Allen Warrior (Osage) points out, this trend has found support among those non-native Christians influenced by the liberation theology movement, who have encouraged native Christians to jump on the liberation bandwagon. "Native American Theology of Liberation has a nice ring to it. . . . There are theologies of liberation for African Americans, Hispanic Americans, women, Asian Americans, even Jews. Why not Native Americans?"[24] Charleston suggests that the absence of native Christian theology from the "theological supermarket" reflects the inordinate demand for native spirituality by "shoppers" from the dominant culture:

> Well-intentioned shoppers may have simply thought that this talk about spirituality was the voice of Native America in the religious dialogue. And up to a point, they're right. Traditional Native spirituality does represent a major and crucial voice for Native People. It is a voice that has frequently been misquoted, distorted, or co-opted, but it's a voice nonetheless. . . . Still, the spirituality section alone does not complete the supermarket. It is still not an expression of a Native Christian viewpoint. As good (or bad) as these works may be at articulating Native tradition, they do not offer a clear voice for Native American Christianity. They are not a Native People's Christian theology.[25]

But many native Christians have also recognized the potential dangers in attempting to express native religious experiences and perceptions using the English language and the formalized conventions of theological writing. They have problematized and deconstructed the Christian theological tradition in the very process of critically appropriating and reconfiguring it for their own purposes. James West (Cheyenne) calls theology a "non-Indian concept," and prefers to describe native religious traditions as a "spiritual way-of-life." "Indian people have a long tradition of words about Maheo [God]," he writes. "But, theology as an intellectual discipline, sometimes very separated from the every day life of people, is a very foreign concept to most Indian tribal experience."[26] Rosemary McCombs Maxey (Muscogee) points out that native religious diversity means that "there is no way of presenting a single homogeneous view" while engaged in theological dialogue with non-native Christians, and that "conveying ideas in our common language of English is incomplete and misunderstood because of our differing world views, which remain largely unexplored and foreign to one another."[27]

Stan McKay (Cree) admits to "a sense of compromise" and "hesitancy in placing images on paper that reflect our spiritual insights," and suggests that this accommodation represents a reasoned response to the important issues facing global society. "The present urgency to come together for a healing vision for the Earth, 'our Mother,' has brought our elders to advise us to share and risk even by writing what has been our oral tradition."[28] Baldridge has issued, in an earlier essay, one of the most serious challenges to the idea of a native Christian theology:

> Doing theology, thinking theologically, is a decidedly non-Indian thing to do. When I talk about Native American theology to many of my Indian friends, most of them just smile and act as if I hadn't said anything. And I am pretty sure that as far as they are concerned I truly hadn't said anything. . . . Theology is not a natural nor a normal product of Native American cultures. I know that some things are reduced, not increased by too much thinking, too much analyzing and many American Indians share my attitude and conviction regarding the relative worth of entering into experience versus thinking about experience. When Indians theologize they must place one foot into the Euro-American culture; and if they are not careful they will soon have both feet outside of their own culture.[29]

If native Christian "theology" were to develop as nothing more than the elite intellectual culture of native Christian leaders, then it would promise only to reinforce colonial configurations by replicating the intellectual elitism that has characterized Western religious discourse since the Emperor Constantine I convened the Council of Nicaea in the year 325 C.E. Most native Christian "theologians" have very different goals in mind, and this is clearly evident from a close reading of their texts.[30]

The ongoing debate among native Christians over the appropriateness of theological conventions highlights two important methodological features of this emerging body of native literature. First, nearly all of these texts are directed at a primary audience composed of non-native Christians. After generations of struggle with church hierarchies over spirituality, liturgical traditions, ordination, congregational finances, community life, morality, biblical interpretation, and doctrine, native Christians are increasingly putting their admonitions in writing. They are engaging the North American religious establishment at the discursive level, articulating their demands for religious self-determination in a form and style comprehensible to those who still exercise some measure of institutional control over native Christians and their churches. Their writings, like many other types of contemporary native literature, cross cultural boundaries in order to facilitate intercultural understanding and respect and to effect structural change; they are cross-cultural epistles to the cross culture. While many of these authors are also intent on dialoguing with other native Christians about their common identity and shared struggle, their central goal is evident in this public act of discursive advocacy. In general, contemporary native Christian literature is apologetic (in the theological sense, meaning defensive or demonstrative) rather than evangelistic. This apologetic literature is also self-consciously contextual and particular; native Christian writers are not proposing just another "universal" theological master narrative.

The contextual orientation of contemporary native Christian literature points to the other important methodological feature of these writings. Most of these texts employ autobiographical narratives as primary methodological techniques for making (and not merely illustrating) theological points, and many of them also make use of stories drawn from a more general collective, cultural context. Native societies are traditionally oral cultures; only a few native communities enjoy a substantive literary tradition and widespread literacy in their native language. Spanish, French, and English have become the primary languages in many native communities, but even in those where European language literacy is commonplace, a high degree of orality still survives, especially in family and ceremonial contexts. Oral cultures typically preserve worldview and tradition in stories, which teach through example rather than by catechism. The prominence and centrality of narrative accounts in contemporary native Christian testimony suggests that native Christians consider personal and collective experience to play a central role in the development of religious insight. While conventional Christian theology is typically doctrinal and rational, native Christian reflection is experiential and performative; while conventional Christian theology is often dogmatic, native Christian discourse is confessional.

Contemporary native Christian writers have problematized and reconfigured the theological tradition, challenged the Christian establishment by articulating their demands through cross-cultural discourse, and used autobiographical and cultural narratives to express their own religious identities. This new genre of native literature resists the interpretive boundaries implied by literary categorization, but it might very well be described as native Christian narrative discourse.

NATIVE CHRISTIAN NARRATIVE DISCOURSE

Contemporary native Christian writers face many of the same challenges that in earlier times circumscribed the lives and writings of Charles Alexander Eastman, Liliuokalani, and William Apess. Native Christian narrative discourse has emerged in recent years as the unanticipated product of several distinct varieties of social change in the United States and Canada; developments taking place in a wide range of popular, institutional, and intellectual contexts have intersected to create new opportunities for native Christians to make their voices heard. Native Christian writers ground their literary work in communities that are struggling to survive, both physically and spiritually.

Many native people, whether living on reservations or in urban areas, face structural and situational obstacles that often prevent them from satisfying their own basic needs in nutrition, housing, health care, education, and employment.[31] Many native communities are also the battlegrounds for intense religious contestation and conflict; religious life in these communities is characterized by unusual forms of religious diversity, involving a variety of tribal traditions, intertribal groups, and denominational churches that often compete for human resources.[32]

Native people responded to these community crises in the 1960s by organizing for social/political and cultural/religious change on tribal, national, and international levels. This period of overt activism (which in many ways continues today) saw the emergence of a new generation of native leaders, who pursued their strategic goals along two parallel and overlapping courses of action. The "Red Power" movement focused on social and political reform, reasserting tribal sovereignty and native legal rights and in the process forcing non-natives to acknowledge the contemporary native presence; the American Indian Movement (AIM) has received a great deal of publicity, though many other tribal and intertribal organizations have accomplished important reforms during this period.[33] Native people also worked for cultural and religious revival through the traditionalist movement, guided by an extensive network of native elders who have successfully reinvigorated and reestablished a wide range of ceremonial and philosophical traditions; the little-known Indian Ecumenical Conference has played a pivotal role in facilitating revival in widespread native communities.[34] Native Christian writers have both responded to and participated in the growing sense of native consciousness this activism has generated.

Contemporary native activism developed against the backdrop of the civil rights and black power movements, which also provided the impetus for important institutional changes that have taken place within Christian churches during the last three decades. Minority Christian constituencies have demanded equitable participation in church governance and resource distribution, forming racial/ethnic caucuses to make their voices heard within religious power structures. Native Christians, many of whom also participate in other activist organizations, have played key roles in this process; the formation of the native Christian caucuses is an important dimension of contemporary native activism that has been almost completely overlooked by academic scholars. For example, native Episcopals organized the National Committee on Indian Work in 1969, one year after Vine Deloria, Jr., completed an important study of native ministries entitled "More Real Involvement"; the Committee was reorganized as an all-native body in 1977.[35] Native Presbyterians formed the Consulting Panel on Indian Ministries in 1969 after an advisory meeting held on the Nez Perce reservation a year earlier proposed a number of significant reforms to mission policy; the Panel became the Native American Consulting Committee in 1974.[36] Native Methodists created the

National American Indian Committee in 1970 after participating in a consultation on native ministries two years earlier; the Committee was reorganized as an all-native body in 1972 and is now known as the Native American International Committee.[37] Native Anglicans established the Sub-Committee on Native Affairs in 1970, a year after the publication of the influential report *Beyond Traplines: Does the Church Really Care?*; the Sub-Committee was reorganized in 1980 and is now known as the Council for Native Ministries.[38] Native Catholics revitalized the Tekakwitha Conference, which had been a support group for missionary priests for more than thirty years, beginning in 1977, and have played a key role in the leadership of the organization since the mid-eighties.[39] These and other native Christian caucuses have engaged in advocacy on a wide range of issues including leadership development and ordination, curriculum design, spirituality and theology, racism, cross-cultural education, healing and reconciliation, health care, women's issues, legislation and public policy, land rights, and tribal sovereignty. Most of the leading native Christian writers are also active participants in these denominational caucuses.

Liberation struggles taking place in North America and throughout Africa, Asia, and Latin America also provided fertile ground for the growth of a radically new variety of Christian theological expression, a diffuse movement of critical, politicized, contextual formulations commonly referred to as theologies of liberation. Black Theology in the United States and Latin American Liberation Theology emerged simultaneously but independently in the late sixties, the former among black Protestant theologians and ministers, the latter among European-trained Roman Catholic theologians and priests.[40] Despite the obvious differences in their religious orientations and sociopolitical contexts, these and other liberation theologians have made surprisingly compatible methodological choices and thematic interpretations. Liberation theologies are the intellectual expressions of Christian life on the underside of history; they are based on rigorous social and cultural analysis and on a personal commitment to solidarity with the oppressed, and they advocate a radical reordering of human relations rooted in prophetic religious critique. North American Christians responded to the growing liberation theology movement by organizing Theology in the Americas, a multiracial coalition of theologians and activists, at a conference held in 1975.[41] A year later, Christian leaders from Africa, Asia, and Latin America gathered at Dar-es-Salaam, Tanzania, and formed the Ecumenical Association of Third World Theologians, which has become the most influential international organization in the global movement.[42] Theologies of liberation are among the most vital and dynamic voices in current Christian intellectual debate; they have set the agenda for the future of Christian theology and have revolutionized the way many Christians understand and express their own religious identities.[43] Black Theology in the United States, which emerged at the intersection of black radicalism and the black church tradition, has played a key role in the global liberation theology movement. In much the same way, native

Christian narrative discourse is the organic product of contemporary native activism and the native Christian caucuses, and has developed in dialogue with theologies of liberation worldwide.

As a veteran of activist organizing, church politics, and theological debate, Yankton Sioux scholar Vine Deloria, Jr., is uniquely qualified to speak from the intersection of these popular, institutional, and intellectual contexts. Deloria is the son and grandson of Episcopal priests and graduated from the Lutheran School of Theology (Rock Island, Illinois) in 1963. He did not pursue ordination, however, and instead embarked on a career in Indian affairs, serving as executive director of the National Congress of American Indians, earning a law degree at the University of Colorado, and teaching American Indian Studies at several major universities. Deloria became a leading spokesperson for native people by publishing a series of important books during the height of the Red Power movement: *Custer Died for Your Sins* (1969), *We Talk, You Listen* (1970), *God Is Red* (1973), *Behind the Trail of Broken Treaties* (1974), and *The Indian Affair* (1974).[44] These works demonstrated Deloria's sophisticated understanding of the symbiotic relationship between politics and religion in American society, as well as his razor-sharp sense of humor; years later, he described his religious affiliation as "Seven Day Absentist."[45] In *God is Red*, Deloria examined a number of Christian doctrines and beliefs in light of native philosophies and argued that these two basic views of reality "appear to stand in direct opposition," especially on the question of whether human existence should be understood primarily in spatial or chronological terms. For example:

> Indian tribal religions and Christianity differ considerably on numerous theological points, but a very major distinction that can be made between the two types of thinking concerns the idea of creation. Christianity has traditionally appeared to place its major emphasis on creation as a specific event while the Indian tribal religions could be said to consider creation as an ecosystem present in a definable place. In this distinction we have again the fundamental problem of whether we consider the reality of our experience as capable of being described in terms of space or time—as "what happened here" or "what happened then."[46]

Furthermore, "the opposition is more than conceptual; it colors the manner in which non-Indians view the world and the people they deal with in that world, particularly Indians."[47] Deloria was also the first native writer to mount a sustained critique of the liberation theology movement, which he found to be methodologically problematic because of its (initially) uncritical dependence on Western philosophical assumptions and modes of social analysis.[48] If we are serious about "the necessity of liberation," he wrote, "we are talking about the destruction of the whole complex of Western theories of knowledge and the construction of a new and more comprehensive synthesis of human knowledge and experience."[49] Deloria's early writings articulated a devastating critique of American cultural and political history that scandalized conservatives and liberals alike, but it is his analysis of religious philosophies that has proven especially challenging for native Christians. By emphasizing the glaring differences between generic native and Christian worldviews, Deloria highlighted the existential dilemma facing contemporary native Christians and implicitly delineated their discursive options. His critical books and essays are foundational texts in the emergence of native Christian narrative discourse.

Native Christians became increasingly outspoken during the seventies and eighties by advocating for native concerns through their denominational caucuses. Some individuals also began publishing articles and essays during this period, though most of these early pieces focused more on historical and social analysis than the complexities of native Christian identity. Two important interdenominational organizations articulated a native Christian voice beginning in the late seventies: the Native American Project of Theology in the Americas and the Native American Theological Association. The Native American Project began in 1978 as an "ecumenical working group" involving both native Christians and traditionalists who were committed to interreligious dialogue, social analysis, and strategic action; this collaboration led to the publication of a number of position papers, essays, and reflection pieces.

> The work of the Native American Project has been to open a dialogue amongst ourselves in the hopes of lessening the gaps between our peoples. It is a job of recreating the true feelings of oneness amongst ourselves and the Creation. It is a job of affirming who we are, in the context of the environments we were born into, and the changes that have occurred that we must analyze and draw the best from.
>
> We are faced with the job of recapturing our humanity for the purpose of our survival as distinct peoples of the Mother Earth. As we proceed with this work we will begin to evolve toward a theology that is owned by the Native peoples, and genuine to their experience. It will also probably mean the restructuring of the institutions that have come to our lands. We recognize that we are not alone in this process, that it is a process being undertaken by many peoples throughout the world.[50]

The active participation of non-Christians in the Native American Project challenged some of the fundamental assumptions on which Theology in the Americas was based. The coalition responded by organizing a series of "Inter-Ethnic/Indigenous Dialogues" during the early eighties, the first of which was hosted by the Haudenosaunee people (the Iroquois Confederacy) in 1981 at their Native Self-Sufficiency Center near Utica, New York.[51]

The Native American Theological Association also sponsored a series of interreligious dialogues during this period, and published the proceedings from two major conferences held in 1979 and 1981. These exchanges facilitated cooperation between native Christians and traditionalists and helped all participants reflect on their own religious identities, though not without some controversy. At the 1979 meeting, Lakota traditionalist Leonard Crow Dog criticized missionary conversion strategies by making unnecessarily broad generalizations that deny native religious agency: "Indians became Christian by force. Often they were killed if they did not convert. Indian Christians have a very hard time these days as they are caught between two ways of seeing the world. I feel sorry for those of you who don't know who you are." Several native Christians who knew who they were challenged Crow Dog, including Sydney Byrd, an ordained Presbyterian minister: "I am a Dakota and I freely chose to be a Christian. I agree that force was used to convert Indian people, but the loving example of my grandparents who were Presbyterian missionaries to our people, made me want very much to be like them, to be a Christian." Dakota traditionalist Joe Rock Boy was asked to make a statement after further discussion the following morning, and he expressed the consensus:

> My mother was an Episcopalian, but my father believed in the Indian way. I was taught in the Christian way to love, to forgive. I became a lay reader and they wanted me to be a priest. I still go to churches some. But I offer prayers. That's my gift. I must be right with my Creator to pray, so I must love people of all denominations. We must try to understand each other's ways! The Creator is understood differently, and called by different names. But there is one Creator, and we all worship this Creator. We must respect each other.[52]

Native Christian narrative discourse has achieved an unprecedented degree of prominence in the last ten years, with new writers and new articles now appearing on a regular basis in religious magazines, scholarly journals, native periodicals, and topical anthologies (see Bibliography). A number of recently published books by native Christian writers are also evidence of this growing literary tradition. Lutherans Paul Schultz (Ojibwe) and George Tinker (Osage/Cherokee) collaborated on *Rivers of Life: Native Spirituality for Native Churches* (1988), the first systematic attempt at a comprehensive overview of native Christian theological perspectives written by and for native people. *Rivers of Life* begins with two chapters devoted to historical, social, and cultural analysis in an attempt to understand why so many native people "do not identify with any expression of faith," whether traditional or Christian, and why so many of these are "still unable to take the risk" involved in exploring "spiritual options. For many those spiritual options are not yet real."[53] Subsequent chapters discuss creation and the creator, Jesus Christ, the doctrine of justification, the significance of land, community ethics, and ceremonial traditions, each topic considered from a native

Christian perspective. The book closes with a challenge to native Christians who want to participate in rebuilding the spiritual life of their communities:

> What is the responsibility that we must then carry in attempting to assure that more and more members of our communities can benefit from the spiritual transformation we have all so longed for? The answer is basically quite simple. We must continue to do all that we can to realize new and individual spiritual growth while at the same time praying for the kind of openness with one another which allows the Creator to become the central focus for other Native American persons and communities. In order to do this we must maintain our awareness that too many of our brothers and sisters have been judged and categorically denied any sense of spiritual worth by many different churches over the years.
>
> Through the process of unpacking inappropriate theological and biblical interpretation, which was only meant to exclude rather than include human differences, we find ourselves in a position to understand better and experience the healing power of God's love for all persons—past, present, and future. Interpretation which maintains theological and biblical integrity can also be focused inclusively in a way which allows and encourages a healthy and dynamic encounter with the Holy Spirit. At last, all of us will be free![54]

Recent books by Owanah Anderson (Choctaw), Homer Noley (Choctaw), and Tinker have focused on the history of missions, while those by George Lee (Navajo), Arthur Holmes (Ojibwe), and Joseph Iron Eye Dudley (Yankton Sioux) have offered autobiographical accounts of contemporary native Christian lives.[55]

THEMES AND PERSPECTIVES

The essays selected for this anthology of native Christian narrative discourse cover the central themes and represent the range of perspectives evident in this emerging literature. These twenty-one selections are arranged in four sections organized around the key questions facing native Christians today.

The essays in part one, "Spirituality and History," focus on the intersection of religious experience and historical tradition. How do native Christians understand the relationship between immigrant and indigenous traditions, between Christian history and the native religious heritage, between written scriptures and oral traditions? How do native Christians critically appropriate these collective, historical realities in light of their own personal, subjective spiritual experiences and perceptions? What are the foundational ideals and values that define what it means to be native and to be Christian, and how do native Christians negotiate the similarities and differences between these distinct identities? What are the theological principles, methodologies, and emphases that determine how native Christians will arrive at their own interpretations of conventional Christian beliefs and practices? These essays introduce the theoretical questions at stake in formulating, expressing, and articulating native Christian identities. Native Christian writers are engaging in historical and social analysis that sheds new light on the history of Christian missions and on the native traditionalist revival, and they are grappling with the implications that each of these influences has for native Christians today. They are relying on foundational native values such as holism, equality, respect, harmony, and balance in articulating native Christian perspectives on important theological doctrines including creation, God, humanity, Jesus Christ, salvation, and scripture. They are also employing methodological techniques that demonstrate the centrality of oral tradition, story, and visionary experience in native Christian narrative discourse. Native Christian writers are theorizing a new paradigm of interreligious interaction grounded in respect, dialogue, and cooperation, which will allow native Christians to nurture meaningful solidarities with other native people and with other Christians while maintaining their own distinctive religious identities.

The essays in part two, "Liberation and Culture," focus on the relationship between religious activism and cultural priorities. How can native Christians respond to the situational and structural injustices perpetrated against their communities without losing sight of the religious ideals that guide their lives? To what extent can native Christians defy the Christian establishment in order to reclaim a greater degree of religious independence, and what are the practical implications of adopting a more or less radical stance? How can native Christians relate to the global liberation theology movement and to liberation struggles in other sociopolitical contexts? Where can native Christians look for a paradigm of liberation that is consistent with native cultural criteria, and what political strategies can they employ? These essays suggest ways in which native Christian conceptions of liberation are grounded in the struggle for survival and the pursuit of religious self-determination. Native Christian writers are engaging in dialogue with liberation theologians throughout the world while struggling with the domineering power of institutional churches in their own communities. They are critiquing the cultural presuppositions behind conventional liberation theologies, particularly the widespread, uncritical reliance on the biblical paradigm of Exodus as a basis for understanding historical process and social praxis. Suggesting new ways of thinking about the relationship between justice and peace, they are challenging Western cultural understandings of history and creation, of rationality and experience. Native Christian writers are issuing a prophetic challenge to the lazy habits of mainstream religious life by calling for an engaged spirituality of personal responsibility and sacrifice.

The essays in part three, "Tradition and Community," focus on the connection between religious heritage and community life. How can native

Christians organize their religious communities in order to promote meaningful participation and to foster reconciliation and unity? To what extent can native Christian leaders incorporate native traditional ways as they preach, teach, pray, sing, worship, celebrate, heal, and share among their people? How do native Christians understand the relationship of their own religious communities to those of native traditionalists and of non-native Christians? How do the answers to these questions change according to the specific context of a native Christian community: reservation or urban, tribal or intertribal, denominational or interdenominational? These essays show how theoretical and political considerations are brought to bear on the practical challenges of native Christian life. Native Christian writers are validating their own religious histories and conceptualizing their own forms of religious community in order to serve the needs of native people. They are addressing the practical consequences of a phenomenon that church administrators and academic scholars variously refer to as indigenization or inculturation, syncretism or acculturation. Native Christians are facing a number of specific issues in developing viable forms of community, including: religious leadership and the ordination process; preaching and teaching; prayer traditions, sacred music, and liturgical forms; physical and spiritual healing; and the tension between institutional affiliation and congregational autonomy. The pervasiveness of tribal and denominational diversity only complicates this situation even further, making native Christian life a highly localized phenomenon. Native Christian writers are drawing attention to the importance of religious sensitivity, dedication, and creativity among native Christian leaders. They are outlining an approach to cultural integrity in religious life that speaks to the problem of identity affecting many other Christian communities around the world.

The essays in part four, "Transformation and Survival," focus on the nexus of religious pilgrimage and personal identity. Why do native Christians make religious choices that, to many other people, appear to be unwise or even irrational? How are these choices influenced by the specific circumstances facing each individual native Christian, such as visionary experiences, personal crises, guidance from elders, parental responsibilities, community affirmation, political conflicts, and institutional support? Is religious growth and change among native Christians an instantaneous event or a lifelong process? How do native Christians sustain or recover a sense of native identity, and how do they maintain or formulate a sense of Christian identity? Are the terms "native Christian" and "Christian native" interchangeable, or does each one imply a hierarchy of identity that represents more than just a linguistic distinction? These essays offer autobiographical insights on the complex religious choices many individual native Christians make. Native Christian writers are illuminating the ways in which religious identity unfolds in response to the challenges of daily life, and they are testifying to the importance of religious motivations and behaviors in maintaining personal, family, and community relationships. They are struggling with institutional churches and private insecurities, social dysfunction and substance addiction, elders' teachings and children's needs. Native Christians are drawing strength from living traditions and actively constructing their own meaningful, viable religious identities.

MOVING FORWARD

What does the future hold for native Christians, and for native Christian narrative discourse? The road gets rough in places; it is hard to be misunderstood by so many people for such a long time. Sometimes the obstacles seem too great and the passion for the journey fades, healing visions become obscured by painful realities, hope gives way to despair. We can take heart in knowing that the spirit of resistance and survival that inspired Dr. Eastman, Queen Liliuokalani, and Rev. Apess is alive today throughout the United States and Canada among native Christians, who are continuing their centuries-long struggle for religious self-determination. Native Christian narrative discourse is only the latest expression of an enduring struggle over worthwhile and honorable goals: respect, equality, independence, peace.

This collective voice represents a reasoned attempt to persuade the dominant culture and the religious establishment to acknowledge the undeniable veracity of native Christian identities. This pluralistic voice expresses the intellectual acumen of an ongoing debate, crossing tribal borders and denominational boundaries, about the nature of native Christian life. This intimate voice alludes to the intensely personal dimension of the struggle, the challenge to find faith in the midst of conflict, described so eloquently by Laverne Jacobs (Ojibwa) as "a lifelong dialogue with self," uncovering "different aspects of that reality like the many facets of a precious gem."[56] Native Christian narrative discourse is native literature; it is liberation theology; it is each of these, and more. Native Christian narrative discourse is a hallmark of patient persistence and a herald of spiritual healing; like Charles Alexander Eastman, native Christians today are helping men and women "of another race" to understand "the religion of the Indian."

NOTES

1. Charles Alexander Eastman, *The Soul of the Indian: An Interpretation* (Lincoln: University of Nebraska, 1980 [1911]), x–xii.
2. Charles Alexander Eastman, *From the Deep Woods to Civilization: Chapters in the Autobiography of an Indian* (Lincoln: University of Nebraska, 1977 [1916]), 1–13; Raymond Wilson, *Ohiyesa: Charles Eastman, Santee Sioux* (Urbana: University of Illinois, 1983), 13–20.
3. Eastman, *From the Deep Woods to Civilization*, 71.
4. Eastman, *From the Deep Woods to Civilization*; Wilson; David Reed Miller, "Charles Alexander Eastman, the 'Winner': From Deep Woods to Civilization," in *American

Indian Intellectuals: 1976 Proceedings of the American Ethnological Society, edited by Margot Liberty (St. Paul, MN: West Publishing, 1978), 61–73.

5. Eastman, *From the Deep Woods to Civilization*, 193–94.

6. Eastman, *From the Deep Woods to Civilization*, 194.

7. Eastman, *The Soul of the Indian*, 19–23. Tewa anthropologist Alfonso Ortiz has summed up the relationship between native people and Christianity by making a similar observation:

> Indian people never, to my knowledge, had any objections to the ideals of Christianity nor to the teachings of Christ. What they objected to was the behavior of alleged Christians on the "frontier"— ruffians who would rob, steal, and defraud them, all in the name of Christianity.

See "Indian/White Relations: A View from the Other Side of the 'Frontier,'" in *Indians in American History: An Introduction*, edited by Frederick E. Hoxie (Arlington Heights: Harlan Davidson, 1988), 6.

8. Eastman, *The Soul of the Indian*, 24.

9. Eastman, *From the Deep Woods to Civilization*, 138.

10. Liliuokalani, *Hawaii's Story by Hawaii's Queen* (Boston: Lothrop, Lee and Shepard, 1898); Haunani-Kay Trask, *From a Native Daughter: Colonialism and Sovereignty in Hawai'i* (Monroe, ME: Common Courage, 1993), 6–21; Helena G. Allen, *The Betrayal of Liliuokalani: Last Queen of Hawaii, 1838–1917*, (Glendale: Arthur H. Clark, 1982).

11. Allen, 93, 241, 19.

12. Liliuokalani, 188, 356, 367.

13. See Barry O'Connell (ed.), *On Our Own Ground: The Complete Writings of William Apess, A Pequot* (Amherst: University of Massachusetts, 1992).

14. O'Connell, 20–21.

15. O'Connell, 8, 19, 33, 49.

16. O'Connell, xlvii, lxvii.

17. Native Christians throughout Latin America are also engaged in this struggle and are confronting many of the same issues facing their North American allies, though their lives and writings are beyond the scope of this anthology.

18. *In the Spirit of the Circle* (New York: Episcopal Church Center, 1989), 26.

19. *In the Spirit of the Circle*, 26.

20. For example, see A. LaVonne Brown Ruoff, *American Indian Literatures: An Introduction, Bibliographic Review, and Selected Bibliography* (New York: Modern Language Association of America, 1990); Duane Niatum (ed.), *Harper's Anthology of 20th Century Native American Poetry* (San Francisco: Harper and Row, 1988); *The Land Called Morning: Three Plays* (Saskatoon: Fifth House, 1986); Louis Owens, *Other Destinies: Understanding the American Indian Novel* (Norman: University of Oklahoma, 1992); Gerald Vizenor, *Narrative Chance: Postmodern Discourse on Native American Indian Literatures* (Albuquerque: University of New Mexico, 1989); Thomas King (ed.), *All My Relations: An Anthology of Contemporary Canadian Native Fiction* (Toronto: McClelland and Stewart, 1990); Hertha Dawn Wong, *Sending My Heart Back Across the Years: Tradition and Innovation in Native American Autobiography* (New York: Oxford University, 1992); James E. Murphy

and Sharon M. Murphy, *Let My People Know: American Indian Journalism, 1828–1978* (Norman: University of Oklahoma, 1981); and Margot Liberty (ed.), *American Indian Intellectuals: 1976 Proceedings of the American Ethnological Society* (St. Paul: West Publishing, 1978).

21. Steven Charleston, "The Old Testament of Native America," in *Lift Every Voice: Constructing Christian Theologies from the Underside*, edited by Susan Brooks Thistlethwaite and Mary Potter Engle (San Francisco: Harper and Row, 1990), 50.

22. Native American Theological Association, brochure, [1979?].

23. William Baldridge, "Reclaiming Our Histories," in *New Visions for the Americas: Religious Engagement and Social Transformation*, edited by David Batstone (Minneapolis: Fortress, 1993), 29.

24. Robert Allen Warrior, "Canaanites, cowboys, and Indians: Deliverance, conquest, and liberation theology today," *Christianity and Crisis*, September 11, 1989, 261.

25. Charleston, 52. The pattern Charleston identifies is readily evident in recently published anthologies and reference works edited by theologians and religion scholars. See, for example: Deane William Ferm (ed.), *Liberation Theology: North American Style* (New York: International Religious Foundation, 1987); Judith Plaskow and Carol P. Christ (eds.), *Weaving the Visions: New Patterns in Feminist Spirituality* (San Francisco: Harper and Row, 1989); Mar Peter-Raoul, et al., (eds.), *Yearning to Breathe Free: Liberation Theologies in the United States* (Maryknoll, NY: Orbis, 1990); Ronald G. Musto, *Liberation Theologies: A Research Guide* (New York: Garland, 1991); and Martin E. Marty (ed.), *Native American Religion and Black Protestantism*, volume 9 of *Modern American Protestantism and Its World: Historical Articles on Protestantism in American Religious Life* (New York: K. G. Saur, 1993).

26. James L. West, "Indian Spirituality: Another Vision," *American Baptist Quarterly* 5, no. 4 (December 1986), 350.

27. Rosemary McCombs Maxey, "Who Can Sit at the Lord's Table? The Experience of Indigenous Peoples," in *Theology and Identity: Traditions, Movements, and Polity in the United Church of Canada*, edited by Daniel L. Johnson and Charles Hambrick-Stowe (New York: Pilgrim Press, 1990), 54.

28. Stan McKay, "An Aboriginal Christian Perspective on the Integrity of Creation," *Ecumenism* 100 (December 1990), 15. This is a risk that not all native elders are willing to take; the author of one of the essays originally selected for this anthology, a Cree Anglican priest in Canada, declined to have his work published on the instructions of his elders, who are growing increasingly concerned about the popularization and commercialization of native spirituality.

29. William E. Baldridge, "Toward a Native American Theology," *American Baptist Quarterly* 8, no. 4 (December 1989), 228.

30. See the selected bibliography at the end of this volume.

31. See C. Matthew Snipp, *American Indians: The First of This Land* (New York: Russell Sage Foundation, 1989); Pauline Comeau and Aldo Santin, *The First Canadians: A Profile of Canada's Native People Today* (Toronto: J. Lorimer, 1990); and Duane Champagne (ed.), *The Native North American Almanac* (Detroit: Gale Research, 1994).

32. See Sam D. Gill, *Native American Religions: An Introduction* (Belmont, CA: Wadsworth, 1982); Janet Hodgson and Jay Kothare, *Vision Quest: Native*

Spirituality and the Church in Canada (Toronto: Anglican Book Centre, 1990); and R. Pierce Beaver (ed.), *The Native American Christian Community: A Directory of Indian, Aleut, and Eskimo Churches* (Monrovia: MARC, 1979).

33. See Alvin M. Josephy, Jr. (ed.), *Red Power: The American Indians' Fight for Freedom* (Lincoln: University of Nebraska, 1991); Stephen Cornell, *The Return of the Native: American Indian Political Resurgence* (New York: Oxford University, 1988); and Boyce Richardson (ed.), *Drumbeat: Anger and Renewal in Indian Country* (Toronto: Summerhill, 1989).

34. See James Treat, "Contemporary Native Religious Identity: The Indian Ecumenical Conference," *American Indian Religions* (forthcoming); and Chief John Snow, *These Mountains Are Our Sacred Places: The Story of the Stoney Indians* (Toronto: Samuel-Stevens, 1977).

35. Owanah Anderson, *Jamestown Commitment: The Episcopal Church and the American Indian* (Cincinnati: Forward Movement, 1988), 129–37.

36. Henry Warner Bowden, "Native American Presbyterians: Assimilation, Leadership, and Future Challenges," in *The Diversity of Discipleship: Presbyterians and Twentieth-Century Christian Witness*, edited by Milton J. Coalter, et al., (Louisville, KY: Westminster/John Knox, 1991), 249–53.

37. Homer Noley, *First White Frost: Native Americans and United Methodism* (Nashville: Abingdon, 1991), 225–30.

38. Council for Native Ministries, Anglican Church of Canada, "Life in Its Fullness," brochure, [1989?]; James A. Treat, "Contemporary Native Religious Identity: The Indian Ecumenical Conference," Ph.D. dissertation (Berkeley: Graduate Theological Union, 1993), 46–58. For recent developments, see Laverne Jacobs, "Let Us Be: Native People's Plea for Self-Determination," *Practice for Ministry in Canada*, November 1991.

39. Tekakwitha Conference National Center, "Tekakwitha Conference: Voice, Presence, Identity of Native American Catholics," brochure, 1993; Robert J. Paul Fox, "Catholic Native Americans: A Church in Renewal," *America*, December 31, 1988, 541–43.

40. See James H. Cone, *Black Theology and Black Power* (New York: Seabury, 1969); James H. Cone and Gayraud S. Wilmore (eds.), *Black Theology: A Documentary History*, 2nd ed., revised (Maryknoll, NY: Orbis, 1993); Gustavo Gutierrez, *A Theology of Liberation* (Maryknoll, NY: Orbis, 1973 [originally published 1971]); and Alfred T. Hennelly (ed.), *Liberation Theology: A Documentary History* (Maryknoll, NY: Orbis, 1990).

41. See Sergio Torres and John Eagleson (eds.), *Theology in the Americas* (Maryknoll, NY: Orbis, 1976).

42. See Sergio Torres and Virginia Fabella (eds.), *The Emergent Gospel: Theology from the Underside of History*, Papers from the Ecumenical Dialogue of Third World Theologians, Dar-es-Salaam, August 5–12, 1976 (Maryknoll, NY: Orbis, 1978).

43. See Theo Witvliet, *A Place in the Sun: An Introduction to Liberation Theology in the Third World* (Maryknoll, NY: Orbis, 1985 [1984]); Deane William Ferm (ed.), *Third World Liberation Theologies: A Reader* (Maryknoll, NY: Orbis, 1986); Virginia Fabella and Mercy Amba Oduyoye (eds.), *With Passion and Compassion: Third World Women Doing Theology* (Maryknoll, NY: Orbis, 1988); and Mar Peter-Raoul, et al (eds.), *Yearning to Breathe Free: Liberation Theologies in the United States* (Maryknoll, NY:

Orbis, 1990).

44. Vine Deloria, Jr., *Custer Died for Your Sins: An Indian Manifesto* (New York: Macmillan, 1969); *We Talk, You Listen: New Tribes, New Turf* (New York: Macmillan, 1970); *God Is Red: A Native View of Religion* (Golden, CO: North American, 1992 [1973]); *Behind the Trail of Broken Treaties: An Indian Declaration of Independence* (New York: Dell, 1974); *The Indian Affair* (New York: Friendship, 1974).

45. Linda Metzger and Deborah A. Straub (eds.), *Contemporary Authors*, New Revision Series, volume 20 (Detroit: Gale Research, 1987), 130.

46. Deloria, *God Is Red*, 78. Also see his later book, *The Metaphysics of Modern Existence* (San Francisco: Harper and Row, 1979).

47. Deloria, *God Is Red*, 283.

48. Vine Deloria, Jr., "A Native American Perspective on Liberation," *Occasional Bulletin of Missionary Research*, July 1977, 15–17, reprinted in *Mission Trends No. 4: Liberation Theologies in North America and Europe*, edited by Gerald H. Anderson and Thomas F. Stransky (New York: Paulist, 1979), 261–70; "A Native American Perspective on Liberation Theology," in *Is Liberation Theology for North America? The Response of First World Churches*, edited by Sergio Torres, et al (New York: Theology in the Americas, 1978), 12–20.

49. Deloria, "A Native American Perspective on Liberation," 269.

50. "Position Paper of the Native American Project of Theology in the Americas," 1980, 14–15. Also see *Theology in the Americas Documentation Series*, no. 9 (New York: Theology in the Americas, 1979); Mike Myers, "The Native Americans and Western Christianity," in *Theology in the Americas: Detroit II Conference Papers*, edited by Cornel West, et al., (Maryknoll, NY: Orbis, 1982), 85-89; and *Doing Theology in the United States* 1, no. 1 (Spring/Summer 1985).

51. *Doing Theology in the Americas* 6, no. 3 (August 1981).

52. Howard Anderson (ed.), *Recalling, Reliving, Reviewing: Creation Theologies in the Dakota-Lakota, Judeo-Christian, Ojibwe and Winnebago Traditions* (Minneapolis: Native American Theological Association, 1979?), 19–20. Also see Anderson (ed.), *Black Hills III: The Spiritual Formation of Native American Youth: Drawing Strength from Native American Traditions to Shape the Youth Ministry of the Future* (Minneapolis: Native American Theological Association, [1981?]).

53. Paul Schultz and George Tinker, *Rivers of Life: Native Spirituality for Native Churches* (Minneapolis: Augsburg Fortress, 1988), 12.

54. Schultz and Tinker, 47–48.

55. Owanah Anderson, *Jamestown Commitment: The Episcopal Church and the American Indian* (Cincinnati: Forward Movement, 1988); Homer Noley, *First White Frost: Native Americans and United Methodism* (Nashville: Abingdon, 1991); George E. Tinker, *Missionary Conquest: The Gospel and Native American Cultural Genocide* (Minneapolis: Augsburg Fortress, 1993); George P. Lee, *Silent Courage, An Indian Story: The Autobiography of George P. Lee, a Navajo* (Salt Lake City: Deseret, 1987); Arthur Holmes with George McPeek, *The Grieving Indian: An Ojibwe Elder Shares His Discovery of Help and Hope* (Winnipeg, MB: Indian Life, 1991); Joseph Iron Eye Dudley, *Choteau Creek: A Sioux Reminiscence* (Lincoln: University of Nebraska, 1992).

56. Laverne Jacobs, "The Native Church: A Search for an Authentic Spirituality," *Ecumenism* 112 (December 1993), 23.

.. 1 . . . .

SPIRITUALITY
AND HISTORY

. . . .

1

JAMES L. WEST

INDIAN SPIRITUALITY
ANOTHER VISION

James West (Southern Cheyenne) is president of Okom Enterprises, a financial services company specializing in tribal economic development and based in Tijeras, New Mexico. An ordained American Baptist minister, he graduated from Andover Newton Theological School in 1971 and was a co-founder of the American Baptist Indian Caucus; he has served the denomination as president of the Board of National Ministries and as a member of the General Board Executive Committee. West has also held positions with the American Indian National Bank, Native American Research Associates, and the Interreligious Foundation for Community Organization, and has specialized in crisis intervention and arbitration in a variety of political and religious conflicts involving native communities. This essay was originally presented at a theological conference exploring cultural diversity within the American Baptist Churches, "Patterns of Faith: Woven Together in Life and Mission," held at the American Baptist Seminary of the West in Berkeley, California. West introduces some of the key issues involved in relating native religious experiences to the Christian theological world, and he suggests an alternative paradigm for Christian mission based on the need for healing and reconciliation. His use of personal narratives to frame his theological reflections highlights the centrality and power of visionary experience in native Christian life.

A BEGINNING . . .

I walked with one of our old people in my mind's eye; His name was Mutsiiuiv and He told me the story of the Medicine Wheel, the sacred circle of the Tsitsitas, the Cheyenne people. And then He told me that the circle had been broken; that the buffalo are gone and that this sacred circle, the symbol of the spiritual life of the Cheyenne people, could never again be as it was. And I was angry and I wanted to blame someone. He saw my anger, the anger of a young man, and He smiled and He told me that we have broken the circle, and I did not understand. He told me that we are responsible for the Medicine Wheel. It was given to us at Bear Butte by Grandfather and Grandmother, and only we can break the circle. No one can break it for us. He told me of the Cheyenne prophecy that one day we the red men and women, would walk with brothers and sisters who are black and brown and yellow and white. And then He gently sent me away, and I was afraid and did not want to go from Him. But, He sent me into the world to share the truth of Maheo's love.

We are each here to search, to teach *and* to learn. The spirit has been at work here with us, and we have quickly joined to celebrate our diversity as Christians. I am amazed at how quickly Maheo's love can weave a pattern of color together. Yet, as Kim Mammedaty pointed out this morning, sometimes we must unweave patterns and start again even though it is frustrating. Paul Nagano challenged us to look, even in this new moment of celebration, as the cloth of color in Christ is just forming, and to look beyond it out into the world where Maheo, where God is the weaver, and we in all our richness of Christian heritage and cultural color are merely threads. We must come to share our diversity, not as an end in itself; not only to seek the spirit of Christ among us, but to be open to the Spirit of God throughout the creation.

BASIC ASSUMPTIONS

The limited purpose of this essay is to outline and discuss briefly the theological issues of Christian mission, which have been barriers to spiritual growth as seen through the spiritual experience of the Native American, both traditional and Christian. If the richness of Indian tradition and personal testimony is to add to our praise of God's name, then the pain of the Christian mission experience should inform our faith and our perception of God's purpose in the creation.

Theo–logos or words about Maheo (God) as a discipline is a non-Indian concept. Indian people have a long tradition of words about Maheo. But, theology as an intellectual discipline, sometimes very separated from the everyday life of people, is a very foreign concept to most Indian tribal experience. Therefore, what will be discussed are certain aspects of the spiritual way-of-life of some Indian nations as well as comparisons between these ways-of-life and Christian theology. . . .

There are several assumptions I must make in this essay. I must assume very limited knowledge of Indian traditional and Indian Christian spiritual life by most people in the United States. . . . I must make some generalizations about Indian spiritual life which will be broad and, therefore, inadequate since there are some 400 Indian nations in the continental United States, each with its separate culture, language, and spiritual way-of-life. I assume that people at this consultation might be able to agree that Maheo (translated from Cheyenne as "Great Mystery" or God) is an attempt to represent a fundamental concept of a transcendent being which is both within this world and, yet, beyond this world or supernatural. I understand the central problem of Christian theology to be the development and refining of criteria in regards to this fundamental concept, so that this concept can be compared, modified, and reshaped so that it is intelligible to people trying to understand it. Finally, I understand mythology to be an important task of spiritual understanding. I shall assume that mythology is the conception of spiritual ideas through images and symbols drawn from within this world and human experience.

With these very simplistic definitions and assumptions, I present this essay on "Indian Spirituality: Another Vision."

REFLECTIONS ON INDIAN SPIRITUAL EXPERIENCE

The spiritual life of Native American peoples developed for thousands of years within the context of the tribe before any contact with non-Indian religions. There was also considerable interaction and dialogue among tribes about spiritual concepts. For instance, most tribes had a tradition of what could be compared to the law of reciprocal hospitality in the tribal history of the Hebrew people. Through the common language of sign-talk, ideas could be shared and compared among Indian tribes including the spiritual concepts that are an intricate part of the Indian's everyday experience.

I characterize Indian spiritual experience in terms of a spiritual way-of-life because the concepts and rituals of this experience are not generally confined or even kept by an institution whose existence is defined for this purpose or in any way separated from other institutions. Traditional leaders of Indian tribes do not just play political, social, or legal roles, but are seen as leaders with spiritual power. Traditional understanding of health and medicine do not separate physical health from social, psychological, or spiritual health. Tribal ritual is not governed or controlled by a church. Socially and spiritually, the Indian experience is a unique combination of a fierce individualism within a tightly knit and communal society. Therefore, the vision or revelation of Maheo is a potential experience for any member of the tribe. Yet, to be born into the life of a certain tribe is to be born into the spiritual life of that people as revealed to them by Maheo or God.

Maheo is the Cheyenne word for Great Mystery and the symbol of the monism that has traditionally been characteristic of the spiritual understanding of most Indian people. One of the most important qualities that Indian people attribute to Maheo is the force of creativity; Maheo is creator. Almost all tribes had a mythology to describe the nature and chronology of the creation of this world, just as Christianity has built on the creation mythology of the early Hebrews. For the Cheyenne people, initial creation took place in four stages and is told in four creation legends.

There are two general understandings of creation shared by many Native American tribes which I would now like to discuss. First, creation is often characterized as a dynamic between Maheo and Escheheman (the earth-Mother of all creatures). Escheheman is characterized as an ongoing creation and, as the earth (or nature or the universe), is understood as a symbol to be loved and accepted, not to be manipulated by any creatures.

All creatures of Escheheman, of this world, share the relationship of brothers and sisters. "Two-leggeds" or human beings are not considered above other creatures. Our nature is different so each creature's "story" focuses on that creature's experience. As brothers and sisters, we accept the nature of Maheo's creation as it is expressed through us. We share in Escheheman, and as brothers and sisters, we do not exploit or use each other or "our Mother."

Indian people have often been characterized as being pantheistic by Christian writers. Christians often give spiritual qualities only to human beings, e.g., the soul or sainthood, yet, these are not considered qualities on the same level as those attributed to Maheo, but are considered a "reflection" or "image" of Maheo expressed by human beings only, and not other "animals." In contrast, Indian people have developed an equal, horizontal, spiritual status for all creatures. Thus, all creatures express the spiritual image of Maheo in creation. This spiritual nature or soul for all creatures has often been misunderstood and thought of as pantheism.

The second concept which is generally shared by many Native American tribes and expressed in a myriad of ways, is that of the vision. The vision may be characterized as spiritual communication either within the experience of this world, Escheheman, or beyond it. In either case, it would be an experience which reveals something of Maheo directly to an individual. As such, it might be understood in Christian terms, as an experience of limited revelation. Each person is capable of achieving this spiritual experience, although many do not. One's life is often characterized as a search for one's vision. Visions are shared with an instructor or teacher who may recommend that the nature of a vision is such that it should be private, shared with another person, the family, or the whole tribe.

The vision experience of the Cheyenne is spiritual experience born of physical discipline through fasting. It represents the Cheyenne understanding that each creature is made up of a physical, intellectual, emotional, and spiritual essence in that ascending order. The spirit includes, but is not limited to, the former three aspects of oneself. Therefore, one's physical, intellectual, and emotional capacities can be utilized to express or search for one's spiritual life. The vision quest as a form of meditation would be similar to the meditation of the Zen Buddhist or the Tibetan Buddhist.

Certain visions have developed as revelations (a Christian theological term) for a given tribe or nation. As an example, Mutsiiuiv (Sweet Medicine or Sweet Root Standing) brought the Cheyenne much understanding of Maheo, Escheheman, and the sacred circle of the Cheyenne. (The sweet root is used to increase the flow of a mother's milk.) Mutsiiuiv's teaching is the revelation by which the Cheyennes have grown in wisdom and is symbolized by the Mahuts or Sacred Arrows. Tradition says that, when Mutsiiuiv left the Cheyenne people, he was transformed into the sacred plant which bears his name. When Mutsiiuiv gave the People the Mahuts, He said, "Do not forget me. This is my body I am giving you. Always think of me."

The vision of Mutsiiuiv is very important for "the people," the Tsitsitas or Suhtaio (the Cheyenne). However, visions are an ongoing spiritual potential, a potential of each Cheyenne. Also, the Cheyenne recognize that each People have visions which have been given to them and which continue to guide them.

THE CHRISTIAN MISSION

Christian theology has often been expressed in symbols that are very personal. The personal acceptance of the Christian faith transcends the history and culture of the human being that is converted or changed. This conversion ethic has been expressed in a political, social, economic, and spiritual theory called "manifest destiny" in regards to the "discovery" or the conquest of the "new world." This theory, simply put, states that God has destined the Christian world to conquer the rest of creation in His name. This has not been an expression of an inevitable fate, but rather a purpose or justification for historic events. The universality of Christ is the positive potential behind this more negative concept of manifest destiny.

Within this context, spiritual conversion is related to social, economic, and political conversion. But, most important for the work of this consultation, is the recognition of the many assumptions that accompany the Christian mission of converting or changing human beings. Conversion is a potential barrier. Conversion is seen as transcending the history and culture of the objects of conversion. Christian mission assumes that, whatever spiritual understandings non-Christian peoples have, they are, at least, inadequate, if not wrong or evil. It assumes that the mythology of the "pagan" is spiritual voodoo or, at most, the wild imaginings of primitive peoples. A mission built on the significant changing of a personal life over and above that person's culture must assume that the spiritual understanding of that culture has not afforded its people communication with or revelation of

God. If such revelation is even recognized, a mission of conversion must assume that the revelation is inadequate and/or in need of replacement.

These assumptions characterize the basis and purpose of mission as exemplified by the Christian mission history of the Church with my people. The "universality of Christ" has meant that the revelation of God by Jesus Christ can and should be applied to all of creation, which seems to reveal more about the nature of the Christian church than of Maheo. This revelation does not just reveal the truth about God but reveals it in some magic way that makes this truth "truer" or "truest" in comparison to other revelations of Maheo to other peoples. "I am the way, the truth and the life; no one comes unto the Father, but by me" (John 14:6). Salvation comes only to the truest. The Christian Church must struggle with the author of the Book of John. Therefore, for many Christians, evangelism has been measured by whether or not souls have been saved and, if so, how many. Despite the efforts of some within the Christian Church to broaden this concept and/or build on it, the assumptions stated above still seem to guide the Christian mission.

To exemplify this point, I would share a particular experience of dialogue with different non-Indian constituencies. Some people are able intellectually to recognize, feel guilty for, and work through the political, social, and economic imperialism which characterized the conquest of this land. However, only a few have ever understood the history and ongoing reality of the spiritual imperialism which is a fundamental part of the continued conquest of this land.

THE INDIAN CHRISTIAN

Simply stated, what this mission has usually meant for the Indian person who has converted to Christianity is a choice, a choice between Maheo or God; a choice between Mutsiiuiv or Jesus Christ; a choice between Christianity or our own people and our spiritual way-of-life. Obviously, not all Native Americans have converted from their tribes' traditional spiritual way-of-life. Some newer expressions of traditional spiritual ways have incorporated parts of Christianity, e.g., the Peyote Religions of many tribes. Most traditional spiritual leaders, recognizing the potential of other truths, see no need for choice at all.

Indian Christians have attempted to face the spiritual dilemma of this choice in many different and individual ways. One is to reject "all except Christ" including their traditional way-of-life or their life as a part of their people. These Indian Christians have in general been unsuccessful in the complete divesting of their identity with their people, thus, the addition of many rich values and traditions into the life of the Christian church. Christian peoples are most familiar with these Indian Christians, who are usually held up as exemplary Indians and are often the subject of church films, filmstrips, books, and magazines.

Many Indian Christians secretly work at integrating the two truths of their life or more often just accepting the reality of two distinct truths within their spiritual experience. Secrecy has been the key to this Christian experience in the past. The experience of openness which has marked traditional Indian dialogue among the tribes has been matched most often in the Christian mission to Indian people by a refusal on the part of most Christians to dialogue at all. An Indian often shares his/her Christian experience in an Indian traditional spiritual context, but he/she is careful to guard the very existence of any Indian traditional spiritual experience from Christians.

The struggle for identity, for a theological understanding of Maheo and an individual role within creation is constant and ongoing for the Indian Christian. If an Indian is a Christian, above all, why does he/she have a special mission to Indian people? The struggle to understand how Christian conversion should affect one's people politically, socially, and economically lurks in the backs of many Indian Christians' minds.

A NEW CHRISTIAN MISSION

The task of defining and/or interpreting the mission of the Christian church is a task that has gone on since the church's very beginnings. In Acts 13:15, the original Christian elders struggled to determine whether the church's mission should include Gentiles or not. The experience of these Christians was that the church had existed only within the context of the nation, Israel, and Jewish culture. Hindsight from the historical perspective of centuries of believing in the universality of Christ should not blind us to the fact that Christianity during the life of Christ was understood within a culture, the Jewish culture. Neither should it blind us to the fact that throughout the Book of Acts, Christians are struggling with a redefinition of the church's mission.

The theological task evolving out of this essay for this consultation and for the entire Christian Church is the redefinition of Christian mission and the theology which supports this mission. We must strive to redefine the mission of the Christian church in a world where God has been revealed to many peoples in many ways; where salvation is possible in many ways. I would suggest that such a mission must be defined in a way that the Christian Church reaches out to dialogue with and work with other religions and spiritual ways-of-life, instead of seeking new ways to conquer.

To redefine the church's mission, one must struggle with what evangelism will mean in the church. This essay can only suggest a simplistic beginning to that task. The context for Christian evangelism to the world must now be a context in which the creation of God is just beginning to be known. The Christian Church does not exist in a world where all spiritual life outside of Christianity is a void. Christian mission exists in a pluralistic world where many rich and ancient spiritual ways-of-life have lived side-by-side. The Christian church is made up of creatures on a planet that revolves around a small sun, in a small galaxy that is only a small part of the cosmos. As our knowledge of our creation grows and as our search for meaning expands, can we really continue to believe that the truth that forms the basis for our faith is exclusive or that God has chosen to reveal truth only to Christians? At the same time, does the realization of other truths have to mean that the rich history, tradition, and faith in the truth of Jesus Christ is any less vital? I do not think so.

As an Indian Christian for whom traditional Cheyenne spiritualism and Christianity have been two realities, two truths, existing side by side within the same spiritual experience, it would seem a hopeless and useless task to measure these truths or weigh them to the purpose of determining which is "truer." It would seem a terrible loss if these truths did not inform each other. It would be a loss if a tightly knit tribal and spiritual understanding of life were not challenged by the Christian concept of universality. In like manner, it would be a loss if a nation built on Christianity and its belief in human "dominion over the earth" was not challenged by the traditional Indian belief that creatures are brothers and sisters and that the earth is Mother especially when such a nation struggles to understand ecology.

The challenge to our mission based on "salvation of the unsaved" is obvious. We can no longer assume that all peoples who have not shared in our particular revelation from God are lacking revelation. Not to recognize the revelations of God to Moslems, Hindus, Jews, Taoist, Buddhists and, yes, even to the Cheyenne and other native tribes of this country, is to cut Christianity off from the potential to grow with our expanding understandings of God's creation. This lack of recognition has caused great destruction in the past and has the potential to continue to destroy in the present and future. We must begin to discover the vast, mutual ethical basis of religious experience and begin carving out theology with peoples of different faiths. We must begin to share our faith, not as a tool of conversion, but as a means of mutual spiritual growth in which learning becomes as important as teaching. We must begin to share in spiritual understandings, spiritual expressions, and even spiritual beliefs, not to convert, but to grow in understanding. We are compelled to do this not only out of self interest (to strengthen our faith) but that in this sharing, we along with others may grow in our understanding of God's purpose for creation.

AN ENDING . . .

I walked with another man in my mind's eye and His skin was dark like mine, for the skin of His people had been darkened for centuries under the desert sun of Nazareth. And He took my hand and His hands were the rough hands of a carpenter. And in His hands were scars and the scars told me that

He loved me. He loved me, not in spite of who my people are, but because of who my people are. And He gently sent me away and I was afraid and did not want to go from Him. But, He sent me into the world to share the truth of God's love.

May we pray . . . Maheo, Escheheman, together you have created all things. You have created the two-leggeds, the four-leggeds, the birds in the sky, the fish in the water, and all the creatures that crawl on the earth.

The circle is broken; the sacred circle is broken. So, we pray that your spirit is with us this day. We pray for the strength to believe that this circle is broken, so that a new circle can be formed by your hand, a larger circle that reaches out to include each of us. And as that circle forms as we reach across a chasm of mistrust and pain to touch one another, and even as we celebrate your love for each of us, give us the courage to turn this circle out-wards. For we are more secure when we gaze across the inside of our circle. We pray to you for the strength and faith to turn our circle outwards—to share in the wonder of all your creation. And as you gently push us out into the world, remind us that you are the weaver and that we are only the threads in your hands.

We pray this in the name of Mutsiiuiv and in the name of Jesus Christ and in the name of each of those who have come to reveal Your love, Amen.

2

ROSEMARY McCOMBS MAXEY

WHO CAN SIT AT THE LORD'S TABLE?
THE EXPERIENCE OF INDIGENOUS PEOPLES

Rosemary McCombs Maxey (Muscogee) is pastor of the Mt. Tabor United Church of Christ in Rocky Ridge, Maryland, and lecturer in philosophy and religious studies at Western Maryland College. She is active as a public speaker in both denominational and ecumenical circles, addressing a variety of native religious and political issues, and is currently preparing a collection of her sermons and lectures for publication by Pilgrim Press. This essay originally appeared in *Theology and Identity* (Pilgrim, 1990), an anthology exploring theological and cultural diversity in the United Church of Christ. Maxey addresses many of the same basic issues facing James West and other native Christians. Exploring the aftermath of the missionization process, she questions the practice of unity in the midst of diversity by considering cross-cultural perceptions of deity, humankind and harmony. Her emphasis on relationships rather than doctrines or institutions suggests a distinctively native Christian understanding of "church" and of the connection between theory and practice.

The purpose of this essay is to explore the place of indigenous peoples' religions within and without the diverse theological stances of the United Church of Christ. Indigenous people are those who today are called American Indians or Native Americans. I intend to recall briefly the history of the Euro-American Christian movement and the indigenous peoples' responses in early "American" history, thereby creating a base for a deeper understanding of Native American particularization of their perspectives as they relate to Christian churches today. The major thrust has to do with relationships, not with classical definitions of ecclesiology as proposed by European and Euro-American scholars. Relationships link the present with past and future and link people with all creation. Theologically, environmentally, and in their holistic understanding of human nature, indigenous people have much insight to offer to those who seem to have garnered the best seats for themselves at the Lord's Table. The United Church of Christ, which carries as its motto "That They May All Be One" and proclaims its unity in diversity, should be especially receptive to the voices of indigenous people who desire room at the table.

HISTORICAL SURVEY

Beginning with the "discovery" made by Christopher Columbus, Christians have struggled with the issue of what should be done with the original inhabitants of the New World. When Columbus returned from his first voyage in 1493, a squabble arose between the kingdoms of Castile and Portugal over possession of the lands of the New World. The Pope intervened with four papal bulls in 1493 and one in 1506, in them demarcating lands, giving most of the New World to Spain, which would convert the pagan indigenous inhabitants. Other European countries denounced or ignored the Pope's bulls, but throughout the sixteenth century theologians, jurists, historians, friars, and administrators debated what to do with the indigenous people.[1] In 1550 the issue was debated by the Catholic Church's Council of Fourteen. Two theological camps emerged. Bishop Bartolome de las Casas debated one side: that the noble savages were developed in the arts, languages, and government. They were gentle, eager to learn, and quick to accept Christianity. The other side, represented by Gines de Sepulveda, argued that these creatures were savage-like, slaves by nature, pagan, uncivilized, incapable of learning, and unable to govern themselves.[2] The issue was what to do with the aboriginal inhabitants, whether they were entitled to the soil, and what could be done to them if they refused the beneficence of "lumbre y doctrina" ("light and doctrine" or "light and teaching"). The debate ended in Las Casas's favor, but when missionaries came from Europe, the results were more closely tied to Sepulveda's argument.[3] And for five hundred years, the primary mission strategy of many mainline denominations has followed or paralleled that early approach.

Common historic interests have always existed between the indigenous people of North America and the forebears of the United Church of Christ. In 1629 the Congregationalists began efforts to include indigenous people in the Christian fold. With well-intentioned, dedicated missionaries, the general thrust was to "wynn and invite the Natives . . . [to] the onlie God and Savior of Mankinde."[4] Missionaries from that time to the present have consistently tried to make indigenous people participate in the church as acculturated Euro-American Christians. Indigenous people have resisted, reacted, and responded in a variety of ways to Christianity as presented by the missionaries. A monograph in the United Church of Christ Heritage Series, *Two Spirits Meet*, traces the process of cultural change and conflict:

> Prof. Robert Berkhofer, in *Salvation and the Savage*, demonstrated that when missionaries successfully converted part of the tribe, they set off a sequence of events through which the tribal unit frequently crumbled. Berkhofer studied Protestant mission history of the one-hundred-year period prior to the Civil War. He outlined a sequence of four stages. After missionaries converted some members of a tribal group, either the traditional or the Christian group was ostracized. The ostracized group usually moved and separated physically from the other members of the tribe. However, both groups frequently reunited physically in the face of common military threats. After they reunited and reestablished common government, political factions emerged, usually based on religion, which prevented the tribe from taking totally effective actions.[5]

The same continues to be true today. Three patterns of participation can be discerned among the indigenous people who relate to the United Church of Christ. The first, occurring in the earliest relationships with the missionaries, was the development of native churches. Using their tribal language in worship and church polity, single tribal churches developed along family, clan, and community lines. These churches exist today among the Dakotas and the Winnebagos.

Second, in 1982, a multitribal congregation was started in Minnesota, called All Nations Indian Church. Incorporating some of the symbols of their ancestors and their native languages, this church worships and provides services to the community. The third pattern involved other indigenous people over the years who joined Anglo churches and became involved in them to varying degrees, sometimes minimizing their identity with the indigenous community, sometimes assimilating in terms of worship but maintaining an identity with the tribal community.

My own relationship with the church as a Muscogee (Creek) Indian Christian has taken me through all three relationships. Three generations of my family have been Christian in a tribal community church affiliated with the Southern Baptist Convention. The Muscogee language is spoken in worship and business. During college and seminary, and immediately thereafter, I attempted to assimilate with the Anglo churches by working in new church development. It was not until I was a member of a multiracial church in New York City that I began to question the Euro-American nature of all Christian churches and to search for a new church relationship where the attempts at pluralism were more intentional. My search ended when I moved to Westminster, Maryland, and became friends with the leaders of a United Church of Christ congregation. In the tradition of my grandfather, who said, "I will be a Baptist because I have met a real good one," I became a member of the United Church of Christ because I met some "real good ones" who shared with me convincing evidence of the United Church of Christ's genuine interest in pluralism and ecumenism.

Since joining this congregation I have been privileged to sit with those in conference and association-level consultations who are serious about theology and serious about ecumenicity. But even they are more apt to cling to investigating "the unity." With furrowed brows, members of theological consultations and study groups pore over an array of theological position papers looking for that shred of evidence that enables them to proclaim, Aha! We are alike after all! Let's celebrate our unity. The fact that the United Church of Christ cannot declare a single or at least a four-strand theological position bothers even the most progressive theologian. The nameless "they" seem to push the panic button. "Other denominations make fun of the United Church of Christ because it is too diverse to take a theological position. . . . The UCC has been accused of a murky Christology," wailed two theologians in my presence recently.

From an indigenous person's perspective, I raise some questions about the denomination's proclaimed inclusivity. One must ask, What exactly is the criteria for sitting diversely together at the Lord's Table? What conditions and limits are placed on such an invitation? Do the indigenous peoples' ways of living and believing keep them marginalized in the United Church of Christ because there is no Euro-American theological or ecclesiastical category for them at the Lord's Table?

Can indigenous people, in their diversity, and others in the United Church of Christ, in their diversity, sit side by side in wholeness to strategize and pray for a realization of an eschatology that restores the unity of a fragmented world? Can we, in our united particularities, prepare our human communities for the wholeness that is more than people, and includes the entire cosmos?

There are difficulties in addressing these questions. In the first place, there is no way of presenting a single homogeneous view of the indigenous peoples. We are as varied and diverse as the United Church of Christ claims to be. We are many tribal groups and nations who vary in culture, thought, government, and language. However, some tribal and national commonalities exist in theological beliefs about the deity, ceremonies that celebrate the relationship between the Creator and the created, the origins of humankind, and the relationship and responsibility for living within the created order.[6] We also have many symbols and rituals that are common to us and parallel those of the Christian church. We often practice parallel Christian/Traditional rituals and rites simultaneously.

The second difficulty is our loss of pure culture. What was ideal and complete culturally cannot be entirely regained. Exploitation, relocation, assimilation, loss of sacred land bases, and loss of many of our languages (our roots of understanding) hinder us from achieving our cultural and religious goals, our ways of being. Most of us have become "diaspora people" in our own homeland.

The third difficulty in presenting the indigenous peoples' perspective is the "majority" audience who will read this essay. Conveying ideas in our common language of English is incomplete and misunderstood because of our differing world views, which remain largely unexplored and foreign to one another.

The motivation for listening to each other should, however, point to our mutual need for understanding, respecting, and living with each other. Indigenous people need the help of Christian churches in advocacy for justice and survival as distinct peoples. Christian churches need the indigenous people to help the church reclaim the activity of a particularly significant and faithful community of believers. That is, Christian people need to undertake their specific mission in the world, understand their possession of a sacred history, and live out their sacred duty to humankind and to the cosmos.

Further, the church needs to hear the indigenous peoples' voices regarding place in the universe and care for the created order. The United Church of Christ is just now doing its exegetical work on environmental theology and stewardship and coming to the same conclusions that the Ancient Ones have proclaimed all along.

IDENTITY VERSUS ASSIMILATION

In December 1978, the Native American Project (now called the Indigenous Peoples Project to avoid confusion of "Native Americans" as a reference to second and third generations of others who have staked a claim in "America") of Theology in the Americas worked out a position paper to describe and analyze the commonalities that exist for indigenous peoples in their religions and the effects Christianity has had on them. The uniqueness of this project lies in the sixty-five indigenous people who participated. They included Catholic and Protestant Christians and traditionalists (those who practice only their tribal religions) from urban and reservation dwelling places and represented some fifteen tribal nations.

The common beliefs or themes that emerged follow:

> We are an ancient people whose religious oral traditions declare that we have lived and evolved in these lands since the beginning of time. Examining our history, our traditions and our beliefs, we find creation stories that point to a time of birth from out of the earth and a covenant relationship with a Creator Spirit that is unique to this part of the world. We know that we have always been integral to this part of the world; we did not come from anywhere else. We know that our covenant with the Life Giving Force did not end and was not negated with the arrival of Christopher Columbus, the Mayflower or any other foreign vessel that has ever come to this continent. Many of our tribal people have clung tenaciously to the ancient beliefs and ritual ceremonies of our people even under persecution: therefore, we have survived as distinct peoples with a history and a place in the cosmos.[7]

With the introduction of Christianity to the tribes, some of our people, regardless of tribal affiliation, found the teachings of Jesus similar and compatible to the ancient moral and ethical teachings of our people. Jesus' teachings were accepted by many who did not give up their understanding of their place in the universe as taught in traditional instruction prior to missionary influence. Indigenous peoples have started churches of their own and conducted the business of the church from a tribal perspective, that is, using the same style of selecting a minister as was used in designating a chief and designing the worship according to the model of traditional religious ceremonies. Accepting "civilization" and Christianity from this orientation was an attempt to maintain separate sovereign nations in the face of Western expansion. Ultimately, the "Indian Church" did not help maintain tribal sovereignty, but it did provide indigenous expression in a Christian mode.

Assimilation attempts by the U.S. government, working in concert with the Euro-American church, have had an impact on many of our people as well. This triumphal church approach led many of us to join the Anglo church and we often find ourselves accepting Americanized Christianity as a way of believing and living. I find that, for me, this is a dangerous way to live. The different perceptions of the ministry of the church and the Euro-American's view about humankind's place in the universe and the church's efforts to universalize and impose its beliefs on all peoples of earth create difficulty and confusion for many indigenous people.

In spite of Christianity's doctrine of original sin and the virtue of humility, the European perception and attitude about their place ("a little lower than the angels") is quite lofty. This is the irony of a pessimistic view of sinful humanity. The contradictions between stated beliefs and the actual life style leave one to compromise and compartmentalize daily living into incompatible units. The belief that Jesus came "that all may have life" and the actual practices of genocide to indigenous peoples are strange bedfellows indeed.

Granted, the United Church of Christ has adopted an impressive and new missiology. It has become common to affirm that "the gospel is in the people and we go to them and discover the gospel in their lives." Evangelism has become more of a witnessing/inspecting mechanism to see the gospel at work and respond with awe. Is this another name for "fact-finding missions" where the church checks to see if God is at work and is surprised to find out that it is so? This missiology may have been slow in coming, but it does make way for cultural diversity within the church and may be welcomed by indigenous people who are outside the church.

Those indigenous people outside the church who maintain their tribal religious ceremonies and ways of being are referred to as the traditionalists. Indigenous people within the church who adore their heritages must express gratitude to those who in the face of adversity have held to the ancient beliefs of our peoples. It is through the efforts of the traditionalists that indigenous Christians stand a chance of regaining identity as a distinct and covenanted people. We must reconsider our old values if not our old practices, even as we take our places at the Lord's Table.

To promote greater understanding and cross-cultural exchanges, traditionalists have invited Anglos to share in ceremonials such as the Vision Quest and Sweatlodges. Recently, some of our brothers and sisters in the United Church of Christ have explored these experiences of Native Americans. Ordinarily, one would welcome these cross-cultural opportunities but two suspicions arise. These ceremonials are about the essence of survival as a covenanted people. When nonindigenous persons bypass the hardships of reservation life and what it means to be Indian in this country and move into the ceremonials for filling a personal spiritual void, are they not exploiting the religious experience for personal gain? What are they contributing back to the survival of a people and our beloved Mother Earth? Another question concerns people like those in the New Age movement. The New Age movement people who have explored Native American spirituality have turned a nice profit by writing and lecturing on Native American spirituality.

I find it odd/interesting that while some Anglos learn and experience Native American roots of spirituality, the United Church of Christ affirms and supports indigenous Christians in their efforts to learn about scripture, tradition, and reason in order to provide leadership for indigenous peoples' church community. Such engaging issues are prime topics for opening dialogue for all of us. Consider Joshua 24:25–28, where God made a covenant with the tribes of Israel:

> So Joshua made a covenant with the people that day, and made statutes and ordinances for them at Shechem. And Joshua wrote these words in the book of the law of God; and he took a great stone, and set it up there under the oak in the sanctuary of the Lord. And Joshua said to all the people, "Behold, this stone shall be a witness against us; . . . lest you deal falsely with your God."

Some of the psalms likewise speak of God's power in created nature. Psalm 96 says, "Sing to the Lord, all the earth! Let the heavens be glad . . . let the sea roar . . . let the field exult, and everything in it . . . the trees of the wood will sing for joy."

PERCEPTIONS OF THE DEITY

In the Muscogee (Creek) language, the name of the creator-spirit deity is *Hesaketvmese*, that is, "Breath Holder." Other meanings include Creator (earth), Sustainer (air), Redeemer (water), Intervener (unexpected events), Lover, Intimate Confidant, and Fun-Loving Friend (gentle breezes and small whirlwinds). The deity is accessible and present throughout the entire cosmos.

The scriptures, in remarkably similar ways, attest to the presence of the deity in what are considered by the Euro-Americans to be inanimate objects. In the Gospel according to Luke, when Jesus was making the triumphant entry into Jerusalem amidst the palm waving and praise, the Pharisees in the crowd spoke to Jesus, saying, "Teacher, rebuke your disciples." He answered, "I tell you, if these [disciples] were silent, the very stones would cry out" (Luke 19:40). Passages such as these resonate vibrantly in the essence of indigenous peoples.

In the history of the church there have been a few individuals, Francis of Assisi, St. Anthony, and Julian of Norwich, for example, who have been especially spiritually alive to the Creator in the created world. In the indigenous peoples' history Black Elk is recorded as a spiritual holy man attuned to the created order, and there are many others, including women, who are known to us by oral tradition.

But greater than the enchantment of mystery in the created order and stones that shout is the recognition that nature is an active participant with human beings and has feelings. Nature may have immortal and inexhaustible qualities, but it can die and it can die at the hands of human beings if human beings are not attuned to the voices and feelings of nature.

Indigenous people call for the recognition of the Breath Holder who through the act of creation permeates all life forms. Native thought has always embraced the philosophy enculturated through our oral traditions that all of the created elements are to be revered as an elder and nurtured as a child. What creation provides is to be cared for and used by all.[8] All of creation is sacred.

PERCEPTIONS OF HUMANKIND

The stories of many tribal nations concerning the creation of human beings are not unlike the Genesis account (2:4a–23). We are created from the earth, made last, not as a hierarchical culmination, but in a more humble position.

The human being is considered the weakest of creation, entirely dependent on all other created life forms for mere existence. Gratitude, nurture, and equality are to be accorded all creation.[9] The Genesis story of the fall from grace and expulsion from Paradise (Genesis 3) should humble us, not make us proud and possessive. Christian faith aims to restore the state of grace with God and creation but Christians have alienated themselves too far from nature, making reconciliation in universal wholeness difficult.

Only in recent biblical scholarship have theologians begun to see that the Hebrew words for dominion (*radah*) and subdue (*kabash*) are antithetical to universal harmony and order.[10] Some ancient manuscripts can be read as either *radah* or as *mashal*. Could it be that substituting the Hebrew verb *mashal* for *radah* would clarify human beings' place in the created order? While the root word of *mashal* is difficult to trace, one of the verb's meanings is "to pattern one upon the other" as in speaking in parables. If humankind could pattern its relationship to the created order in the way the Creator is related to creation, humankind could be cocreators with God in God's world. God-likeness would generate harmony and order rather than dominion and subjugation.

Contrast that to the Euro-American distortion of the concept of "man" naming, subduing, and having dominion over the earth. This forces the earth to produce rather than allowing the earth to flourish under the rhythm of life. Western European technological arrogance has jarred the harmony of the cosmos and thwarted the Creator's intention. The drive to possess the land, rather than act as God's cocreators, further adds to the imbalance. Christianity's influence in this regard affects all humanity. The earth and every living entity have been objectified, depersonalized, and made inanimate. The concept of humankind being patterned after God, the Breath Holder and Gardenkeeper, is lost.

The United Church of Christ has exhibited concern for the environment and a desire to uphold a theology of stewardship rather than dominion. It seems, then, that one of the areas that indigenous peoples have in common with the United Church of Christ is the goal of restoring harmony with each other and the natural order. But how do we overcome our diverse perceptions of what that means?

I had the privilege of attending the first Theodore Roosevelt Environment and Conservation Symposium (Fall 1986) sponsored jointly by Grace Reformed Church in Washington, D.C., the United Church Board for Homeland Ministries, the Central Atlantic Conference of the UCC, the UCC Office for Church in Society, the Stewardship Council, and the National Wildlife Federation. While the goal of preserving creation was common to all, the contrast in approach between the United States Forestry Service and the United Church of Christ was interesting. The theological approach was that the problem is people taking over the function of God instead of recognizing that God is at home in God's world, and that God has shared God's home with nature and humankind alike as a household. The Forestry Service representative called for persons to exercise their responsibility to be God's stewards and use and renew resources as appropriate to the technology that has been developed by humankind. In other words, to the Forestry Service it seems that people have found a way to care for the world in God's absence.

The perspective of the UCC theologian is in harmony with indigenous peoples' goal of restoring and maintaining harmony with each other and the natural order. But we have a lot of work to do to overcome our diverse perceptions of what that means. Over a century ago, Chief Seattle spoke of the indigenous peoples' perspective of our human relationship to earth and the environment, the indigenous sense of harmony, and the problem with the Euro-American world view. In 1854, at a time when the president of the United States was trying to negotiate a treaty, Chief Seattle said,

> So we will consider your offer to buy our land. But it will not be easy. For this land is sacred to us. . . . We may be brothers after all; we shall see. One thing we know, which the white man may one day discover, our God is the same God. You may think now that you own him as you wish to own our land, but you cannot. He is the God of man, and his compassion is equal for the red man and the white. This earth is precious to him and to harm the earth is to heap contempt on its Creator. Continue to contaminate your bed, and you will one night suffocate in your own waste.[11]

A PERCEPTION OF HARMONY

> For God so loved the world that God gave God's only Son, that whoever believes in him should not perish, but have eternal life. (John 3:16, RSV adapted)

This famous verse that the missionaries taught us, but often neglected to analyze or assess for themselves, contains real truth in the word "world." The Greek word is *kosmos*, or universe. The intention of the deity seems to be to offer salvation to all of creation. The offered salvation is not limited to the people in the church, to those who have strands of unity, but salvation is opened to the entire cosmos. Cosmic balance, harmony, and longevity belong to all of the created order in their particularities and even when there seems to be no common thread among them! Justice, ethics, and morality flow from the intertwined, interdependent, and intimate relationships of Creator and created.

Genocide, extermination, exploitation, pollution, contamination, and oppression are the acts that most upset the natural order and upset the deity. When harmony is disrupted, the Creator is sad, hurt, angry, and vengeful (in the sense that the disrupters must suffer the natural consequences of their deeds). Sometimes the deity turns away from, does not favor, those who are disruptive. Sometimes, in a manner reminiscent of Jesus' Beatitudes, the deity intervenes with those least likely to appear worthy and orthodox.

Learning the lessons of restoring harmony involves individuals and their community as they participate in the ceremonies of the tribe. It is in the seasonal, temporal, geography-centered, rigidly followed ceremonies that one learns the ways of worship, gratitude, and well-being.[12] Ceremonies always begin with prayer. Many tribes use a sacred pipe filled with special tobacco. First, offering the pipe to the four directions, then to the sky and the earth, then to "all my relatives" symbolizes the inclusion of all creation. Then, the smoking of the pipe by every person in the circle symbolizes communion and accepting the gift from the Creator and Mother Earth. Dances, such as the hoop dance of the Ojibwe, represent the circle of the universe. Other dances remind the tribe of its dependency on and relatedness to the Creator and the created.[13] In the ceremonies harmony is restored and perpetuated for the future. In the ceremonies indigenous nations express their connection with primordial time and space, with cosmic reality.

Yet the very ceremonies that ground our beings were hindered and outlawed with the arrival of Europeans. The attacks on our ways of life are unparalleled in human history and our ability to regain and restore these ceremonies in their fullest sense is all but lost.

WHAT CAN WE DO AT THE LORD'S TABLE?

Vine Deloria, Jr., says, "Tribal religions have a very difficult time advocating their case (in the courts)... They may have to wait for the radical changes now occurring within Western religious institutions to take root and flourish before much progress can be made. Protestantism is increasing its ceremonial/ritual life, and Catholicism is becoming more secular, so that behavior comparable to tribal ceremonial behavior among Christians may not be far off."[14]

The United Church of Christ is noted for its diversity within the Euro-American theological tradition, in its historic pluralism and flexibility, its ecumenical interest, and its being on the cutting edge of social issues as a prophetic voice in the world. If this church can relinquish its defensive power posture and assume a listening posture, then we can sit at the Lord's Table as I believe God intends us to do. Let the United Church of Christ forthrightly say, We don't see one strand of commonality on which to base our unity, but let's be our unique selves at the Lord's Table. At the Lord's Table there is room to be, to be included, to be fed, to be forgiven, to be acknowledged, and to be at home in God's world.

At the Lord's Table, there is a theology of listening toward mutual hearing. Our various voices, the voices of all creation, and the voice of the

Creator can speak and be heard. In mutuality, we can examine our motives for listening, our motives for hearing, our motives for talking—if we can risk being heard. Indigenous peoples' ceremonies and ceremonial grounds and the worship centers of the United Church of Christ have community-building opportunities that are mandated by our sacred histories and sacred obligations.

Each of us, indigenous peoples and the United Church of Christ, must learn how to authenticate our relationships with our own people. It is one thing to stand on the side of justice in Central America, South Africa, the Philippines, and the "uttermost parts of the earth" (Acts 13:47), but it is quite another to do justice with the victimized of our own people and the contamination of the environment in which we are blessed to dwell. Community building and living requires rebirth and relinquishment in the present in this place as well as in other lands and in the future so that "all may have life" at the Lord's Table. Paulo Freire wrote,

> Those who authentically commit themselves to the people must re-examine themselves constantly. This conversion is so radical as not to allow ambiguous behavior. To affirm this commitment but to consider oneself the proprietor of revolutionary wisdom—which must then be given to (or imposed on) the people is to retain the old ways. The [person] who proclaims devotion to the cause of liberation yet is unable to enter into communion with people, whom he [or she] continues to regard as totally ignorant is grievously self-deceived. Conversion to the people requires a profound rebirth. Those who undergo it must take on a new form of existence; they can no longer remain as they were.[15]

May it be so.

NOTES

1. J. Leitch Wright, Jr., *The Only Land They Knew* (New York: MacMillan Free Press, 1981), 29.
2. *Ibid.*, 30–33.
3. Vine Deloria, Jr., *God Is Red* (New York: Delta Books, 1973), 3.
4. Stuart Lang, *Two Spirits Meet,* Heritage series, ed. Edward A. Powers (Philadelphia: United Church Press, 1976), 3.
5. *Ibid.*, 18.
6. Position paper of the Native American Project of Theology in the Americas, 475 Riverside Drive, New York, N.Y., 1978.
7. *Ibid.*
8. *Ibid.*
9. "Recalling, Reliving, Reviewing," a report on a religious dialogue sponsored by the Native American Theological Association and the Minnesota Humanities Commission, October 1979.

10. David Jobling, "Dominion Over Creation," in *Interpreter's Dictionary of the Bible*, supp. vol. (Nashville: Abingdon Press, 1976), 247–48.

11. The words of Chief Seattle were quoted by Adam Cuthand, in "The Spirituality of Native Americans," a speech given at the Toronto World's Future Conference (July 1980).

12. Deloria, *God is Red*, 262ff.

13. *Ibid.*

14. Vine Deloria, Jr., "Indians and Other Americans: The Cultural Chasm," *Church and Society* (Presbyterian Church U.S.A.) (Jan.-Feb. 1985): 11–19.

15. Paulo Freire, *Pedagogy of the Oppressed* (New York: Seabury Press, 1969), 47.

3

AN ABORIGINAL CHRISTIAN PERSPECTIVE ON THE INTEGRITY OF CREATION

Stan McKay (Cree) is an ordained minister in the United Church of Canada and is from the Fisher River Reserve in Ontario. He was elected to a two-year term as moderator of the United Church in 1992, the first native person to lead a mainline denomination in Canada, and he is the subject of a recent biography by Joyce Carlson, *Journey from Fisher River* (United Church, 1994). In 1994 he returned to his position as director of the Dr. Jessie Saulteaux Resource Centre in Winnipeg, Manitoba, an ecumenical training program that prepares native church leaders for full-time ministry and also offers cross-cultural educational opportunities for non-native Christians. McKay wrote this essay on the basis of his personal involvement with native elders for more than fifteen years; he wanted to articulate some insights that he has learned and that have contributed to his spiritual journey, insights that were not included in his formal theological education. In discussing the tensions involved in expressing these spiritual insights in writing, he suggests a way for Christians to understand native religious history by foregrounding parallels with ancient Israel, where religious identity was rooted in a special relationship to creation and the Creator. McKay shows how this theological starting point can lead to a healthy emphasis on stewardship, harmony, and respect.

There is a sense of compromise in doing this essay as well as hesitancy in placing images on paper that reflect our spiritual insights. The present urgency to come together for a healing vision for the Earth, "our Mother," has brought our elders to advise us to share and risk even by writing what has been our oral tradition.

Art Solomon is an Ojibway (Ontario, Canada) spiritual elder who attended the World Council of Churches' meeting on the Island of Mauritius in February 1983. Art wrote this prayer for the diverse group of people representing various faith communities gathered there to prepare for the Vancouver meeting.

> Grandfather look at our brokenness.
> Now we must put the sanctity of life as the most sacred principle of power, and renounce the awesome might of materialism.
> We know that in all creation, only the family of man has strayed from the sacred way.
> We know that we are the ones who are divided, and we are the ones who must come back; together to worship and walk in a sacred way, that by our affirmation we may heal the earth and heal each other.
> Now we must affirm life for all that is living or face death in a final desecration with no reprieve.
> We hear the screams of those who die for want of food, and whose humanity is aborted and prevented.
> Grandfather, the sacred one, we know that unless we love and have compassion the healing cannot come.
> Grandfather, teach us how to heal our brokenness.

It would be possible to say no more than what Art Solomon has shared in the prayer and allow you to ponder how simple our spiritual world view is and how profound. The purpose of this article is to develop some themes that are supportive of the emphasis now being placed on the integrity of creation by the World Council of Churches.

ALL MY RELATIONS
(ANTS AND UNCLES)

For those who come out of the Judeo-Christian background it might be helpful to view us as an "Old Testament People." We, like them, come out of an oral tradition which is rooted in the Creator and the creation. We, like Moses, know about the sacredness of the earth and the promise of land. Our creation stories also emphasize the power of the Creator and the goodness of creation. We can relate to the vision of Abraham and the laughter of Sarah. We have dreams like Ezekiel and have known people like the Pharoah. We call ourselves "the people" to reflect our sense of being chosen.

The comparisons with the spirituality of indigenous peoples around the world may be centered on the notion of relationship to the whole creation. We may call the earth "our Mother" and the animals "our brothers and sisters." Even what biologists describe as inanimate, we call our relatives. We can understand the power of Christ's statement that the stones would cry out. This calling of creation into our family is an imagery of substance but it is more than that, because it describes a relationship of love and faithfulness between human persons and the creation. This unity as creatures in the creation can- not be expressed exclusively since it is related to the interdependence and connectedness of all life.

Because of our understanding of the gift of creation we are called to share in life. It is difficult to express individual ownership within the Native spiritual understanding. It follows that if the creatures and the creation are interdependent, then it is not faithful to speak of ownership. Life is under- stood as a gift and it makes no sense to claim ownership of any part of the creation. Our leaders have often described how nonsensical it is to lay claim to the air, the water, or the earth, because these are related to all life.

Reference to the earth is not singular in our culture to indicate owner- ship. Our words indicate sharing and belonging to the earth. The coming of Europeans to the land which we used in North America meant a conflict of understanding which centers on the ownership of land. The initial misun- derstanding is not surprising since the first immigrants were coming to take "possession" of a "vacant, pagan, land." The incredible fact is that this per- ception continues after five centuries. Equally surprising has been the historic role of the Christian Church in this process of colonization which consisted in a dividing up of the earth so it could be a possession.

We are into a time of survival which will not allow people to pursue ownership of the earth without perceiving that the path leads to destruction of life, including their own. The most obvious example is the nuclear threat for the world. More important for Native people is the depletion of resources and pollution of the environment. We understand this activity to be insane, since we live in an environment which gives life but is sensitive to abuse.

Our elders have told stories about the destruction of Mother Earth. In their dreams and visions they have known from time immemorial about a deep caring and reverence for life. Living in very natural environments they taught that we are to care for all life or we may die. The elders say: "If you see that the top of the tree is sick you will know that it is dying. If the trees die, we too will die." The earth is our life. It is to be shared and we know the Creator intends it for generations yet unborn.

We maintain the earth is to be shared and we continue to challenge face- less corporations to be faithful to their humanity. Even as we are being pushed into a "land claims" process, we maintain our heritage and are motivated by a love of the earth, a concern for the survival of the creation. Our Earth Mother is in a time of pain and she sustains many thoughtless children.

IN HARMONY WITH CREATION

From what has been described in this reflection, it may not be sufficiently clear as to what the spiritual relationships to earth are for us. It is thus necessary to say that we have a sense of Amen about the psalmist saying, "The earth is the Lord's and the fullness thereof. . . . "

The value that comes from the spirituality of my people is one of wholeness. It certainly is related to a view of life which does not separate or compartmentalize. The relationship of health with ourselves, our community and with all creation is a spiritual relationship. The need of the universe is the individual need to be in harmony with the Creator. This harmony is expressed by living in the circle of life.

There is an awareness that the Spirit moves through all of life. The Great Spirit is in fact the "Cosmic Order." The aboriginal North American spirituality draws together this cosmic order in human experience in a very experiential way. The view of the creation and the Creator are thus an attempt to unify the world view of human beings who are interdependent. We are a part of all life and the need for dogmatic statements is not relevant since the spiritual pilgrimage is one of unity in which there are many truths from a variety of experiences.

The image of living on the earth in harmony with the creation and therefore the Creator, is a helpful image for me. It means that "faithful" living on the earth will be moving in the rhythm of the creation. It will mean vibrating to the pulse of life in a natural way without having to "own" the source of the music. It allows the Creator to reveal truth to the creation so that all may share in it. We have ceremonies and symbols of what may be true for us. We have developed myths and rituals which remind us of the centrality of the earth in our experience of the truth about the Creator. We seek to integrate life so that there will not be boundaries between the secular and religious. For us, the Great Spirit is in the daily earthly concerns about faithful living.

Each day we are given is for thanksgiving for the earth. We are to enjoy it and share it in service of others. This is the way to grow in unity and harmony. There is a word that is central to the movement into harmony with other communities and that is respect. In Christian teachings the word used is love. It allows for diversity within the unity of the Creator. The dialogue can then take place in a global community which does not develop defensive arguments to protect some truth. The situation will be one of sharing stories instead of dogmatic statements and involves listening as well as talking.

MENDING THE HOOP

There are many teachings in the aboriginal North American Nations that use the symbol of the circle. It is the symbol for the inclusive caring community, where individuals are respected and interdependence is recognized. In the wider perspective it symbolizes the natural order of creation in which human beings are a part of the whole circle of life. Aboriginal spiritual teachers speak of the reestablishment of the balance between human beings and the whole of creation, as a mending of the hoop. In the Church we speak of renewal or rebirth when we describe balance. In his prayer, Art Solomon precisely states that only we have wandered from the sacred way and we must learn again about our place in the circle. It is faithful to reflect that the Christ came to save the world, but we make that statement anthropocentric in the Church, and for hundreds of years our theology denied the integrity of creation.

The pressure for short term economic gain has reduced human beings and everything in the creation to disposable commodities. Materialism and the related military programs are served by what is described as science and technology. The words "potentially hazardous" do not reflect the present critical imbalance in the circle of life. Our ecological proposal often does not encompass the wholistic and inclusive vision that aboriginal Christians hold. The words "the well-being of all people" should be changed to "of all creation" and the references to "our physical environment" should include the mental and spiritual environment. Christian faith is based on the power of love incarnate. We are called to understand the integrity of creation, to live love in the world.

4

PAUL SCHULTZ AND GEORGE TINKER

RIVERS OF LIFE
NATIVE SPIRITUALITY FOR NATIVE CHURCHES

■

George Tinker (Osage/Cherokee) is associate professor of cross-cultural ministries at Iliff School of Theology and pastor of Living Waters Indian Church in Denver, Colorado. He is the author of *Missionary Conquest: The Gospel and Native American Cultural Genocide* (Fortress, 1993) and numerous essays and articles. Tinker is an ordained Lutheran minister and during the early 1980s founded the Bay Area Native American Ministry (BANAM), a community-based program now funded by both Lutheran and Presbyterian denominations. In 1985 he was succeeded as director of BANAM by Paul Schultz (Ojibwe), an educational administrator and community activist from the White Earth Reservation in Minnesota. Schultz was a founding member of the National Indian Lutheran Board in 1970 and served as its chair 1978–84. This essay is excerpted from *Rivers of Life: Native Spirituality for Native Churches* (Augsburg, 1988), an educational resource written for a series on multicultural issues produced by the Lutheran Church in America. *Rivers of Life* is the product of a collaborative process; Schultz and Tinker co-authored this work on behalf of a National Indian Lutheran Board committee, which reviewed and edited the entire manuscript. This excerpt includes chapters three, four and five of the nine-chapter publication, the core of its theological argument. Like many other native Christians, Schultz and Tinker make the act of creation their theological starting point, then move to a discussion of Jesus in light of native religious traditions and the missionization process. They offer a reinterpretation of the doctrine of justification based on the importance of community among native people, which suggests that native Christian identity is not something to be worked out strictly on individualistic terms. Schultz and Tinker wrote *Rivers of Life* in an effort to promote spiritual healing in native communities, though today they both believe that this reconciliation is a more difficult and complex process than they envisioned in 1988.

CREATION CIRCLES OF THE WORLD

> When he inscribed a circle upon the face of the deep, when he made firm the skies from above, when the foundations of the deep were given their force, when he gave to the sea its bounds, that the waters should not transgress his spoken word, then I (Wisdom) was beside him, a master builder (Proverbs 8:27b–30, paraphrased).

THE BEGINNING OF ALL THEOLOGY

"In the beginning God created the heavens and the earth" (Genesis 1:1). The God we confess is a God of grace, of love, of beauty—the Creator. The hills and mountains themselves and the splendor of all creation shout forth with joy proclaiming the Creator's goodness (Psalm 148). All Christian theology should begin here.

This is where the Bible begins to tell the story of salvation, and so also begins our own confession at Holy Communion: "We believe in one God, the Father, the Almighty, maker of heaven and earth, of all that is, seen and unseen."[1] The Confessions of the Lutheran churches begin here, too, and so every Christian should begin his or her confession of faith by remembering God's act of creation.

Yet even as we proclaim the glory of God, the Creator, we must also admit that the mystery of creation is enormous. The Creator we worship has not been seen by any of us. The presence of God in the world can only be experienced by us in mysterious ways—ways as mysterious as the Creator. Nevertheless, we are certain in our confession, certain when we acknowledge the graciousness of the Mysterious One who created heaven and earth.

It is the same graciousness of God that we proclaim in Christ Jesus. The same creative power that God exercised in the beginning is the power that functions in Christ to create a new spirit, to re-create, to redeem all of us and set us on the right path once again. But there is a curious insight here that must not go unnoticed. That is, until we introduce the name Jesus into this theology of creation, we have said nothing that was not fully understood by our Native ancestors in all of our tribes long before the missionaries came to teach us the truth.

Our ancestors had a relationship with God as Creator that was healthy and responsible long before they knew about Jesus. They had a relationship with the Creator that was solidified in the stories they told around the camp fires in each of their tribes, in their prayers, and especially in their ceremonies. This relationship began with the recognition of God as Creator, the creative force behind all things that exist, and long predated the coming of the missionaries. In that relationship, the people saw themselves as participants within creation as a whole, as a part of creation, and they celebrated the balance and harmony of the whole of the universe in all that they did together.

In all that they did our ancestors acknowledged the goodness of the Creator and of all creation including themselves. That was the point of the stories, the focus of their prayers, and the purpose of the ceremonies. They recognized the balance and harmony that characterized all of the created universe: winter and summer were held in balance with one another. So also were hunting and planting, sky and earth, hot and cold, sun and moon, female and male, women and men. Our ancestors recognized all this as good, just as did God. In Genesis 1, at the end of the sixth day, God saw all that God had made and God said, "It is good."

BALANCE AND HARMONY:
GOD'S ACT AND HUMAN RESPONSE

There are different places to start for any group of people to create a theology—that is, people talking about what it is they are doing when they pray. Many of America's churches use original sin as that starting point. The argument runs as follows: All have sinned; all have fallen short of the glory of God (Romans 3:23). Since all have sinned, there must be some way to make amends for that fallenness. Either we develop a theology of works and argue that people can make good for former sins by personal achievement, or, as Christians, we look to the grace of God to forgive us our sins through the death and resurrection of the Lord Jesus Christ.

Now this starting point clearly makes an important assumption, namely, that all human beings are fallen creatures, that is, basically evil and sinful, and in need of divine salvation. While this certainly has a solid biblical ring to it, it is not the Bible's starting point, and it may not be the appropriate starting point for Christian theology in a Native context.

Before the missionaries came, the Native Peoples had little theoretical sense of sin, no sense of fallen humanity, and no sense of basic inclination in every human being to do evil. To the contrary, the primary sense that our peoples had of themselves in those early days was not a sense of individual fallenness, but the sense of community belonging as a whole group who were in relationship to God as Creator, who together participated in and celebrated the balance and harmony of creation. God created harmony and balance. The people's response was to participate with the Creator in maintaining the harmony and balance of all things.

This is not to say that Native People had an image of themselves as some sort of perfect beings who did not need any divine salvation like that proclaimed in the Christian gospel. Of course, our ancestors understood the existence of evil. That was and is a fact of life. What the insight does underscore, however, is that Native Christians need a different theological starting point.

Our starting point would have to be one shared by many other Christians, namely, God's gracious act of creation. From there we can proceed to God's gracious act of redemption in Christ Jesus. Now this will make sense to a lot of Native Persons. Even those who are not Christians can respect and understand this kind of an approach to spirituality. For we celebrate first the gift of wholeness and life that God has bestowed upon us and all the rest of the world. If we take that seriously, we have to image ourselves not as somehow above creation and in charge of it, but instead as one of God's created beings, related to all the rest of God's creatures: other people, the four-leggeds, the winged, and even the trees and streams and mountains.

If this, then, becomes our theological starting point in a Native context, then we can go on to celebrate God's other acts of grace and especially the act of grace in Jesus Christ in our behalf. But the primary value for Native People has always been the need for harmony and balance, health and wholeness, not just for the individual, but for the community, for all people, for all of creation. This is the work to which our ancestors committed themselves, because it was and is the response the Creator demands to the gracious act of creation.

As Native American Christians, then, we need to discuss with one another what it means to hold onto the value of balance and harmony of creation in our communities. And, with that in mind, what does it mean to be a Native Person and also a Christian?

To what extent are we being asked by our churches to compromise our American Indian or Native Alaskan identity by giving up those values our peoples have always held dear? Are the new values we are being asked to affirm really rooted in the gospel itself? Or are not many of them rooted in the culture of the missionaries who converted us to the gospel? If we decided that many of our values are still important to us, can we blend our values with the Christianity we have come to embrace? Is it possible to weed out those values which came with the missionaries but are not necessary for the gospel?

The second thing we need to discuss with one another is whether we can also continue to respect those Native People who have chosen to hold onto those ancient values, like the balance and harmony of creation, by maintaining their participation in the traditional stories, prayers, and ceremonies and declining our invitation to them to become Christian. Can we affirm the life and wholeness our sisters and brothers find there?

TRADITIONAL RELATIONSHIPS WITH
CREATOR AND NATIVE CONGREGATIONS

Many Native People today have been converted to Christianity and belong to a variety of denominations on their reservations or in the cities. We rejoice that God has blessed our people with salvation in Jesus Christ. Nevertheless, this raises an important question for all of us: what became of our ancestors who died without benefit of the Christian faith? And what happens to our brothers and sisters today who choose to follow the traditional ways and not to follow Christianity? One answer is we can and should continue to affirm those Native American people today who have become Christian, yet still respect the traditional stories; our Christian prayers may often reflect these traditional ceremonies, and many Native American Christians continue to participate in them.

The institutional churches to which our congregations belong will have to learn to make allowances for the different ways that we as Native People pray and relate to God as Creator. Some of us might even argue that the appropriate Old Testament for Native American people is not the Hebrew Old Testament with that people's stories and history, but the stories that each of our tribes tell and our histories. Thus, our starting point for coming to faith in Jesus Christ is not a history imposed on us, but our own history first of all and our own understanding of the world, our own celebration of God's gracious act in creation.

In the sections that follow we will begin to discuss different ways in which our Native congregations might choose to identify themselves both as Christians and as Native Peoples.

NATIVE AMERICANS AND JESUS

The Spirit of the Lord is upon me, because he has appointed me to preach good news to the poor.

He has sent me to proclaim release to the captives and recovering of sight to the blind, to set at liberty those who are oppressed, to proclaim the acceptable year of the Lord (Luke 4:19).

NATIVE RESPECT FOR JESUS:
RESPONSE TO THE MISSIONARY FAITH

Native Peoples of North America are naturally very spiritual people. So when the missionaries first came to our tribes, many of our ancestors received the missionaries' story with keen spiritual interest. They listened attentively and found it quite easy to embrace the new religion that had been brought to them. For most Native Peoples this did not mean leaving one religion to embrace a new religion. At first it meant living with both sets of stories and becoming more conservative in their missionary faith. As a result, it has become more and more difficult for our people to distinguish between respect, love, and commitment to Jesus Christ, and that part of the missionary faith that asks us to embrace not just Jesus, but a new culture and a new set of values—to change our way of living life.

TRADITIONAL RESPECT FOR JESUS:
A SPIRITUAL LEADER

Among a great many Native People there is definite animosity felt towards Christianity. Many have chosen to remain true to their tribe's traditional ways and have found life, strength, and wholeness for themselves and their communities. Among many there is deep-seated resentment towards any attempt to criticize those traditional ways as pagan or heathen, or worse, as Devil worship. It is interesting, however, to talk to many of the older, traditional, spiritual leaders. These people can say some very derogatory things about the Christian churches on their reservations and about brothers and sisters who have become Christians. Nevertheless, these traditional spiritual leaders show nearly a universal respect for Jesus as a spiritual person and leader. Even as Christianity is rejected and the missionary faith is disparaged, Jesus is respected.

The questions we as Native Christians have to raise are, What is it about this Jesus that commands respect from many of our relatives, even those who choose not to stand with us in our Christianity? What is it about this Jesus that has won our hearts over as well and has brought us into the Christian fold? And finally, can we find new ways to talk to our non-Christian sisters and brothers, those who respect Jesus and those who are angry at the institutions of Christianity?

THE WHITENESS OF THE MISSIONARY JESUS

A group of Christian people were gathered together for a study. One of them began to pass around four pictures of the crucified Jesus. The first was by an African artist, a Black Jesus hanging from an African cross, and everything about this Jesus was African. His hair was short and curly; his facial features reflected the tribal characteristics of the artist. The second picture was of an Asian Jesus, perhaps Chinese or Korean, a yellow-skinned Jesus reflecting a culture from half a world away from us. The third picture was a red-skinned Jesus with long, straight black hair. Instead of a loincloth he was wearing a breechclout; from his crown of thorns there dangled a feather hanging toward the back of his head. The last Jesus was taller than the others. He had long, naturally curly reddish brown hair. This Jesus clearly had blue eyes and white skin. Those in this study group were asked to pick out which Jesus they most clearly and comfortably identified with. Which Jesus did they recognize as their own? Of course, the Blacks identified with the African Jesus, the Whites picked the White Jesus, and so forth.

We could ask a number of questions about this incident. We might even ask which Jesus is the real Jesus. Which Jesus is it who calls us into faith, calls us into a new and vibrant relationship with the Creator? Which Jesus is it that gives us an experience of the grace of God?

For many American Indians and Alaskan Natives and in too many of our Native congregations, the image of Jesus that we have learned to hold dear is the image of the White Jesus. Of course we have learned to insist with our denomination that Jesus indeed has no color, that the gospel is color blind, and that God makes no distinction among people. Yet if we look closely, the Jesus we have embraced is too often a White Jesus. We need to ask ourselves, how can this be?

If we accept a White Jesus, if that is the image we see, have we not also adopted an image of salvation, of health, wholeness, happiness, that also comes to us via a White culture and comes to us with a White value system that may require us to compromise the value system and culture that is our heritage, and with which our people may feel most comfortable?

At another level we can address the question by answering that none of those images of Jesus is the real Jesus. They are all just images of Jesus that come out of a variety of contemporary communities. The real Jesus was in fact not White, that much we know. The real Jesus was a Mediterranean Jew and had darker skin, olive complexion, perhaps, or at least, swarthy. Jesus, in fact, was not even a "Christian." He was a good and faithful Jew who participated in all those Jewish ceremonies, and proclaimed a gospel from God to his Jewish brothers and sisters, calling them to repentance, calling them into a new, restored relationship with God, the Creator.

THEOLOGICAL FOUNDATIONS FOR A NATIVE CHRISTOLOGY

The word *Christology* really has nothing to do with our faith or the way we pray. Christology is what theologians do when they talk theologically about the meaning of Jesus Christ in our religion. It is what theologians do when they talk about what the rest of us are doing when we pray and live out our lives of faith. But it might be helpful for us to think about Christology for a bit—helpful because the way we understand Jesus, the way we image the Christ in our own hearts does, indeed, affect the way we pray and the way we believe.

The first thing that we as Native People must understand about the modern church scholars' discussion of the Christ is that Christianity is a Western faith and is primarily rooted in a world that is time oriented. Most Native Americans, on the other hand, are still rooted in a world where space is more important than time. As time-oriented people, modern Christian scholars must take history seriously and the "facts" that "probably" can be ascertained. For many Native People a story is important in itself because it is a source of truth. For the Western world, history and historical facts give the story its ultimate importance. Hence, modern scholars must ask questions like, What can we really know about the actual Jesus?

This is a strange question for any Native Person to begin with, because Native Peoples tend to think of the world not in temporal terms but in spatial terms. No self-respecting Lakota would ever raise the question, What can we know about the historical White Buffalo Calf Woman? The question would probably not occur to such a person. No self-respecting Navajo would even think of asking, Is this or that story a true story? For if we tell the story it must convey truth. But the Western intellectual tradition deals with truth from a perspective that Native intellectual traditions do not have. The Western intellectual tradition (and the church is a part of it) must deal with the level of facts as a way of getting at truth, facts rooted especially in time as well as in space.

So modern Christian scholars have indeed raised the question, What can we know about the actual historical Jesus? They are all convinced that what we have in the four Gospels (Matthew, Mark, Luke, and John) are not historical accounts in the strict sense, but something more like the portraits of Jesus that we mentioned above. Each one of them gives us a different picture of Jesus, a meaning-filled picture of how some people understood Jesus in the earliest church. It is not that these pictures are without spiritual meaning; they are rich with spiritual meaning. But for the Western mind we have to go one step further and try to look behind those pictures to discover what the real Jesus was actually like. In fact scholars are convinced that there is precious little that we can finally agree to about this actual Jesus. Strangely enough, they finally conclude that our faith must be built not on this actual historical Jesus but on the stories about Jesus that were proclaimed in the sermons of the earliest Christian community and resulted in the pictures of Jesus that we now call the four Gospels of the New Testament.

But there are some things scholars agree that we can know about the historical Jesus, and it might help us in our faith to understand those things. The first thing that we can affirm is that Jesus was interested in the poor and the outcasts of his day. He is consistently pictured in all the Gospels as associating with the sinners and tax collectors, the poor and the needy. For Jesus, salvation is much more than a spiritual blessing to be enjoyed at the end of life. Salvation must also include spiritual and physical liberation in this world. So Jesus heals the sick, feeds the hungry, and struggles for the dignity of every human being. He upsets some people, too. Jesus told many of his stories in order to confront the complacency of rich and powerful people. Salvation for these people may mean a new attitude toward the poor and oppressed, learning to see the world the way Jesus does.

This picture of Jesus might be more convincing to our non-Christian brothers and sisters. It might even encourage our own congregations to act even more boldly in our faith. When we remember that Jesus died on the cross for us, and was resurrected on Easter morning, that can bring us a real sense of peace and contentment. But that peace and contentment will fade away like any other experience if it is not used for good. It can become a useless thing. If our people are to live, our peace and contentment must become a source of power to act. And the model for the Christian's actions must always be Jesus. His life gave his death meaning. His death gives our lives meaning today. Now we must live for the good of our people and all people—so that the people may live!

BALANCE AND HARMONY OF LIFE:
JUSTIFICATION BY FAITH AND COMMUNITY EXISTENCE

> I am not ashamed of the gospel; it is the power of God for salvation to every one who has faith, to the Jew first and also to the Greek. For in it the righteousness of God is revealed through faith for faith; as it is written, "He who through faith is righteous shall live" (Romans 1:16–17).

JUSTIFICATION BY FAITH:
THE CENTRAL LUTHERAN DOCTRINE

We are saved by God's grace. We are made righteous, or justified, by faith alone. So proclaimed the German reformer Martin Luther in the early sixteenth century. And that proclamation is the high-water mark of the doctrine of justification, a doctrine which had always been of some importance to Christian theology and the church. Since Luther's own day, justification has become the central doctrine of the Lutheran churches in particular. St. Paul probably never intended that it become a doctrine of the church. For him it was simply a convenient figure of speech to help explain the relationship between human beings and the Creator.

As a doctrine or as a figure of speech, *justification* can only be understood when we know what the world meant in its original cultural setting; that is, the first century A.D., Greco-Roman world of St. Paul. Today, the word has become a religious word and has lost much of its meaning.

In its original cultural setting, *justification* was a Greek legal term used in courts of law. And it has a quite simple meaning. When a person was "justified" or declared "righteous," that person was being proclaimed "innocent" in a court of law.

That is what Paul means when he says we are justified. God is the judge, and God has declared us legally innocent. That is good news indeed. The scandal of the gospel for Paul is that in reality none of us is truly innocent. Quite to the contrary, Paul says, "None is righteous, no, not one" (Romans 3:10). The gospel message is that God, in spite of our lack of innocence, has proclaimed us innocent.

This is a very powerful message, one that can set people free who feel bondage to their past, that is, their sin. The gospel has a power which can set people free to live once again meaningful lives in their communities.

JUSTIFICATION AND THE RISE OF THE "INDIVIDUAL" IN THE WESTERN INTELLECTUAL TRADITION

There is one problem we cannot overlook. The Western church's interpretation of the doctrine of justification has emphasized the relationship between the Creator and each person. It proclaims balance and harmony between God and each individual, between God and me.

A Native Christian congregation will find this interpretation appealing up to a point, but a true Native interpretation will speak of justification as an act of God that brings whole communities or congregations into a healthy relationship with their Creator. Hence any Native American interpretation of justification would understand the justification of the person in the context of a whole community's relationship to the Creator. When we understand God in relationship with the whole community, then the community must see itself in relationship with one another—and even with all of creation.

The Western church's interpretation of justification in individual terms is quite natural. In Western thought there has been a steady trend toward individualism since early Greek philosophy. The individual has become more and more important in the course of Euro-American history until it has been reduced to an absurdity in modern American society. Unfortunately, when the justification of the individuals is emphasized, the nature and structure of the community suffer a loss. It becomes vitally important to ask what St. Paul intended. It is certainly valid for Native Peoples to suggest that Paul's own understanding had a strong community aspect built into it, and that the Western church has long overlooked this community aspect because of its own cultural bias.

THE PRIORITY OF COMMUNITY AMONG NATIVE PEOPLES

There are two problems with the doctrine of justification by faith for Native Peoples of North America. We have already hinted at both of them. First of all, there is a problem with understanding sin the way the Euro-American churches have understood it. In all our traditional stories there was no doctrine of sin, per se. Yes, there was always an understanding of evil in human existence. We are not arguing here from some sort of romantic life of the noble savage where there was no evidence of evil or wrongdoing. In all of our traditional tribal stories, sin or evil is treated as a fact of life. It is not explained theologically or philosophically. Sin is not turned into a doctrine, and our people were never oppressed with a doctrine of their own sinfulness in ways that coerced them to do or engage in certain behavior patterns that would atone for their sinfulness. There was imbalance and disharmony in community existence, and the people did act—in prayers and ceremonies and so on—to help restore balance and harmony. Even today, for most Native People sin must be understood in this way, as community imbalance and disharmony.

This brings us back to the priority of community existence for Native People. For all our tribes, life has been measured most significantly by the needs of the whole community. On the whole, individual identity has always been measured by participation in the community. And still today we honor and respect the structure of the whole community above the accomplishments of individuals. In fact, individual accomplishment is measured in terms of contribution to the whole. This is a traditional, Native American value that continues to live for all of us in American Indian and Alaskan Native communities.

There is an old story about an early missionary that illustrates the importance of community wholeness very nicely. This missionary came out into Indian country, settled in with one tribe, and began to work first of all, and many missionaries did, on the tribe's leadership. After many long and patient months of conversations, the missionary finally won the conversion of the chief. With great excitement the missionary planned a great celebration for the chief's Baptism the following Sunday in the little church that he had built but had not yet begun to fill. The missionary was more shocked than surprised when the chief showed up with the entire tribe expecting that all of them would be baptized together into this new religion. Of course, the missionary tried to explain that he could not baptize all those people, because they were not yet Christians; they had not yet been instructed and had not yet learned to accept Jesus as their Lord and Savior. Not understanding, the chief responded that they would all learn soon enough. When the missionary finally refused, the chief sadly said that he too would have to wait until all of his people were ready and acceptable before he would be baptized. We live together, we work together, we pray together, and either we become Christian together or we will not become Christian at all.

The point here is the value of community wholeness for Native Peoples. The needs of the community come before the needs of the individual, even spiritual needs. If the doctrine of justification is to speak to the greatest number of Native Peoples, it must speak not only to those who have become so acculturated that they have learned to feel individual guilt, and learned that they must atone for their individual sins, but it must also speak to those Natives who still identify themselves first with their tribe as a community whole.

BALANCE AND HARMONY:
A NATIVE INTERPRETATION OF JUSTIFICATION

If the doctrine of justification by faith is a proclamation of innocence over human beings which brings us back into a healthy relationship with the Creator, then perhaps we can say this means that God has proclaimed us whole, healthy, sane, and capable. That we can rejoice in. That we can celebrate: My wholeness and your wholeness; my capabilities and your capabilities.

But perhaps the Native American witness to Western Christianity is to expand the meaning of that doctrine in a significant way. Perhaps even as we expand it, we can all reclaim some of the original meaning that may have been lost over the centuries as the West shifted away from a community understanding of human existence to an individual understanding of human existence. Perhaps God's proclamation of grace over us is a proclamation to the whole community and to the whole world. We can argue that this is the point in John 3:16: "God so loved the *world*." Then the doctrine of justification by faith must mean that God has once again proclaimed the whole world to be healthy, sane, capable, and whole, and *me* a part of it.

Now we are back once again to the Native value of seeing in creation a necessary balance and harmony in all of life. If that is the kingdom of God that Jesus intended to bring into existence, then I think Native People can not only accept Jesus Christ as their Lord and Savior for their personal salvation, but they can become excited about committing themselves to working for the good of all creation in this new Christian faith: working for the balance and harmony of all creation, working for the good of the whole of the community, whether it be the congregation or the tribe or the village or city in which they live. If we can start our mission, our proclamation about the goodness of God's creative acts from the vantage point of saying the world is okay, and I am okay because God is gracious, then we have generated a power that is far greater than ourselves and a power that can effect good for all things.

NOTES

1. Nicene Creed, *Lutheran Book of Worship*, p. 64.

5

STEVE CHARLESTON

THE OLD TESTAMENT OF NATIVE AMERICA

Steve Charleston (Choctaw) was consecrated as the sixth bishop of the Episcopal Diocese of Alaska in 1991. He has served as the national director of American Indian/Native Alaskan ministries for the Episcopal Church and as director of the Dakota Leadership Program, a training program for native church leaders in the Dioceses of North and South Dakota. Most recently, Charleston was associate professor of systematic theology at Luther Northwestern Theological Seminary in St. Paul, Minnesota, and priest at Holy Trinity/St. Anskar Episcopal Church in Minneapolis. This essay was originally published in *Lift Every Voice* (Harper and Row, 1990), an anthology of multicultural and liberationist methodologies in Christian theology. Charleston begins with his own struggle as a native Christian in order to ground his theological proposals in personal experience. Arguing that interpreting native religious traditions as an alternative Old Testament can be a useful strategy, both for affirming native Christian identity and for establishing the native Christian presence in the "theological supermarket," he develops this idea further by pointing out a number of theological and cultural parallels between native people and ancient Israel. Charleston concludes by empha-sizing—and modeling—the power of prophetic critique in religious discourse.

CONTEXT AND COMMITMENT

I come from Oklahoma. I was born in the southern part of the state in a small town called Duncan. My grandfather and great-grandfather were Presbyterian ministers. Like most people in our tribe, the Choctaw Nation, they were Presbyterians who preached and sang in Choctaw. My own family was tied up with the oil fields. We moved out of Duncan and went up to Oklahoma City as the jobs changed. That means that I experienced a number of different churches. I was baptized a Southern Baptist, but I've known everything from Roman Catholic to Unitarian to the Baha'i faith. I think that's partly because Oklahoma Indian life can be so eclectic. There are dozens of tribes to go along with dozens of churches. Things are very mixed in Oklahoma. It's a cultural patchwork quilt laid down over ranch land, red dirt, and eastern timberland. I've inherited some of that mixture and it's followed me around wherever I've gone.

I am an Indian. I am a Christian. Being both hasn't always been easy. Like many other Native People, I've known my share of confusion, frustration, anger, and struggle. But I've also known a lot of hope, joy, and visions. So the two balance each other out. Today I feel comfortable talking about Christianity as a faith that emerges from Native America. I came to that feeling after many years of travel through different Native communities. I would credit a great many Native men, women, and children (Traditional, Christian, and a little of both) as being my real teachers. They helped me to grow up and find the sense of spiritual balance that I think is central to life. Of course, keeping the balance takes a lifetime, but at least I have a place to stand.

The place I stand is in the original covenant God gave to Native America. I believe with all my heart that God's revelation to Native People is second to none. God spoke to generations of Native People over centuries of our spiritual development. We need to pay attention to that voice, to be respectful of the covenant, and to be unafraid to lift up the new covenant as the fulfillment of the ancient promise made to the Native People of North America. That means not seeing Jesus as a white plastic messiah taken off the dashboard of a car and dipped in brown to make things look more Indian, but as a living Christ that arises from the Native covenant and speaks with the authority and authenticity of Native America.

I have been talking about what I call a Native People's Christian theology for over fifteen years. I started when I was one of only four Native People in seminary and I am still doing it today. So I feel a deep commitment to this new theology. I want to do all that I can to help bring Native People together. That means healing the false divisions brought into our tribes by Western colonialism. It means helping Native People who think of themselves as being either Traditional or Christian find a common ground, a common center. In time, it will mean carrying the voice of Native America around the world to join with millions of other Christians in a second reformation. I may not be around for that time, but I want to help make it happen by proclaiming the indigenous theology of this continent.

That brings me full circle, because I also believe that theology is autobiography. If we are really honest about all of this, about all of the millions of words we produce each year on theology, we have to admit that when we start out trying to talk about God, we usually wind up talking about ourselves—at least, between the lines. So, I think you can read Oklahoma in what I have to say; and Presbyterian preachers baptizing Native People in the river, and Choctaw camp meetings, and some struggle to be made whole. I also hope that you can hear commitment, energy, and strength, and that you recognize the power of God to help and to heal and a messiah who is changing the world.

CONSTRUCTION

Imagine a supermarket—not one of the small local convenience stores, but a really big supermarket, the kind of place with aisle after aisle of things from which to choose. The shelves are loaded. There are hundreds of different brands. There are different departments or sections. The merchandise is carefully organized to make shopping easier. This is a real American store, a place that testifies to our abundance and our right to choose for ourselves.

Now imagine that instead of groceries, this supermarket sells theologies. As you roll your cart along the aisles, what do you see? Dozens of different brands—a theology for every taste. There is a department for basic Western theologies, the old standbys. There are sections reserved for feminist theology, for Black theology, for liberation theology. There are shelves for African theology and Asian theology. There is even a gourmet section for New Age theologies. At first glance, it seems that this supermarket has a Christian theology from every culture and community. Almost. But not quite. Something is missing. As strange as it may seem, the Great American Religious Supermarket is incomplete. It has some shelves that are standing empty. Go down the aisles and try to find the section for a Native People's Christian theology. It isn't there. Look for a department called Native American or American Indian Christian theology. Still not there. The fact is, in all of the abundance of Christian theologies flooding the religious marketplace in contemporary America, one is conspicuous by its absence. There is no strong presence of Native American Christians in the theological marketplace.

Why? That's the simple but profound question that needs to be answered. Why have Native People not entered visibly into the Christian debate? Why is there no quickly recognizable Christian theology from Native America? Why not several brands for Native Americans to choose from? Why not a whole shelf of theologies from Native Christian theologians? Is it because they are content to let others do the talking for them? Or are there other reasons that need to be examined, understood, proclaimed?

"Conspicuous by their absence." That's the phrase I used and I wonder if you caught it? There is an irony in using those words, because I doubt if Native People have really been conspicuous by their absence. I doubt it, because I have rarely heard the question "Why?" asked before. Not too many Christians seem troubled by the absence of a Native People's Christian theology. I think if we are honest with one another, we will admit that most religious shoppers have gone down the aisles and never even noticed that Native People were missing. They assumed that the supermarket was complete as new products arrive daily, old products are repackaged—new and improved theologies, special sales on hot items. In all of the abundance, in all of the excitement, I don't believe many people have noticed a few empty shelves. This fact alone raises another question. Why have so very few people questioned the absence of Native Americans? Given the proliferation of theologies from many racial, cultural, ethnic, and economic communities, given the rise of theologies from the feminist community, given the increased awareness on the part of consumers of theology—why has the absence of Native People's theology gone unnoticed?

If we tackle that question first, we may find that we are starting to uncover some clues to the more fundamental reasons for Native America's silence in the Christian debate. Many people may have overlooked the absence of a Native People's Christian theology because they assumed it was covered by the supermarket sections reserved for spirituality. I think that's a fair guess. After all, there are many shelves these days loaded with works on Native American spirituality. Some are historical, others are anthropological or biographical; some are journalistic accounts by white authors who went to live with the Indians and returned to share the exotic secrets they discovered. In fact, there has been something of a minor gold rush in Native American "spirituality," with lots of people writing about it. What is described as Native American spirituality crops up in all kinds of places, especially in the gourmet section of the theological supermarket. In a style not too far removed from the 1960s and early 1970s, it has become chic to be Indian again, or, at least, to know an Indian, particularly if that Indian is a medicine person. It's romantic, earthy, "creation-centered."

The Native spirituality craze, therefore, may account for the neglect of a Native People's Christian theology. Well-intentioned shoppers may have simply thought that this talk about spirituality was the voice of Native America in the religious dialogue. And up to a point, they're right. Traditional Native spirituality does represent a major and crucial voice for Native People. It is a voice that has frequently been misquoted, distorted, or co-opted, but it's a voice nonetheless. I am certainly not prepared to argue against a legitimate role for that spirituality. In fact, I am going to argue that this spirituality is something extremely central to Native America, and to the Christ, and faith. Still, the spirituality section alone does not complete the supermarket. It is still not an expression of a Native Christian viewpoint. As good (or bad) as these works may be at articulating Native tradition, they do not offer a clear voice for Native American Christianity. They are not a Native People's Christian theology. Instead they are the source for materials for that theology—they are reference points, or commentaries.

THE OLD TESTAMENT OF NATIVE AMERICA

So far, we've said that the answer to why most people have ignored the absence of a Native People's Christian theology is because they thought they were getting it through Native "spirituality." But that still doesn't explain why the theology itself is missing. Now, we have a clue to follow. What would happen if instead of speaking about Native American spirituality we began speaking of an Old Testament of Native America? What would that do for us?

Well, first of all, it would give us a new vocabulary in dealing with what we've been describing as Native spirituality. For example, a great many of those books in the supermarket would become Old Testament commentaries. They would be books about the source material of Native America's Old Testament. Books about the traditions of Old Testament times, about the culture of Old Testament times, about the personalities of Old Testament times, and the theology of Old Testament times. We might start treating them more seriously and critically, since they would be describing the foundational theology for a contemporary Christian theology. They would have to be weighed and judged on a much finer scale than we have become accustomed to. The authors of these books would begin to seem like Old Testament scholars, not hack writers. Their standard of scholarship would be open to public inspection and criticism. Tossing off a book about "living with an Indian medicine woman" might not qualify as research so easily anymore. We would want to know how accurate the work was. How genuine. How consistent with any tradition. If Ralph Nader were a theologian, he would be proud of us for our new sense of comparison shopping.

What about the Old Testament scholars themselves? Who would they be? My own guess is that the gold rush would be over. Instead of Western writers hacking away at Native spirituality, we would begin to see the emergence of more theologians from within the Native community itself. That might not be as romantic, exotic, or exciting as what we've been used to, but I expect it would be a great deal more valuable. Native American women and men could finally speak for themselves, not as gurus for Western theological science fiction, but as reputable scholars for an Old Testament tradition. Their voices would be clear and distinct. They would be listened to seriously. These speakers would not necessarily be Christian, but they would be treated with respect by the Christian community, just as Jewish scholars are respected. Their contribution to the larger interfaith dialogue would be profound. It would change us. It would open us up to a whole new dimension in theological exploration.

As a result, attitudes toward Native People and their Tradition would alter. Naming that Tradition an "Old Testament" is a powerful statement of recognition for Native America. It says that Native People are not just historical curiosities, footnotes for Western colonial expansion, but the living members of a world-class religious heritage. Since the first Western missionary or anthropologist walked into a Native community, the Tradition of Native America has been called everything but an Old Testament. It has been named by others. It has been named by the West, not the People themselves. It has been called "superstition," "tribal religion," "nature worship," "animism," "shamanism," "primitive," "Stone Age," "savage," "spirituality," anything and everything, but never an Old Testament. The namers themselves have had mixed motives, some innocent, some racist, some just ignorant. But the results have been the same: the names attached to the Old Testament of Native America have consigned that Tradition to the backwaters of serious Christian scholarship. Native American spiritual tradition has been considered the proper study of historians, ethnologists, anthropologists, or even the gourmet writers of the New Age, but not for most Christian theologians. There is a big difference for Western theologians between a "spirituality" and a "theology," just as there is between a "tradition" and the "Old Testament." By claiming the right to name the Tradition an Old Testament, Native America would be walking into the private club of Christian theology, even if that means coming uninvited.

Finally, shifting our vocabulary to Old Testament language gives us an answer to that original question: Why hasn't there been a Native People's Christian theology? The whole purpose of such a theology would be to talk about the New Testament. It would be the Native perspective on Jesus and the gospels, on Paul, eschatology, redemption, salvation, sin, resurrection, community, grace, love, and God. To truly be a "Christian" theology, it would have to cover the whole range of ideas that form the Christian understanding of the New Testament. It would also have to be directly related to what we have always called the "Old Testament," i.e., the Old Testament of Israel. You can't have one without the other.

And there's the problem—you can't have a "new" testament if you don't have an "old" testament. Christians have invented those adjectives to distinguish between the original covenant relationship between God and the people and the "new" relationship established through the person of Jesus as the Christ. For Western People those distinctions work. For Native People they don't work.

Why? Because Native People also have an "old" testament. They have their own original covenant relationship with the Creator and their own original understanding of God prior to the birth of a Christ. It is a Tradition that has evolved over centuries. It tells of the active, living, revealing presence of God in relation to Native People through generations of Native life and experience. It asserts that God was not an absentee landlord for North America.

God was here, on this continent among this people, in covenant, in relation, in life. Like Israel itself, Native America proclaims that God is a God of all times and of all places and of all peoples. Consequently, the "old" testament of Native America becomes tremendously important. It is the living memory, the living tradition of a people's special encounter with the Creator of life.

So what are Native People supposed to do with that memory when they pick up the New Testament? Forget it? Pretend it doesn't matter? Assume that millions of their ancestors were just ignorant savages who didn't have any ideas about the reality of God in their lives? Was God just kidding around? Was the Creator passing off disinformation onto Native America? Was it just a joke?

It should be painfully obvious that Native People have only one choice to make. To erase the collective memory of Native America would not only be a crime against humanity, but a macabre theological position that would so limit the nature of God as to cease to be Christian. Or Jewish. God is the God of all time, of all space, of all people. Moreover, God relates to humanity through love, not through disinformation. When God spoke to Native America, it wasn't a joke. It wasn't primitive. It wasn't Stone Age. It wasn't nature worship. It wasn't superstition. It was the call of God to all people to draw near, to listen, to believe, and to love. Did Native America hear this call? Yes. Did Native America encounter God? Yes. Did Native America remember that encounter and try to explain it to their children? Yes. Did they always get it right? No. Like any human community, Native America is finite and fallible. Its "old" testament is full of mistakes, false starts, guesses, hopes, dreams, wishes, just like any other Old Testament. And yet it is also full of truth, prophecy, and promise. It reveals something genuine and precious. It tells us a little more about the Creator we call God.

When Native People were denied access to that religious legacy, when they were told that their Old Testament was nothing more than a grab bag of primitive superstitions, when they were forbidden to share the memory with their own children, when they were commanded to undergo spiritual amnesia, to lose their memories, to go blank, to forget their own story and let others do the naming for them, it was exactly at this moment that any "new" Testament was jerked away from them. We need to press this point again; you cannot have a "new" testament if you do not have an "old" testament. You cannot fulfill what you do not have. The shelves are empty of a Native People's Christian theology because the theologians who would fill them have been brainwashed. They have been told to be content with another People's story, and to forget their own. They have been reduced to silence. It is the silence of any man or woman who cannot remember their own name. Who cannot remember where they came from. Who cannot remember having a family. Who cannot remember having a home. It is a silence of terror and of dread. An insane silence. A silence of isolation. The silence of a People who have been exiled from the love of their God.

74

THE TRIBE OF ISRAEL/THE TRIBE OF AMERICA

The reason for proclaiming an Old Testament of Native America is to break the silence. It is my intention to be a Christian theologian. To be a Native Christian theologian. But I cannot do that if I am not allowed to name myself. To name my tradition, and to use it. I cannot write about the Jesus of the gospels or the letters of Paul if I don't interpret them through the truths as I try to understand it. That means the truth of the original covenant that God maintained with Israel, the truth of the witness of Jesus as the Christ as upheld in the "new" covenant, and the truth of the covenant between God and the Native People as revealed in the ancient testimony of Native America. Like any theologian from any community that retains its memory of God through tradition, I have to work with at least three primary sources; the Old Testament of Israel, the New Testament of the Christian scriptures, and the Old Testament of my own People. The three are integral. They cannot be separated.

I am very aware of the negative reaction this proclamation can produce among Christians, Jews, and Native People themselves. The words "old" and "new" testaments account for part of that reaction. The words certainly are not accurate, nor do they promote interfaith understanding. The term *Old Testament* is too pejorative; it leaves the impression that it is something we can dismiss, something that has been replaced, something secondary. I know that within the Jewish community there is a strong reaction when Christians describe the Bible in this way. And yet, I feel bound by the words, as they have become a shorthand for signifying distinctions. At least for now. At least until people begin to accept the Native Old Testament for what it is. Then in a few years' time, we can bypass the words "Old Testament of Native America" and begin to speak of the Native Covenant.

Until that time, I want to push for recognition of a Native American Old Testament, even if it evokes a strong reaction from all directions. To be honest, *because* it evokes a strong reaction. The kind of silence I describe is not going to be broken by whispers, but by shouts. Therefore, I announce the Old Testament of Native America and invite others to do the same. Even if the language is imprecise, it is familiar language. It sends a clear message. It makes Christians, Jews, and Native People uncomfortable.

The discomfort arises because all of us have been conditioned to think of the Old Testament. Good, bad, or indifferent; we all know what we mean. We say *the* Old Testament and we know that we are referring to the first thirty-nine books of the Bible. That's the Christian position, of course, but it is understood by both Native People and the Jewish community when Christians use the term in conversation or discourse. We all assume that there is only one Old Testament, just as Christians assert that there is only one New Testament. Challenging that assumption makes people nervous. To use the term *Old Testament* conventionally seems to question the validity of the traditional canon.

It also opens a closetful of theological and doctrinal issues. Can there be more than one "Old Testament"? If so, then what is the relationship between them? What is their relationship to the "New Testament"? Does one supplant the other? Where is the final claim on truth? Can the Christ be said to fulfill other Old Testaments? Wouldn't that be heresy at best and syncretism at worst? I doubt that I will be able to answer all of these questions here, anymore than I may be able to reassure all concerned that the Old Testament of Native America is a valid idea. Still, I think there are some basic points that may prove to be helpful.

First, my own awareness of a Native American Old Testament began growing while I was sitting in an introductory Old Testament class during my first year of seminary. The professor described what was unique about the religious worldview of ancient Israel. He said that Israel, unlike its neighbors, had a special understanding of the relationship between God and humanity. This was the covenant between a single God and a particular People. It involved the promise of a homeland. It was sustained by the personal involvement of God in history. It was communicated through the prophets and the law. It made Israel a nation. It brought them together as a People.

It was the most simple, important understanding of the Old Testament that we share as Christians. And yet, during that lecture, I couldn't help but make a list of comparisons in my mind. Each time the professor mentioned some aspect of the Old Testament story that was "unique" to early Israel, I was reminded of my own Tradition and People. To help you understand what I mean, I include the basic elements of that list here in abbreviated form:

God is one.

God created all that exists.

God is a God of human history.

God is a God of all time and space.

God is a God of all People.

God establishes a covenant relationship with the People.

God gives the People a "promised land."

The People are stewards of this land for God.

God gives the People a Law or way of life.

The People worship God in sacred spaces.

God raises up prophets and charismatic leaders.

God speaks through dreams and visions.

The People maintain a seasonal cycle of worship.

The People believe God will deliver them from their suffering.

God can become incarnate on earth.

These points highlight the fact that the religious worldviews of ancient Israel and ancient Native America have much in common. This is not to say that their understandings were identical. There are many variations on the theme not only between the two communities, but within them as well. What is striking, however, is that for many key concepts the two traditions run parallel. Like Israel, Native America believed in the oneness of God; it saw God as the Creator of all existence; it knew that God was active and alive in the history of humanity; it remembered that the land had been given to the people in trust from God. Native People accepted the revelation from God as it was given to them through prophets and charismatic leaders; they recognized sacred ground and holy places in their worship; they maintained a seasonal liturgical calendar; they had a highly developed belief in the incarnational presence of God and expected that presence to be revealed in times of strife or disaster. Is it strange, therefore, that Native Americans would consider themselves to be in a covenant relationship to their Creator or that they would think of themselves as a People "chosen" by God? Take the names which the People used for themselves in their own languages and you get a clear sense of this: in the tribal languages, the many nations of Native America announced their identity as "The People" or "The Human Beings." Moreover, they tied this identity to the land given to them by God. It was this land-based covenant that gave them their identity as "The People," as the community special to a loving God.

Comparisons, of course, and especially sketchy ones, don't "prove" any claim to an Old Testament for Native America. I don't intend for them to. Their function is only to illustrate the depth of the Native Tradition itself. Talking about an Old Testament which emerges from the genius of Native America is not a wild leap into the unknown. There are sound theological reasons for taking the Native heritage seriously. It embodies the collective memory of an encounter with God that should cause any theologian to stop and think. As with Israel, this memory was transmitted through all of those channels that make up any Old Testament—through stories, histories, poetry, music, sacraments, liturgies, prophecies, proverbs, visions, and laws. The mighty acts of God in North America were witnessed and remembered. They were interpreted and passed on. Taken all together, they constitute an original, unique, and profound covenant between God and humanity.

If this is true then we are confronted with a problem. Suppose that we do allow Native People to claim an "Old Testament" status for their Tradition. Then what do we do with *the* Old Testament? What is the relationship between the two? What is the relationship to the "New" Testament?

An immediate answer is that we will have to be more concise when we speak of the original covenant with ancient Israel. We won't be able to use that word *the* in quite the same way. As Christians, we're going to have to make some elbow room at the table for other "old testaments." Not only from Native America, but from Africa, Asia, and Latin America as well. That's another door opening up in Christianity, and I doubt that anyone is going to be able to close it again. The fact is, Christians must permit the same right for other peoples that they have claimed for themselves. God was as present among the tribes of Africa as God was present among the tribes of America, as God was present among the tribes of Israel. Consequently, we must be cautious about saying that God was "unique" to any one people; God was in a special relationship to different tribes or in a particular relationship with them, but never in an exclusive relationship that shut out the rest of humanity.

This understanding broadens our dialogue about the connections between old testaments. It allows us to say that while there was nothing "unique" about God's relationship to either Native America or ancient Israel, there are elements to both that were special or particular. Obviously, for Christians, the concern focuses on christology. As a theologian of Native America, I can feel comfortable (not to mention orthodox) in saying that it was into the Old Testament People of Israel that God chose to become incarnate. Consequently, the story of this community becomes of primary importance to me. I need to honor, as well as understand, the Old Testament of Israel as the traditional culture into which God came as a person. In this way, the Old Testament of the Hebrew People remains central to my faith as a Christian and vital to my reading of the Christian scriptures.

At the same time, I can stand on my own Old Testament Tradition and let it speak to me just as clearly about the person, nature, and purpose of the Christ. I maintain that this Christ fulfills both Old Testaments. In the Pauline sense, I can assert that while as a man Jesus was a Jew, as the risen Christ, he is a Navajo. Or a Kiowa. Or a Choctaw. Or any other tribe. The Christ does not violate my own Old Testament. The coming of the Christ does not erase the memory banks of Native America or force me to throw away centuries of God's revealing acts among my People. But let me be careful about this. I am not glossing over the Old Testament of Native America with the Western whitewash of a theology that gives out a few quick platitudes about the "Christ of all cultures." When I speak of a fulfillment of Native America's Old Testament, I mean just that—a Christ that emerges from within the Native Tradition itself; that speaks of, by, and for that Tradition; that participates in that Tradition; that lives in that Tradition. Grounded in the Old Testament of Native America, it is the right of Native People to claim fulfillment of Christ in their own way and in their own language. I am not looking simply to paint the statues brown and keep the Western cultural prejudices intact. I am announcing the privilege of my own People to interpret the Christian canon in the light of Israel's experience, but also in the light of their own experience. Whether this interpretation is compatible with Western opinions is open for discussion.

The Old Testament of Native America, therefore, does not replace the Old Testament of Israel. It stands beside it. The Native People's claim to truth is not a competition with other traditions. The answer to the question about the relationship between the two Old Testaments is this: they do not cancel one another out (anymore than they are cancelled out by the New Testament); rather they complement each other. I firmly believe that if the Christian faith is ever to take root in the soil of Native America, both testaments will be needed. Native People can read through the New Testament from both perspectives and see the gospel far more clearly for themselves. In turn, the gospel can speak to the Tradition with far more clarity. And here's a critical point: when we talk about the "fulfillment" of the Old Testament by Christ, we are describing the dual role of Christ in both confirming and correcting a People's memory. There was much in the memory of Israel that Jesus confirmed; there was also a great deal that he sought to correct. The same applies to the Old Testament memory of Native America. There is much that the Christ confirms and much that stands corrected. No Old Testament has a monopoly on perfection. The two traditions stand side-by-side under the fulfillment of Christ. As Native People begin to actively use their own Old Testament in reading the Christian scriptures they will find strengths that were missing from the experience of Israel, just as they will find weaknesses that need to be changed.

In the end, the naming of an Old Testament of Native America should not be cause for alarm among any group or People. It is not a threat, but a hope. Our knowledge of God will not be diminished by this act of a People to regain their memory, but enhanced. The testimony of Israel will remain central to all Christians, Western and Native alike. The Tradition of Native People will be as changed by the gospel of Christ as it changes our understanding of that gospel. Native People will discover that they can read and understand both the Old and New Testaments of the Bible with a much clearer vision. Suddenly, they will start to make sense. Not the sense of the West perhaps, the imported versions of truth handed down from a community that fears it has lost its own Old Testament, but the common sense of any People that remembers, that recounts, that reasons, that reveals, and that responds. The "old" and the "new" will merge. They will enter deeply into the Kivas and Lodges of Native America and come back out stronger than we ever dreamed possible.

THE SECOND REFORMATION

In the next century, the Christian church is going to experience a second major reformation. It will be far more powerful than the one we knew in sixteenth-century Europe. For one thing, it will be international, not just regional. It will cross over not only denominational lines, but also over lines of color, class, gender, and age. It will be more important than the last reformation because it will change the way people think and feel about themselves. While the West will participate in this reformation, it will not play a dominant role. The leaders of the coming reformation will be women.

They will be from Africa, Asia, Latin America, and Native America. They are being born right now.

One of the guiding theologies of the second reformation will be the Christian theology of Native America. The emergence of that theology is already taking place, although not too many people have noticed. In the centers of Western religious power, the revolution occurring in Native America is far too distant and obscure to be disturbing. It only shows up occasionally, for example, at meetings to discuss "Indian ministries," at conferences on racism or spirituality, and in books like this one.

The Native People's Christian theology is being overlooked, because it is being born in silence. That silence is so strong, so pervasive, so smothering that even the shout of a human voice cannot escape it. Not alone. But with each day that passes, more and more voices are beginning to take up the cry. In little backwater reservation chapels. In urban slums. In Arizona and Alaska and Minnesota and California and Manitoba. In sweat lodges and camp meetings. In Christian homes and Traditional homes. In Cheyenne homes and Mohawk homes. In Tribes all across Native America.

Native People are shouting into the silence of Western colonialism. They are shouting their names. They are saying that they are still the Tribe of the Human Beings. The Memory is coming back and with it the voice of a whole nation. Against that kind of power, no silence will long endure.

The midwife to the Native Reformation is the Old Testament of Native America. It is going to give birth to a cry of freedom. Old divisions between the People will be healed. The Traditional and the Christian People will once again become whole. The spiritual center of the Tribe will be regained and the People will unite as a family once more. With their combined strength they will begin to reclaim their rightful Tradition. It will not be "old." It will not be "new." It will be alive—right here and right now.

In the next century, the Old Testament of Native America is going to be fulfilled.

2

LIBERATION
AND CULTURE

WILLIAM BALDRIDGE

Reclaiming Our Histories

■

William Baldridge (Cherokee) is professor of pastoral ministries and cross-cultural theology at Central Baptist Theological Seminary in Kansas City, Kansas. As an ordained American Baptist minister and the first American Indian to be certified as a clinical pastoral education (CPE) supervisor, he served as chaplain and CPE supervisor at several midwestern hospitals before pursuing an academic career. Baldridge wrote this essay for *New Visions for the Americas* (Fortress, 1993), an anthology on the relationship between religion and social change. Like Steve Charleston, he believes that native Christians have an important role to play in the future of the Christian church. He analyzes the legacy of "colonial Christianity" as it affects both native and non-native participants in the missionization process, and he identifies the need to reaffirm the native spiritual heritage as the first step in the struggle for religious self-determination. Baldridge calls for a spirituality of sacrifice and personal transformation in the search for liberating conceptions of religious faith and practice.

In the middle of one of Jesus' sermons in Capernaum, Mark's Gospel relates, four people battered a hole through the roof of Jesus' home and lowered a paralytic into the crowded room. I wonder if Jesus had to stop talking when the banging and busting started, or if he just talked louder while the dust and chunks of roof began to rain down on his head. I wonder what the disciples were doing while all this was happening. Ever vigilant to keep the children away from Jesus, what were they doing while strangers were dismantling his family's house? I would have thought that somebody around there, perhaps old Joseph, who presumably was going to have to do the reroofing, or impetuous Peter, or just anybody who wanted to hear Jesus, would have been up on that roof pronto.

Anyway, these men made a hole in the roof big enough to lower a man through. What they did, so pleased Jesus that he began to bait the scribes, who with all the dust flying must have looked like coal miners at the end of a double shift. Without a word to the demolition crew, Jesus looked down and forgave the paralytic. Taking the bait, the scribes questioned the right of Jesus to forgive sins: "It is blasphemy. Who can forgive sins but God alone?"

Jesus boldly reinforced the terms of their challenge: "Which is easier, to say, 'Your sins are forgiven,' or to say, 'Get up and take care of yourself?'" In other words, the authority to forgive sin rests on the authority to define sin. Then, to demonstrate that he had the authority to do both, Jesus defined the man's sin by prescribing its cure, "Get up and take care of yourself." Called to live out his potential, the man got up and walked, presumably at a speed fast enough to keep ahead of the four men who had been carrying him.

From a Native American's perspective, one way to describe the spiritual significance of 1492 is to realize that for the last half-millennium Columbus and his spiritual children have usurped the role of God and imposed their definitions of reality onto this continent. People now go through life believing that trees went unidentified until Europeans came to name them, that places could not be distinguished and directions could not be given until Europeans arrived to designate one place New York and another Los Angeles. People in the United States accept as self-evident that this continent could not produce food until row cropping was introduced, that water was not pure before filtration plants were introduced, and that conservation is a concept introduced by the U.S. Forestry Service. It is believed without question that this land was godless until the arrival of Christianity.

For Native Americans, perhaps the most pervasive result of colonialism is that we cannot even begin a conversation without referencing our words to definitions imposed or rooted in 1492. The arrival of Columbus marks the beginning of colonial hubris in America, a pride so severe that it must answer the charge of blasphemy.

COLONIAL CHRISTIANITY

A central agent in the colonization of this hemisphere has been the C church. Whatever the church likes to believe its intentions were o making us the object of its missionary endeavors, history shows the missionary system to be colonialism in the name of Christ. The foundation of colonial Christianity rests on its power to monopolize definitions: who is godless, godly, and most godly, all stemming from Christianity's definition of the essential nature of God. When Christians confuse their confessions of faith with absolute knowledge of reality, they invite a challenge of hubris. When Christians confuse the limitations of their humanity with the nature of God, they invite a challenge of blasphemy. Who can claim absolute knowledge of reality but God alone?

Native Americans have not been passive toward Christian colonialism. Today's generation of Native Americans, like the generations that preceded us and those to follow, are bound by the spiritual power of freedom and dignity, gifts from our Creator. We are often dismissed as trying to change the past or trying to return to the past. Having our intelligence questioned is a familiar experience. But being underestimated is one of our most effective and constant weapons. We are not denying history or the weight of the forces pushing us down. We are also not willing to forsake our spiritual birthright as children of God. Colonial Christian definitions to the contrary, we will not label our ancestors nor teach our children that they are spiritually illegitimate. So, as well as resisting we are retrenching, reaching down, down to the bedrock of our continent, down where our spiritual vitality is grounded. Native people's thoughts need not be determined by the definitions of the colonizer if they know who they are and where they stand, if their identity is anchored in bedrock. We are the embodiment of this hemisphere. God made us and placed us here.

Identifying and attacking the enemy is a time-honored means to gain respect and admiration within one's community. As a Native American Christian I have done my warring with the missionaries. They are a target as easy to hit as dirt and just as difficult to eliminate. I am not making claims to be a seasoned veteran missionary fighter, but I do know the taste of battle. In my first firefights I joined those presenting a more balanced picture of the Christian missionary work. Many of the missionaries were people of good faith who sacrificially brought us the gospel of Christ. I was raised on the praise and publicity generated by the churches concerning these people.

On the other hand, many missionaries served as federal agents and in that role negotiated treaties which left us no land. Most missionaries taught us to hate anything Native American and that of necessity included hating our friends, our families, and ourselves. Most refused to speak to us in any language but their own. The missionaries functioned and continue to function as "Christ-bearing colonizers." If it were otherwise the missionaries would have come, shared the gospel, and left. We know, of course, that they stayed, and they continue to stay, and they continue to insist that we submit to them and their definitions. The vast majority of Native people have experienced the missionary system as racist and colonial, and our most prevalent response has been passive resistance: A very small percentage of Native Americans are practicing Christians.

I realize that such language makes some people anxious and others quite indignant. If Native American Christians do not use colonial formulas for confessing Christ such people claim that we are not "real Christians," they believe that we are questioning the ability of these formulas to satisfy *their* spiritual needs, and they bristle at being defined as "Christ-bearing colonizers" when they "were only trying to help." Still, the list of injuries to hurl back at the missionaries is long, yet it remains essentially unknown outside of Indian communities. I continue to be impressed by the number of people, active in the life of their various denominations, who are shocked to hear about the realities of current mission programs to Native Americans and who assumed that "we stopped doing missions like that a hundred years ago."

One of the spin-offs of the quincentennial celebration of the European invasion of this hemisphere was a proliferation of information, produced by non-Indian historians, concerning the church's role in colonialism. When whites turn on themselves with their technological expertise—graduate degrees, computers, data banks, ethno-histories, and such—a defiant arrow from an Indian becomes a flame amidst laser beams. Furthermore, as the new official history continues to roll off the press, some of us warriors are realizing that the power of our arrows comes not so much from the historical evidence as it does from the anecdotal experience we own. We Indians lived the missionary history, we continue to live this history, and the power of our stories cannot be matched by "the cold hard facts." It is encouraging to watch the academic historians revisit history, and bring a greater degree of balance to the subject. At the same time, it is discouraging to remember that such "objectivity" typically comes at a point in a political struggle when the issues have been decided and the victors, that is, the ones writing the history, can afford to admit that "nobody is perfect" without any real threat to their power base.

In the 500-year war against Christian colonialism we have had our successes. If on no more than a few occasions of hit-and-run skirmishes, we have had our moments. For me, the sense of camaraderie with brothers and sisters has become a lasting satisfaction. Yet the spoils of our small victories have faded into an ironic lesson: the very act of fighting the missionary system concedes too much to colonialism. It concedes too much because it accepts the premise that our dignity must be granted to us rather than be recognized in us. It accepts the premise that God loves one people more than God loves all people. It accepts the premise that a God of justice would condemn a people to hell because of where they were born and when they were born. Fighting missionaries has taught me that the end of the missionary system begins with a change of heart, my heart, not the heart of the missionary nor the heart of the institutions that commission missionaries. Fighting the oppression of the missionary system is a struggle for justice that unavoidably becomes a struggle for power. Power lies at the core of Christian colonialism. Refusing the terms of the struggle is an essential first step in regaining the spiritual perspective of Native America.

REAFFIRMING OUR SPIRITUAL HERITAGE

Before the Europeans came the Cherokee were taught the following story as spiritual truth. The Daughter of God loved her children. Loving them, she provided food so that they never knew hunger. The day came when her children realized that their mother fed them without labor; it was miraculous. Human nature being what it is, the children developed an insistent need to know the source of the food that sustained them. When their mother retreated to the private place from which she brought them food, they followed her and from their hiding place they witnessed the miracle that gave them life. The food came from their mother's body. "She is a witch!" they whispered to each other. "She is evil! We must kill her! Kill her!" Their mother knew their thoughts and said to them, "When you kill me, take my body and place it in the ground. I will rise from the dead and you will be given life and never hunger." So the children killed their mother and placed her in the ground and in the fullness of time, corn, the source of bread for the Cherokee, rose from the grave.

When the Christians came we were taught a second story as spiritual truth. The Son of God loved his brothers and sisters. Loving them, he provided food for them so that they never knew hunger. On one occasion he fed a great multitude with five loaves and two fish; it was miraculous. Human nature being what it is, his brothers and sisters developed an insistent need to know the source of the food that sustained them. When they questioned him he responded, "I am the living bread that came down from heaven. Whoever eats of this bread will live forever; and the bread that I will give for the life of the world is my flesh" (John 6:51). One day his brothers and sisters brought to him a man who was blind and mute and he cured him. His brothers and sisters said, "It is only by Beelzebul, the rule of the demons, that this fellow casts out the demons." The Son of God knew what they were thinking (Matt. 12:22–25). After that the Son of God began to show his brothers and sisters that he must be killed and on the third day be raised (Matt. 16:21). So, in time, his brothers and sisters killed him and placed him in the ground, and on the third day the bread of life rose from the grave.

Having reaffirmed our spiritual heritage, some of us who are both Native American and Christians have lost the ability to distinguish "us" from "them." When we hear again the words of the Daughter of God and the Son of God we look in vain for the children either one would not feed. We cannot identify the injured brother or sister either one would pass by on the other side of the road. When we recall how we have abused those whom the Creator has sent to us, we find ourselves looking with less hate and more compassion toward those who have abused us.

THE SACRIFICIAL NATURE OF THE SPIRITUAL LIFE

How could we sing the Lord's song in a foreign land?
If I forget you, O Jerusalem, let my right hand wither!
Let my tongue cling to the roof of my mouth, if I do not remember you,
if I do not set Jerusalem above my highest joy. (Psalm 137)

As a Native American Christian, I find it helpful to remember the experience of the people of Jerusalem during their exile in Babylon. The people had so identified God with the place of their origin and with the shape of their temple they could not recognize that God was present in all times and in all places. None of us can know God directly. All of us experience God as through a darkened glass. The color, the shape, and the size of that glass is always a mirror of our particular culture and our particular time and place. Having never seen a ship, some of us Native people believed that the first ones we saw were floating islands. Having never seen a man riding a horse, some of us believed horse and rider were one entity. Having never experienced God except through their own cultures, those who came in ships believed that God had only been revealed to them and that God must be brought to this place. We who first mistook the Daughter of God for a witch must not be too eager to condemn European Christians who did the same. Somehow, Native Americans must find the means to forgive our white brothers and sisters and accept that they too did not know what they were doing.

Whether one eats only at the table of the Corn Mother or only at the table of the Son of Man, both are compelled to come to terms with the sacrificial nature of the spiritual life. Those who refuse to give up all that they have cannot move from death into life. Those who hoard their spiritual life lose it and are left with nothing but religion. Those who refuse to die become the agents of death.

After five hundred years of battle, Native American people are in danger of forsaking the lesson of the Corn Mother and of hoarding her seeds. The lesson—to plant in faith—is being lost in the shouts of our fears and anger. When the Europeans first came we met them and freely shared. We shared because we knew that what we had did not belong to us; it was a gift from our Mother. When the Europeans ignored the spiritual basis of life on this continent and made claims that as creatures they could own the creation, we refused to cooperate with their witchery. Now we are in danger of adopting the fear that produced their greed.

More and more, Native people protest that non-Indians are stealing the only thing we have left: our spiritual lessons. My Native brothers and sisters, spiritual lessons cannot be owned any more than the source of those lessons can be owned. All that we have has been given to us. If we have wisdom about the waters of this land it is because the waters have taught us. If we have wisdom about the rocks and trees it is because the rocks and trees have spoken to us. If we have wisdom about the rhythms of this land it is because the seasons have sung to us. We do not own the voice of the wind, we do not own the light at dawn, we do not own the colors of the grasses, we do not own a single thing. All that we have of value has been given to us by God.

For five hundred years the missionaries have been trying to save us. Look at the water, look at the sky, look at all the hungry children, look at all the machines of war. Brothers and sisters, it is now time for us to save the missionaries; it is time for us to return to sharing.

The way of sharing is sacrifice. The lesson of both the Daughter of God and the Son of God is sacrifice. Not only must the evil be sacrificed, but the good must also be sacrificed. Sacrificing the gains of evil is but the first step toward following the Corn Mother or the Christ. The temptations of evil came to Christ early in his life and were not difficult for him to reject. It was the temptation to hold on to the good that caused his sweat to become like great drops of blood. He had fed the hungry, healed the sick, raised the dead! So much good called to him to reject the final sacrifice. As the old ones have taught us, good, not evil, is the most powerful enemy of the beast. That is also the lesson of Jesus in Gethsemane.

It is good and just to struggle for the right to practice Christianity within the context of our Native cultures, and we will struggle on. Affirming sweat lodges as appropriate places for Christian prayers is good and just, and we will continue to make our claims. The use of Native symbolism in Christian churches is good and just, and we will continue to bring them into our sanctuaries. The insistence that Native Americans do not have to acculturate before they can become Christians is good and just, and we will not abandon our cultures.

As Native people, we have as much right to our heritage as any other people. As Native American Christians, we have a right, as well as an obligation, to express the coming of Christ in a manner that is meaningful within our cultures, and that is what we will do. A unique Native American expression of Christianity, a Native American theology, is a worthy, a good, and a just goal, and we will continue to develop it. Evangelical theology, liberal theology, black theology, feminist theology, liberation theology, why not Native American theology? Still, as desirable and just as all these agendas are, they fail to reach the ultimate goal of a gospel that proclaims neither Jew nor Greek, male nor female, European nor Native American.

Justice, when defined as "our getting ours as you have yours," does not rise above the level of "an eye for an eye." In light of our colonial history, claiming the moral high ground tempts us to the hubris of "owning" our own version of the gospel and of claiming that our definitions are the only ones that belong here. But there are greater spiritual needs than getting a higher place within the ecclesiastical hierarchy or getting a piece of the theological power pie. Life on this planet cannot survive if our, and your, and their, and everyone's spiritual agenda does not move beyond colonialism, nationalism, racism, tribalism, sectarianism, and denominationalism. The form of Christianity that has served the needs of separation and has promoted a disdain of the earth is now a deadly anachronism. In this light, for the follower of Christ justice as law or justice as "equal but separate" are continuations of colonial values, and both must be transcended by love.

Today, Christianity stands in need of the courage to fulfill the work of Christ. We stand in need of the courage to follow him into self-sacrifice. The fulfillment of Christianity will come, indeed it is coming, through the sacrifice of colonialism for hospitality, through the sacrifice of imperialism for invitation, the sacrifice of power for service, the sacrifice of fear for fellowship, the sacrifice of isolation from the world for the joy of living at peace with mother earth. Through self-sacrifice, Christianity can fulfill the promise of Christ's birth: glory to God, peace on earth, good will throughout creation.

TRANSFORMING IMAGES OF GOD

We know that Almighty God, the Ground of Being, is neither defined nor confined by the limits of our imagination. Still, all but the mystics are forced to pray to the Great Mystery through familiar associations. The Hebrew laws forbidding graven images address the tendency to confuse an image with the unimaginable and thus to slip into material idolatry. The laws forbidding even the writing or speaking a name for God address the tendency to slip into conceptional idolatry, "Father" has become a conceptional idol for colonial Christians. "Father" has, to this point, defined the limits of the Christian understanding of God.

But the term has never defined God. The colonial experience of this continent is a witness that "Father God" is not only inadequate but destructive. The god of military conformity, violence, and brutality thundering from the pulpit has suffered neither a witch to live nor a country the size of Grenada to threaten the national insecurity. God is not confined to "Father," but confining our concept of God to "Father" distorts, skews, and throws out of balance our relationship with God and the fullness of God's creation. For example, consider this early colonial representation of "Father God":

> The God that holds you over the Pit of Hell, much as one holds a Spider
> or some loathsome Insect over the Fire, abhors you, and is dreadfully

provoked; his Wrath towards you burns like Fire; he looks upon you as Worthy of nothing else but to be cast into the Fire; he is of purer Eyes than to bear to have you in his Sight; you are Ten Thousand Times so abominable in his Eyes as the most hateful venomous Serpent is in ours. . . . "[1]

The time has come for the sacrifice of seeing God as only Father for a concept that allows the next generation of children to live. The time has come for the emerging Christian experience of God as Father and Mother. Transformation of our images from God the Father to God our Parent(s) will not destroy Christianity but fulfill it. Mother God is not an alternative to Father God; she is an expansion of our possibility to experience God. God as Father will not be lost by including the experience of God as Mother. Father images of God will still tend to discipline, order, history, progress, judgment, duty, transcendence, and all that the masculine has to offer. Mother images of God will make more available God's acceptance, creativity, eternity, grace, enduring nurture, immediacy, and all that the feminine has to offer.

We who are Native American can contribute to Christianity's transformation and fulfillment by sharing our experience of God as both Mother and Father. Even so, we Native Americans do not "own" the experience of God as Parent(s), for many other peoples join in the sharing. In fact, God as Mother as well as Father is not something that colonial Christians do not know; they just do not have images or the security that would allow them comfortable familiarity.

Within the Native American Christian community our history must be owned, our pain must be acknowledged, the present must be realized, and a future for our children must determine how we spend our energy. Our anger must be sacrificed to love as we reaffirm our spiritual heritage and offer it up for the benefit of all our relations. I do not suggest that this will be an easy task, but I am suggesting that our spiritual heritage, as well as our spiritual health, demand it.

The challenge for the larger Christian community is one that is impossible to meet without the grace of God. It is a call to sacrifice what has been good for what can be better. It is a call to sacrifice the good that has allowed us to come to this time and place along the paths of "us" and "them." It is a call to follow Christ to the cross, placing our faith in the power of God to raise us from the dead. The colonial history of the church contains much pain, suffering, and harm. As a community, the body of Christ has never attained the level of sacrifice expressed through the spirit of Christ. The saving news is that we do not have to make the way; we must, however, be willing to follow the way. The path has been well marked whereby we, too, can pass from death into life. The time and the place have come for us to follow the Christ, to share sacrificially, so that all our children might live.

Come spring rains. Come new life. Come Lord Jesus.

NOTES

1. Cotton Mather, *On Witchcraft, Being the Wonders of the Invisible World* (1693, reprint, Mount Vernon, NY: Peter Pauper Press, 1950), 22. See also C. Mather, *Another tongue brought in to confess the great Saviour of the world or, some communication of Christianity, put into a tongue among the Iroquois Indians, in America. And put into the hands of the English and the Dutch traders: to accommodate the great intention of communicating the Christian religion, unto the savages among whom they may find anything of this language to be intelligible* (Boston: Printed by B. Green, 1907).

7

ROBERT ALLEN WARRIOR

CANAANITES, COWBOYS, AND INDIANS
DELIVERANCE, CONQUEST, AND
LIBERATION THEOLOGY TODAY

Robert Warrior (Osage) is assistant professor of English at Stanford University. He is the author of *Tribal Secrets: Recovering American Indian Intellectual Traditions* (University of Minnesota, 1995) and numerous articles, interviews, essays and reviews. He has also worked as a freelance journalist and as a consultant on several educational projects. This influential essay was originally published in the religious journal *Christianity and Crisis*. Warrior points out that the biblical paradigm of liberation used by most liberation theologies is based on an uncritical reading of the Exodus narrative, an interpretation that overlooks the experience of the indigenous Canaanites, and he argues that native people may need to look elsewhere for a compelling and meaningful vision of liberation. Warrior's essay has circulated widely and has provoked a variety of responses, including William Baldridge's letter to the editor. Baldridge answers Warrior's challenge by suggesting another perspective on the historical and religious significance of the Canaanites. Jace Weaver (Cherokee) also responded to Warrior's essay, in a short piece published several years later in *Christianity and Crisis*, in which he outlines an alternative biblical paradigm for the liberation of indigenous peoples. Weaver is a doctoral candidate at Union Theological Seminary in New York City and an accomplished author, and he is active in the Native American International Caucus of the United Methodist Church.

Native American Theology of Liberation has a nice ring to it. Politically active Christians in the U.S. have been bandying about the idea of such a theology for several years now, encouraging Indians to develop it. There are theologies of liberation for African Americans, Hispanic Americans, women, Asian Americans, even Jews. Why not Native Americans? Christians recognize that American injustice on this continent began nearly 500 years ago with the oppression of its indigenous people and that justice for American Indians is a fundamental part of broader social struggle. The churches' complicity in much of the violence perpetrated on Indians makes this realization even clearer. So, there are a lot of well-intentioned Christians looking for some way to include Native Americans in their political action.

For Native Americans involved in political struggle, the participation of church people is often an attractive proposition. Churches have financial, political, and institutional resources that many Indian activists would dearly love to have at their disposal. Since American Indians have a relatively small population base and few financial resources, assistance from churches can be of great help in gaining the attention of the public, the media, and the government.

It sounds like the perfect marriage—Christians with the desire to include Native Americans in their struggle for justice and Indian activists in need of resources and support from non-Indians. Well, speaking as the product of a marriage between an Indian and a white, I can tell you that it is not as easy as it sounds. The inclusion of Native Americans in Christian political praxis is difficult—even dangerous. Christians have a different way of going about the struggle for justice than most Native Americans: different models of leadership, different ways of making decisions, different ways of viewing the relationship between politics and religion. These differences have gone all but unnoticed in the history of church involvement in American Indian affairs. Liberals and conservatives alike have too often surveyed the conditions of Native Americans and decided to come to the rescue, always using *their* methods, *their* ideas, and *their* programs. The idea that Indians might know best how to address their own problems is seemingly lost on these well-meaning folks.

Still, the time does seem ripe to find a new way for Indians and Christians (and Native American Christians) to be partners in the struggle against injustice and economic and racial oppression. This is a new era for both the church and for Native Americans. Christians are breaking away from their liberal moorings and looking for more effective means of social and political engagement. Indians, in this era of "self-determination," have verified for themselves and the government that they are the people best able to address Indian problems as long as they are given the necessary resources and if they can hold the U.S. government accountable to the policy. But an enormous stumbling block immediately presents itself. Most of the liberation theologies that have emerged in the last twenty years are preoccupied with the Exodus story, using it as the fundamental model for liberation. I believe that the story of the Exodus is an inappropriate way for Native Americans to think about liberation.

No doubt, the story is one that has inspired many people in many contexts to struggle against injustice. Israel, in the Exile, then Diaspora, would remember the story and be reminded of God's faithfulness. Enslaved African Americans, given Bibles to read by their masters and mistresses, would begin at the beginning of the book and find in the pages of the Pentateuch a god who was obviously on their side, even if that god was the god of their oppressors. People in Latin American base communities read the story and have been inspired to struggle against injustice. The Exodus, with its picture of a god who takes the side of the oppressed and powerless, has been a beacon of hope for many in despair.

GOD THE CONQUEROR

Yet, the liberationist picture of Yahweh is not complete. A delivered people is not a free people, nor is it a nation. People who have survived the nightmare of subjugation dream of escape. Once the victims have been delivered, they seek a new dream, a new goal, usually a place of safety away from the oppressors, a place that can be defended against future subjugation. Israel's new dream became the land of Canaan. And Yahweh was still with them: Yahweh promised to go before the people and give them Canaan, with its flowing milk and honey. The land, Yahweh decided, belonged to these former slaves from Egypt and Yahweh planned on giving it to them—using the same power used against the enslaving Egyptians to defeat the indigenous inhabitants of Canaan. Yahweh the deliverer became Yahweh the conqueror.

The obvious characters in the story for Native Americans to identify with are the Canaanites, the people who already lived in the promised land. As a member of the Osage Nation of American Indians who stands in solidarity with other tribal people around the world, I read the Exodus stories with Canaanite eyes. And, it is the Canaanite side of the story that has been overlooked by those seeking to articulate theologies of liberation. Especially ignored are those parts of the story that describe Yahweh's command to mercilessly annihilate the indigenous population.

To be sure, most scholars, of a variety of political and theological stripes, agree that the actual events of Israel's early history are much different than what was commanded in the narrative. The Canaanites were not systematically annihilated, nor were they completely driven from the land. In fact, they made up, to a large extent, the people of the new nation of Israel. Perhaps it was a process of gradual immigration of people from many places and religions who came together to form a new nation. Or maybe, as Norman Gottwald and others have argued, the peasants of Canaan revolted against their feudal masters, a revolt instigated and aided by a vanguard of escaped slaves from Egypt who believed in the liberating god, Yahweh. Whatever happened, scholars agree that the people of Canaan had a lot to do with it.

Nonetheless, scholarly agreement should not allow us to breathe a sigh of relief. For, historical knowledge does not change the status of the indigenes in the *narrative* and the theology that grows out of it. The research of Old Testament scholars, however much it provides an answer to the historical question—the contribution of the indigenous people of Canaan to the formation and emergence of Israel as a nation—does not resolve the narrative problem. People who read the narratives read them as they are, not as scholars and experts would *like* them to be read and interpreted. History is no longer with us. The narrative remains.

Though the Exodus and Conquest stories are familiar to most readers, I want to highlight some sections that are commonly ignored. The covenant begins when Yahweh comes to Abram saying, "Know of a surety that your descendants will be sojourners in a land that is not theirs, and they will be slaves there, and they will be oppressed for four hundred years; but I will bring judgment on the nation they serve and they shall come out" (Genesis 15:13,14). Then, Yahweh adds: "To your descendants I give this land, the land of the Kenites, the Kenizzites, the Kadmonites, the Hittites, the Perizzites, the Rephaim, the Amorites, the Canaanites, and the Jebusites" (15:18–21). The next important moment is the commissioning of Moses. Yahweh says to him, "I promise I will bring you out of the affliction of Egypt, to the land of the Canaanites, the Hittites, the Amorites, the Perizzites, the Hivites, and the Jebusites, a land flowing with milk and honey" (Exodus 3:17). The covenant, in other words, has two parts: deliverance and conquest.

After the people have escaped and are headed to the promised land, the covenant is made more complicated, but it still has two parts. If the delivered people remain faithful to Yahweh, they will be blessed in the land Yahweh will conquer for them (Exodus 20–23 and Deuteronomy 7–9). The god who delivered Israel from slavery will lead the people into the land and keep them there as long as they live up to the terms of the covenant. "You shall not wrong a stranger or oppress him [sic], for you were strangers in the land of Egypt. You shall not afflict any widow or orphan. If you do afflict them, and they cry out to me, I will surely hear their cry; and my wrath will burn, and I will kill you with the sword, and your wives shall become widows and your children fatherless" (Exodus 22:21).

WHOSE NARRATIVE?

Israel's reward for keeping Yahweh's commandments—for building a society where the evils done to them have no place—is the continuation of life in the land. But one of the most important of Yahweh's commands is the prohibition on social relations with Canaanites or participation in their religion. "I will deliver the inhabitants of the land into your hand, and you shall drive them out before you. You shall make no covenant with them or with their gods. They shall not dwell in your land, lest they make you sin against me; for if you serve their gods it will surely be a snare to you" (Exodus 23:31b-33).

In fact, the indigenes are to be destroyed. "When the Lord your God brings you into the land which you are entering to take possession of it, and clears away many nations before you, the Hittites, the Girgashites, the Amorites, the Canaanites, the Perizzites, the Hivites, and the Jebusites, seven nations greater and mightier than yourselves, and when the Lord your God gives them over to you and you defeat them; then you must utterly destroy them; you shall make no covenant with them, and show no mercy to them" (Deuteronomy 7:1,2). These words are spoken to the people of Israel as they are preparing to go into Canaan. The promises made to Abraham and Moses are ready to be fulfilled. All that remains is for the people to enter into the land and dispossess those who already live there.

Joshua gives an account of the conquest. After ten chapters of stories about Israel's successes and failures to obey Yahweh's commands, the writer states, "So Joshua defeated the whole land, the hill country and the Negeb and the lowland and the slopes, and all their kings, he left none remaining, but utterly destroyed all that breathed, as the Lord God of Israel commanded." In Judges, the writer disagrees with this account of what happened, but the Canaanites are held in no higher esteem. The angel of the Lord says, "I will not drive out [the indigenous people] before you; but they shall become adversaries to you, and their gods shall be a snare to you."

Thus, the narrative tells us that the Canaanites have status only as the people Yahweh removes from the land in order to bring the chosen people in. They are not to be trusted, nor are they to be allowed to enter into social relationships with the people of Israel. They are wicked, and their religion is to be avoided at all costs. The laws put forth regarding strangers and sojourners may have stopped the people of Yahweh from wanton oppression, but presumably only after the land was safely in the hands of Israel. The covenant of Yahweh depends on this.

The Exodus narrative is where discussion about Christian involvement in Native American activism must begin. It is these stories of deliverance and conquest that are ready to be picked up and believed by anyone wondering what to do about the people who already live in their promised land. They provide an example of what can happen when powerless people come to power. Historical scholarship may tell a different story; but even if the annihilation did not take place, the narratives tell what happened to those indigenous people who put their hope and faith in ideas and gods that were foreign to their culture. The Canaanites trusted in the god of outsiders and their story of oppression and exploitation was lost. Interreligious praxis became betrayal and the surviving narrative tells us nothing about it.

Confronting the conquest stories as a narrative rather than a historical problem is especially important given the tenor of contemporary theology and criticism. After 200 years of preoccupation with historical questions, scholars and theologians across a broad spectrum of political and ideological positions have recognized the function of narrative in the development of religious communities. Along with the work of U.S. scholars like Brevard Childs, Stanley Hauerwas, and George Lindbeck, the radical liberation theologies of Latin America are based on empowering believing communities to read scriptural narratives for themselves and make their reading central to theology and political action. The danger is that these communities will read the narratives, not the history behind them.

And, of course, the text itself will never be altered by interpretations of it, though its reception may be. It is part of the canon for both Jews and Christians. It is part of the heritage and thus the consciousness of people in the United States. Whatever dangers we identify in the text and the god represented there will remain as long as the text remains. These dangers only grow as the emphasis upon catechetical (Lindbeck), narrative (Hauerwas), canonical (Childs), and Bible-centered Christian base communities (Gutierrez) grows. The peasants of Solentiname bring a wisdom and experience previously unknown to Christian theology, but I do not see what mechanism guarantees that they—or any other people who seek to be shaped and molded by reading the text—will differentiate between the liberating god and the god of conquest.

IS THERE A SPIRIT?

What is to be done? First, the Canaanites should be at the center of Christian theological reflection and political action. They are the last remaining ignored voice in the text, except perhaps for the land itself. The conquest stories, with all their violence and injustice, must be taken seriously by those who believe in the god of the Old Testament. Commentaries and critical works rarely mention these texts. When they do, they express little concern for the status of the indigenes and their rights as human beings and as nations. The same blindness is evident in theologies that use the Exodus motif as their basis for political action. The leading into the land becomes just one more redemptive moment rather than a violation of innocent peoples' rights to land and self-determination.

Keeping the Canaanites at the center makes it more likely that those who read the Bible will read *all* of it, not just the part that inspires and justifies them. And should anyone be surprised by the brutality, the terror of these texts? It was, after all, a Jewish victim of the Holocaust, Walter Benjamin, who said. "There is no document of civilization which is not at the same time a document of barbarism." People whose theology involves the Bible need to take this insight seriously. It is those who know these texts who must speak the truth about what they contain. It is to those who believe in these texts that the barbarism belongs. It is those who act on the basis of these texts who must take responsibility for the terror and violence they can and have engendered.

Second, we need to be more aware of the way ideas such as those in the conquest narratives have made their way into Americans' consciousness and ideology. And only when we understand this process can those of us who have suffered from it know how to fight back. Many Puritan preachers were fond of referring to Native Americans as Amelkites and Canaanites—in other words, people who, if they would not be converted, were worthy of annihilation. By examining such instances in theological and political writings, in sermons, and elsewhere, we can understand how America's self-image as a "chosen people" has provided a rhetoric to mystify domination.

Finally, we need to decide if we want to accept the model of leadership and social change presented by the entire Exodus story. Is it appropriate to the needs of indigenous people seeking justice and deliverance? If indeed the Canaanites were integral to Israel's early history, the Exodus narratives reflect a situation in which indigenous people put their hope in a god from outside, were liberated from their oppressors, and then saw their story of oppression revised out of the new nation's history of salvation. They were assimilated into another people's identity and the history of their ancestors came to be regarded as suspect and a danger to the safety of Israel. In short, they were betrayed.

Do Native Americans and other indigenous people dare trust the same god in their struggle for justice? I am not asking an easy question and I in no way mean that people who are both Native Americans and Christians cannot work toward justice in the context of their faith in Jesus Christ. Such people have a lot of theological reflection to do, however, to avoid the dangers I have pointed to in the conquest narratives. Christians, whether Native American or not, if they are to be involved, must learn how to participate in the struggle without making their story the whole story. Otherwise the sins of the past will be visited upon us again.

No matter what we do, the conquest narratives will remain. As long as people believe in the Yahweh of deliverance, the world will not be safe from Yahweh the conqueror. But perhaps, if they are true to their struggle, people will be able to achieve what Yahweh's chosen people in the past have not: a society of people delivered from oppression who are not so afraid of becoming victims again that they become oppressors themselves, a society where the original inhabitants can become something other than subjects to be converted to a better way of life or adversaries who provide cannon fodder for a nation's militaristic pride.

With what voice will we, the Canaanites of the world, say, "Let my people go and leave my people alone?" And, with what ears will followers of alien gods who have wooed us (Christians, Jews, Marxists, capitalists), listen to us? The indigenous people of this hemisphere have endured a subjugation now 100 years longer than the sojourn of Israel in Egypt. Is there a god, a spirit, who will hear us and stand with us in the Amazon, Osage County, and Wounded Knee? Is there a god, a spirit, able to move among the pain and anger of Nablus, Gaza, and Soweto? Perhaps. But we, the wretched of the earth, may be well-advised this time not to listen to outsiders with their promises of liberation and deliverance. We will perhaps do better to look elsewhere for our vision of justice, peace, and political sanity—a vision through which we escape not only our oppressors, but our oppression as well. Maybe, for once, we will just have to listen to ourselves, leaving the gods of this continent's real strangers to do battle among themselves.

NATIVE AMERICAN THEOLOGY: A BIBLICAL BASIS
BY WILLIAM BALDRIDGE

Robert Allen Warrior's article precipitated an intellectual and spiritual crisis for me as a Native American Christian. Through the linking and analysis of the Exodus and Conquest narratives he raised a serious challenge not only to those of us who would attempt a Native American Theology of Liberation, but to any Native American who would call him or herself a Christian. Warrior points out that "The obvious characters in the story for Native Americans to identify with are the Canaanites. . . . " He argues that "the Canaanites should be at the center of Christian theological reflection and political action." We need to know the history of how the conquest narratives have merged into Americans' consciousness and ideology. And "we need to decide if we want to accept the model of leadership and social change presented by the entire Exodus story." He answers his questions with the conclusion. "We will perhaps do better to look elsewhere for our vision of justice, peace, and political sanity. . . . "

Warrior's arguments had a powerful impact on me as I could dispute neither his emphasis on the story nor his reading of the story. He convinced me that the most enlightened historical criticism, itself another form of explanation, was ineffectual as a counterbalance to the power of story. If there was to be any more Native American theology coming from me it would be in the form of story.

Having resolved my relationship to story and theology, I found myself still struggling with Warrior's conclusion that we Native Americans should abandon the stories of the Christians and the role available to us through those stories. I was on the verge of joining Warrior's camp, shaking the dust of the history and the present reality of Christianity and Native American people off my feet, when I remembered another Bible story with a Canaanite as a central character. Warrior is right . . . as far as he goes. Truly we Native Americans are the Canaanites of biblical stories, but Warrior drops the story of the Canaanites and Yahweh sooner than I. The story continues as follows.

Many years after the conquest of the Canaanites and their subjugation and scorn by the Children of Israel, the Son of Yahweh comes to live with the Israelites. A Canaanite woman comes to him and begs him to help her daughter. Remembering his Father's words he dismisses the Canaanite with a lesson. "I was sent only to the lost sheep of the house of Israel."

But the woman has a little girl in great pain, and she falls to her knees and again begs Jesus to help her daughter. Jesus will not spare a blessing. "It is not fair to take the children's bread and throw it to the dogs." With these words Jesus refuses even to grant her the dignity of being a human being.

A million people have been killed for talking back in such a situation. The Canaanite mother dares to speak one last time. "Yes, Lord, yet even the dogs eat the crumbs that fall from their master's table."

What happens next is a miracle: The Son of Yahweh is set free. The son of the god of Canaanite oppression repents. Jesus not only changes his mind, he changes his heart. He sees her as a human being and answers her as such. "O woman, great is your faith! Be it done for you as you desire." And her daughter was healed instantly . . . and so, I believe, were the wounds of bitterness in the Canaanite woman.

The story of the Canaanite mother leads me to claim that the Canaanites of this country, the Canaanites of the Christian community, have a foundation for our Christian faith and our theology in the biblical narratives. This foundation is both rooted in our oppression yet moves beyond our oppression. The story tells us that if we Canaanites will live out our faith, we can change the very heart of God. And if we can change the heart of God we can hope to change the hearts of his chosen people, even those who identify themselves as Christians.

Having learned through a story that Jesus will bless us, we Canaanite Native American Christians find a way to affirm our identity. We find a way to follow Jesus: to drink the cup that he drank, to bear the stripes that he bore, to endure the death that he endured. We also find a way to get off our knees and walk like human beings. Through an encounter with Jesus we have been set free. And when the members of the new House of Israel are ready to hear us, we are ready to speak the words that will set them free.

ROBERT ALLEN WARRIOR RESPONDS:

Bill Baldridge's response to my "Canaanites" essay is a welcome one. Many have regarded the essay highly, but largely missed the point. They are glad to read my "perspective" on the Conquest stories and say that different people need different stories (biblical or otherwise) to be motivated to political liberation. In other words, you have your stories and I have mine: you have your perspective and I have mine. My point, however, was more than the assertion that Exodus-centered theologies are not useful to me. Rather, I had hoped to call into question the assumptions about liberation that may be lurking beneath the theologies of people working for lasting, genuine justice. Baldridge seems to have understood this in a profound way.

What I take to be Baldridge's main points of contention with "Canaanites, Cowboys, and Indians" is my own post-Christian position and my failure to take the story into the Christian New Testament. Others have also pointed to the lack of New Testament analysis as a weakness in what I wrote, arguing that the new covenant in Jesus Christ removes the onus of holy-war violence and favoritism of one people at the expense of another from Yahweh the Conqueror. Somehow, they contend, the bad stories and the good ones balance each other out.

In this regard, I think it important to remember the strength of the Hebrew Bible's influence on political theology in the Reformation, the development of apartheid in South Africa, among the Puritans and Spanish *conquistadores*, and present-day liberation theologies, to name a few. If political theologies are going to be more than ideological subjectivism, biblical interpretation must admit the oppression present in even the narratives of the god who seemingly stands with the oppressed. Too many liberation theologians interpret everything in the Hebrew Bible through overly optimistic christological lenses, obscuring the deep and abiding problems of racism, bigotry, and sexism in both Testaments. I was simply reminding everyone that oppressive narratives of conquest, anti-Semitism, sexism, heterosexism, imperialism, and racism remain in the canonized text even if certain Christians or Jews don't agree with them.

Baldridge allows that there might be something wrong with the Christian god—something requiring conversion and repentance. His use of the Canaanite woman's story is interesting, as far as it goes. Indeed, it is my hope that the force of American Indian humanity can do a lot to humanize both the people who oppress and the gods they brought with them across the water.

I think it is important to note that in the story the woman does not become a follower of Jesus. Having received what she desired from Jesus, she walks away and is never mentioned again. Yes, she changes Jesus, but she does not become a disciple. She seeks him out because he has something she needs. She is persistent to the point where he can no longer deny her humanity and the legitimacy of her pain. The question of what happened to her is left open. Perhaps she later joined the church (if indeed she actually existed) or maybe she went back to her people and fought against the colonizing Romans in her own way with her own gods. The importance of the story is not whether she followed, but that without her, on Baldridge's reading, Jesus would have remained a narrow-minded bigot who viewed indigenous people as inhuman.

Isn't this where we American Indians find ourselves? Like the Canaanite woman, we must go begging to the people who colonized us in order to secure the bare minimum of justice. Like her, our healing has become wrapped up in changing the colonizer's mind about our right to be self-determined, legitimate nations of people. Thus we must confront them in strength with our humanity. We have been doing so for 500 years, to little avail. Yet we remain persistent and hope someday to change their minds, or at least their actions.

I am glad to have a fellow traveler in Bill Baldridge to join in the battle, and I respect his choice to follow the god he is trying to convert. But, if we are able to convert the son of the Christian god and his followers, my choice will still be to go home to the drum, the stomp dance, and the sweatlodge.

A BIBLICAL PARADIGM FOR NATIVE LIBERATION
BY JACE WEAVER

Robert Allen Warrior has written that the Indian experience is that of the biblical Canaanites, dispossessed of their homeland and annihilated by a foreign invader. Natives therefore read the Bible with "Canaanite eyes." Warrior's argument takes on added force in the case of my own people, the Cherokees, who were subjected to a genocidal reverse Exodus from a country that was for them, literally, the "the Promised Land."

Warrior goes on to maintain that the story of the Exodus, the paradigm for liberation theology, cannot be severed from the story of the conquest of Canaan and the destruction of the Canaanites. Colonialism and genocide are at the base of the texts themselves. Unless another paradigm can be found and the biblical witness redeemed, no Native Christian theology of liberation can exist.

Such a redemption is possible. A biblical paradigm for Native American/ Canaanite liberation can be found in the account of the daughters of Zelophehad (Numbers 27 and Joshua 17).

In Numbers, just as Moses and Eleazar have completed the census of the Israelites that will determine allocation of land in the Promised Land, Zelophehad's five daughters approach. They say that their father has died in the wilderness, leaving no sons, only daughters. They are worried that because women cannot inherit, they will be deprived of their place when land is allotted. Moses seeks the guidance of God; God says, of course the daughters should have their place when land is allotted. Zelophehad's children inherit his portion.

In the book of Joshua, when Eleazar and Joshua actually carry out the allocation, they forget about Zelophehad's offspring. The daughters step forward again, pointing out that God commanded Moses to allow them to inherit on the same basis as their male kin. Thus reminded, Joshua allots the promised portion to them.

The story illustrates that all, even the most powerless and oppressed of a society, have the right to share equally in the promise of God. It says also that the oppressed must not remain silent or inactive in the face of their oppression: at every turn it is incumbent on them to remind the oppressor of God's promise and to be the heralds of their own salvation. Most important, the story has direct meaning for the story of the Canaanites.

The names of the five daughters were, in fact, the names of five towns in northern Canaan in the land of Hepher. The names were taken from Numbers 26, where they were meant as towns, and reinterpreted for purposes of the allotment story. The Hepherites were not destroyed or dispossessed, moreover, but formed a religio-political alliance with the Israelites.

The story in Numbers and Joshua is the story of the maintenance of the Hepherites' cultural and territorial integrity—an integrity that, according to the biblical witness, survived at least until the time of Solomon.

Indians are the Hepherites, Zelophehad's daughters, sharing a god with, and living in the midst of, a foreign people, yet preserving our own identity.

VINE DELORIA, JR.

VISION AND COMMUNITY
A NATIVE AMERICAN VOICE

■

Vine Deloria, Jr. (Yankton Sioux) is professor of history at the University of Colorado, Boulder. He is the author of *Custer Died for Your Sins* (Macmillan, 1969), *God Is Red* (Grosset and Dunlap, 1973), and numerous other books and articles on native philosophy, history, and legal rights. As one of the leading native intellectuals since the 1960s, Deloria holds advanced degrees in theology and law and has worked with a number of church organizations on native issues. Deloria wrote this essay for *Yearning to Breathe Free* (Orbis, 1990), an anthology of liberation theologies in the United States. He considers the possibilities for a native contribution to the liberation theology movement by surveying the religious situation among contemporary native people, and draws conclusions that some people will find surprising. He then critiques liberation theology on the basis of the fundamental differences between tribal and Western worldviews, an argument he first articulated nearly two decades ago.

In the last decade liberation theology has moved considerably beyond its original Christian moorings to become an important perspective in addressing the problems of human societies. Even as social, economic, and political institutions tighten their grip on the lives of people and military adventurism runs rampant, there is an identifiable current of spiritual energy flowing through the events and attitudes of our times. Ecological concerns, peace protests, the movement back to small communities, shamanism, inter-religious dialogues, and the widespread perception of the common humanity of our diverse peoples are but elements of an emerging vision of wholeness that promises to deliver us from the particularities of history and to present us with a truly planetary view of our common destiny.

In discussing the impact of liberation theology on the American Indian community, it is necessary to see the four segments of this community in its contemporary expression. There are, unfortunately, a good many American Indians who have accepted, without criticism, the premises of materialistic capitalism and who, in spite of the best efforts of the elders and traditional leaders, insist upon salvation through intercourse with transitional corporations and commodities markets. Although they do not constitute a majority in any Indian tribe, these people are favored by the federal government and their demands are accepted as the valid yearnings of the American Indian community for economic freedom. Their basic activity; the exploitation of the reservation's natural and human resources as a means of generating capital for projects, is anathema to the majority of Indians, and consequently every project they undertake is bitterly and sometimes violently opposed by the majority of the people. Unless and until these Indians forsake the entice-ments of materialistic capitalism, the horn-of-plenty of the consumer society, ultimate American Indian liberation will be a long time coming.

American Indians have been converted, devoted, and practicing Christians for many generations. A good estimate of the number of Indian Christians is difficult to make because of the great and persistent fluidity of the Indian population. Indians living in the urban areas may not attend church regularly or participate in the various outreach programs established by the major Christian denominations. But most certainly these people return to their old reservation churches for the important holidays and look upon themselves as members of century-old missions and parishes. These Indians are more directly related in a fundamental kind of liberation theology. For most of this century Indian churches and chapels have been classified as missions because they have not had sufficient income to be self-supporting in the same manner as prosperous non-Indian parishes. Mission, however, connotes a status in which the immediate human environment is hostile to the church or overwhelmingly lethargic. Indian missions are theologically sound; they represent generations of faithful church attendance; and it galls Indian

Christians considerably to be seen as unchurched and needing conversion simply because they lack large parish budgets.

In the last decade Indian clergy and dedicated and active laypeople have made great strides in overcoming this image which has been unfairly thrust upon them by bookkeeping church bureaucrats. New programs for clergy recruitment and retention have been initiated and the Native American Theological Association, although now financially depleted, has worked to create additional opportunities for Indians in Christian seminaries. Charles Cook Theological School—once a Bible-based coloring book program of enhancement for the native religious leaders who were presumed to be serving at the convenience of the white missionary—has expanded its programs and added sophisticated theological content to its activities. It now serves as a focal point for intellectual adventures of Native Americans wishing to reach beyond the traditional confines of the institutional church programs and engage in dialogue with other people dealing with pressing social, political, and religious issues.

Liberation, for this group of American Indians, is a desperate effort to gain sufficient footholds within the institutional church so that (1) Indian program budgets will not be destroyed in the annual reshuffling that the major Protestant denominations seem to enjoy, and (2) the heritage of American Indians in the spiritual realm will be respected and understood by non-Indian Christians. For these people, freedom and liberation must be seen based in respect. They have no plans for moving outside the institutional ecclesiastical framework and don't seem to understand that liberation from the clutches of non-Indian ecclesiastical bureaucrats inevitably requires them to withdraw from the major denominations and create a Native American Christian church in which both administrative policies and theological content reflect the Indian traditions and experiences.

An equally devoted group of American Indians practice the old ways, and their numbers are probably roughly similar to those of the committed Indian Christians. The twentieth century has seen a massive erosion of traditional tribal religions because of substantial outmigration from the reservation communities and the extensive importation of the electronic media in the form of telephones, radios, television, and videocassette recorders. With outmigration, kinship responsibilities have declined precipitously as missing relatives make it necessary for people to substitute other relatives in roles and functions which they would not otherwise undertake. The electronic entertainment media have become surrogate parents and grandparents and consequently it has become increasingly difficult to pass down the oral traditions of the tribe to the proper people and in the properly respectful context.

In many ways the practice of traditional religion today is somewhat akin to the practice of Christianity, being available to meet life crises and to provide the colorful context for social events, but not dominating the day-to-day life of the people in the communities. In the summertime today many reservations are in a state of constant flux as competing medicine men sponsor their own Sun Dances or Sweat Lodges or Sings. Concern for the continuing well-being of the community or tribe is thus expressed in a situation in which the participants withdraw from the community rather than represent it, thus individualizing a religious tradition that had its most powerful influence in its ability to synthesize diverse feelings, beliefs, and practices.

This segment of the Indian community is showing amazing strength in some obscure places in the United States and is attracting the younger people. The chief characteristic of this strength is the voluntary withdrawal from tribal politics, educational programs, and secular activities and the effort to live on a subsistence basis away from the confusion and disorder that mark the modern agency settlements. Rigorous traditionalism, therefore, is a threat not simply to organized Christian efforts to extend the influence of reservation churches but to the programmatic schemes of the materialistic capitalist Indians who see the reservation primarily as a resource to be exploited. Unfortunately many of the people who have been adopting this mode of life have already been through years of alcoholism, unemployment, and sometimes crime of various kinds. There is a real question, therefore, whether the old traditionalism has a message for young people embarked on the road of personal and professional dissolution or whether it can serve only as a spiritual rescue mission for people who have no other place to turn.

The last identifiable group of Indians, considerably smaller in number than any of the groups already discussed, are those people who have experienced traditional tribal religion to some degree, who have significant knowledge of and experiences with the white people's world, and who now insist that they have been commissioned to bring the tribal religions to the aid and assistance of the non-Indian. As a rule these people live and work far from their own reservations where they would be severely chastised by people for commercialization of tribal rituals. They form a reasonably close network of people who travel the conference and psychological workshop circuit performing for whoever is willing and able to pay the sometimes exorbitant entrance fees.

This group is very interesting. Some of the practitioners are unquestionably fraudulent and their message can be found in any of the popular books on Indian religion such as *Black Elk Speaks* or *Book of the Hopi*.[1] To a white populace yearning for some kind of religious experience it is enough that they speak kindly and administer a message of universal fellowship during a friendly ceremonial occasion. Few people have any extensive knowledge of the ways of any tribal religion and so the ceremonies used by these practitioners, which would be instantly discredited within the reservation context, are taken as real expressions of religious piety by their followers. But it cannot be denied that on many occasions what these people have done has helped the people they have served. There is sufficient evidence that some kind of religious energy is present in these modernized versions of tribal ritual so that the movement cannot be discredited on the basis of its commercialism alone.

It is in the objective vision possessed by this last group of Indians that the importance of the American Indian contribution to liberation theology can be found. Obviously the materialistic capitalists possess only the idea of accumulating wealth and power, and their view—for it can hardly be called a vision—of reality is hardly an improvement on the speculations of English political and economic thinkers of the eighteenth century. Indian Christians also lack a unifying vision; basically they attempt to fit themselves into a two-thousand-year-old paradigm of salvation which has little relevance to the longstanding tribal traditions. The purist reservation traditions are bound in the same way, using the old images and visions as a framework within which present realities can be judged. While there is considerably more power and familiarity in these old visions, nevertheless there is very little in them that addresses the modern social and physical context in which people live. And so we are left with the vision of the new Indian missionaries/entrepreneurs, partly by default, partly by the emphasis on outreach.

The new vision is not without its faults and, like other things of the Spirit, is hardly predictable. But an examination of its positive aspects is necessary before its negative attributes can be considered. First, within this context the vision is one of a unified and *experiencing* humanity. We must emphasize the element of experience because the philosophical message of the Indians who participate in the workshop network is as much a demand for new ceremonial and ritual participation as it is an explanation of the basis for the experiences. So the justification for sharing some of the tribal ceremonies and philosophies is that these beliefs and practices have a universal applicability and the practitioners have a divine commission to share them.

The positive second dimension is the emphasis placed upon the living nature of the universe. This belief is solidly tribal in origin but has been given an added value because it is now being connected to the beliefs of other traditions and to the findings of modern science. In this respect the modern shamanism teaches its adherents to develop once again an understanding of the animals and to cultivate relationships with them. Primarily this is now accomplished by a variation of Jungian active imagination, but within the Indian context. People who would otherwise have a reverence for birds and other animals, except for their lack of familiarity with the natural world, come to see that in the most profound sense humankind cannot live alone. Not only do humans need a companion and community but they also need the fellowship, help, and sense of community of all living things. Surprisingly this idea is strikingly powerful when it is experienced in ceremonies and made concrete in people's lives.

The third point of positive stature in the Indian missionary thrust is a corollary of the second point but must be stressed in this context because it carries with it a call to action that makes it a unique experience in itself. Companionship, in the religious sense, is stressed by these outgoing religious representatives so that people following their directions find themselves dealing with higher and/or different spiritual personalities in both a healing and personal-vocational sense. In the old traditional way of handling these experiences there was an alliance between the Vision Quest participants and higher spiritual personalities, but this kind of alliance was generally restricted to those who had successfully endured the ordeal and for whom the spirits had shown pity. The experiences of people today are not nearly as powerful as they were in the old days, but they are more precisely tuned to the needs of average persons. It helps them deal with the many minor personal vocational and ethical choices which, taken together, make up the consistency of human social life. It is almost as if the spiritual energies inherent in the American Indian tribal universe were deliberately expanding, losing some of the potency they enjoyed in the restricted traditional context, but in turn providing spiritual guidance for an increasingly numerous group of people.

In contrast to these positive aspects of the modern effort to extend the influence and practice of the traditional tribal religious into the non-Indian world, there are a number of negative things that can be identified and which, unless they are corrected, can abort this kind of spiritual expansion and reduce it to simply another American fad, a fate which too many spiritual and artistic energies suffer in our society. Most important in this respect is that these experiences, while helpful to most people attending the workshops and conferences, are not held in or responsible to any identifiable community. A network is not a community, it is simply an elongated set of connections held together by common interests or experiences. A network can easily become a set of highly charged spiritual dominoes unless it finds a center, becomes sedentary and indigenous, and begins to exert a constant influence on a group of people whose lives and actions are thereby changed for the better. Here we need not so much institutionalization as we need to find a means of stabilizing religious experiences within a definite geographical context so that as people accumulate spiritual insights and powers, they can have a community in which these powers can be manifested. Community is essential because visions are meant for communities, not for individuals although it is the special individual who, on behalf of the community, undertakes to receive divine instructions for the community.

The second danger is that as people gain in spiritual understanding they run the danger of misusing what they have received in the constant effort to spread the word of the realities they have experienced. Many of the Indian practitioners who tread the workshop network today are very close to falling into this trap. Surveying the progress and accomplishments of the ten most popular and respected of the Indians who work the non-Indian social networks will show that there is virtually no individual spiritual progress. The feats which they are able to accomplish are basically those gifts which first enabled them to gain a measure of respect and a following in the non-Indian world. Thus while there is progress in bringing the substance of tribal religious experiences to non-Indians, the workshops, Sun Dances, and Sweat Lodges are becoming something akin to the Christian Mass. These presentations on the non-Indian circuit are not only repetitious but lack potential to probe spiritual realities at any increasing depth of experience or understanding.

The traditional religious revelation of the tribes was very people-specific. That is to say, tribes held their religious secrets very firmly to themselves because the nature of the original revelation required the people to follow certain paths, to act in certain ways, and to fulfill a specific covenant with higher powers. Unlike Jews and Christians, who have interpreted their religious mission in terms of absolute divine commissions to oppose other religious traditions, regardless of value or content, the tribal-specific revelations did not spawn religious intolerance. Rather the Indians rigorously followed the universal admonition to remove the mote from their own eyes before they arrogated to themselves the power to correct their neighbors' practices and beliefs. There is not one single instance of wars or conflicts between or among American Indian tribes, or between Indians and non-Indians, which had as its basis the differences in religious practices or beliefs.

Given this tradition, there is a real concern among the reservation traditionals of the impact and meaning of spreading the tribal teachings to anyone who has a spiritual or emotional need. The belief has always been that the Great Spirit and/or the higher spirits are also watching others and they will provide the proper religious insights and knowledge to others. Therefore it behooves Indians to obey the teachings of their own traditions and hold them close. If they were meant for other people, the other people would have them. Such thinking has prevented most tribes from engaging in religious imperialism, and the humility underlying this attitude is admirable. But what happens today when individuals of the various tribes spend their time on the lecture-workshop-conference circuit indiscriminately instructing non-Indians and non-tribal members in a variety of beliefs, some giving simple homilies and others offering deep and profound truths? Will not this kind of behavior, which in traditional terms is utmost sacrilege, ultimately call down the wrath of the spirits on the tribe? These concerns are real and pressing for many American Indians and there is no easy or certain answer to them.

The present situation of American Indians speaks directly to the context in which liberation theology is being done. It is not difficult to trace the paths which liberation theology must inevitably tread, and consequently an intersection between other people and American Indians can easily be discerned sometime in the future. Liberation theology first and foremost seeks to help human beings overthrow or deflect the tremendous oppression that is visited upon us by our own institutions which, in the name of a variety of false deities, have taken control of our lives and emotions. For the first two groups of American Indians there is no question that liberation theology has an immediate and profound message. The sabbath is made for human beings; human beings are not made for the sabbath; and so it is with all of our institutions. To the degree that oppression exists because of ill-informed or ill-intentioned use of human social, religious, and economic structures, to that degree people must act to take control of their lives. Institutions must be responsible to people and people must take responsibility to eliminate institutions and replace them with the free-flowing and spontaneous positive energy of love that flows from deep within themselves.

As liberation theology energizes and inspires people to become what they are intended to be, the task will be shifting from the need to escape from oppressive institutions and situations to the responsibility to free oneself from oppressive doctrines and beliefs and the corresponding practices which keep them in the forefront of our spiritual and emotional lives. Eventually liberation theology must engage in a massive critique of itself and its historico-theological context and inheritance. Here, as the issues become sharper and more profound, liberation theology will encounter traditional American Indian religions and their practitioners, first the modern Indian missionaries of the workshop network and then at last the few remaining traditionals on the reservations. Liberation theology must not only confront these representatives of American Indian religion but it must have a message for them which transcends their experiences and practice *and* makes sense of the Indian tradition in a more universal and comprehensive manner.

At this point of interaction liberation theology must dig deep into the Christian-Judeo tradition and bring forward whatever insights into the nature of reality it may have to present to the traditional Indians. It is not difficult to see that the cupboard is exceedingly bare at this level and that liberation theology must, perhaps inevitably, depart from its historico-theological moorings and deal with important philosophical questions. Is the world dead or alive? And what does that mean for the daily lives of people? What is the place and status of the human being in a world filled with sentient and powerful spirits? Is the world a fallen world from the beginning of time or does it simply have a set of historical difficulties which have been nearly impossible to resolve? What are the purpose, task, and meaning of human existence? The questions and issues which divide traditional American Indian religions from the world religions are many and profound and not capable of resolution through reference to a pre-existing set of doctrines and dogmas.

The basic philosophical difference between the American tribal religions and the world religions, Christianity being the world religion most likely to come into direct contact with the tribal religions, is the difference between time and space, between times and places, between a remembered history and a sacred location. At this point Christianity, and by extension liberation theology, is in mortal danger. History is a highly selective interpretation of the events of our lives loosely strung in sequence to prove the validity of the argument. That is to say, by arranging certain kinds of facts in a certain sequence, it is not difficult to prove to the disbeliever that certain spiritual truths and realities exist. But in performing this arrangement of human memories and experiences, a good deal has to be omitted and a great many facts have to be given a specific twist in order to fit the pattern. We hear from the Christians that God works and is working in history. But this history does not reflect humanity's complete and comprehensive experiences. This history is valid only if the listener surrenders his or her critical self inquiry and accepts the many premises that history, any particular history, requires for validation.

The tribal religions, however, bound as they are to specific places and particular ceremonies, do not need to rely upon the compiled arguments of history. It is only necessary that people experience the reality of the sacred. The attraction of the Indian missionaries on the lecture circuit is that they do provide new kinds of experiences, and in the world today people crave their own experiences and judge the truth of a proposition by the manner in which it helps them understand themselves. Consequently in the conflict or competition between Christianity and the other world religions and the tribal religions, a competition that is approaching on the horizon, there is no question which tradition is capable of speaking meaningfully to the diversity of peoples. A Sweat Lodge, a Vision Quest, or a Sing performed in a sacred place with the proper medicine man provides so much more to its practitioners than a well-performed Mass, a well-turned sermon argument, or a well-organized retreat. Christian rituals simply have no experiential powers.

Ultimately religions ask and answer the question of the real meaning and purpose of human life. The fatal flaw in the world religions is their propensity to try to provide answers to these questions knowing full well that both questions and answers must come from honest and open participation in the world. The Apostle Paul, filled with the Spirit and zealous to pass on his received theological truths, found no audience in Athens because no one was asking questions. Consequently his answers, already pre-formed in his mind and pushing for expression, had no relevance to his situation. Tribal religions do not claim to have answers to the larger questions of human life. But they do know various ways of asking the questions and this is their great strength and why they will ultimately have great influence in people's lives.

American Indians should wish liberation theology well in its endeavors. There is no question that humanity needs liberation from the many ills that plague it. But even the sacralization of the institutions, governments, and economic systems that are represented in our various human societies could not answer the ultimate questions that we must answer in our lives.

Sacralization would only provide a benign and comfortable context in which these questions could be asked. It would always be up to the Great Spirit and the higher spirits, to the community of living things and to the humans themselves to derive cooperatively the proper answers. Liberation theology, however, can and must clear out the underbrush which we have carelessly allowed to obscure our vision of the forest, and this task cannot be accomplished too quickly. All living things now stand on the brink of oblivion and extinction. Mass destruction cannot be allowed to be the answer to all of our other questions, or, for that matter, to foreclose the possibility of asking the proper questions.

An old Crow chief, asked about the difference between the Indian way of life and that of the whites, responded that for the Indian there were visions, for the whites there were only ideas. Visions, in the Indian context, require action and this action manifests itself in the community, enabling the people to go forward in confidence and obedience. The vision is complete, it is comprehensive, it includes and covers everything, and there is no mistaking its applicability. Ideas, on the other hand, have only a limited relevance. They explain some things but not all things; they are rarely comprehensive and there is great difficulty in finding their proper application. Most important, however, the idea never reaches the complete community—it only reaches those who have the ability to grasp it and it leaves the rest of the community struggling for understanding.

It is difficult to discern, at the present time, whether liberation theology is an idea or a vision. It has the requisite characteristics of praxis and community, and in the struggle for freedom from oppression it even has the experiences. But within its larger theological context it is tied to a narrow and historical understanding of the human experience. When and whether it can transcend this foundation and provide the context in which the ultimate questions can be asked is an exciting and perilous possibility that hangs over us today. Hopefully we can glimpse a vision of community through the praxis that liberation theology asks and demands of us.

NOTES

1. See John G.Neihardt, *Black Elk Speaks* (Lincoln: University of Nebraska, 1979); and Frank Waters, *Book of the Hopi* (New York: Penguin, 1977).

9

GEORGE TINKER

SPIRITUALITY, NATIVE AMERICAN PERSONHOOD, SOVEREIGNTY, AND SOLIDARITY

George Tinker (Osage/Cherokee) builds on Deloria's critique of the Western intellectual tradition and offers one of the most developed analyses of liberation theology by a native Christian. He first presented this essay in Nairobi, Kenya, as one of the keynote addresses at the 1992 General Assembly of the Ecumenical Association of Third World Theologians, of which Tinker is a member. He begins by pointing out that the oppression of "fourth-world peoples" involves a spiritual dimension, what might also be called cultural genocide. He examines four important themes of liberation theology that have emerged from the conventional social and historical analysis typified in the work of Gustavo Gutiérrez. Emphasizing the centrality of cultural factors in collective identity and political praxis, Tinker imagines an alternative paradigm for justice and peace that is rooted in indigenous relationships to creation and the Creator.

A boriginal peoples in North America today are, if you will, a fourth world.[1] As fourth-world peoples, we share with our third-world relatives the hunger, poverty and repression which has been the continuing common experience of those overpowered by the expansionism of European adventurers and their missionaries five hundred years ago.

What distinguishes fourth-world indigenous peoples from other third-world peoples, however, are the particular repercussions of conquest and genocide as they impacted our distinctive indigenous cultures. While the immediately obvious effects of conquest and genocide seem similar for third- and fourth-world peoples—poverty, unemployment, disease, high infant mortality, low adult longevity—there are deeper, more hidden but no less deadly effects of colonialism which impact third- and fourth-world peoples in dramatically different ways.[2] These effects are especially felt in the indigenous fourth-world spiritual experience, and we see our struggle for liberation within the context of this distinctive spirituality. This has been often overlooked, until recently, in third-world liberation theology models of social change which often remained inappropriate and ineffective in the struggle of indigenous peoples for their right to self-determination. In fact, the themes of much liberation theology have been derived from the very modes of discourse of the Western academy against which indigenous peoples have struggled for centuries. These modes of discourse—whether theological, legal, political, economic, or even the so-called social sciences—have structured colonial, neo-colonial, and now Marxist regimes which, in the name of development, modernization or even solidarity, have inflicted spiritual genocide on fourth-world peoples. It is from this perspective that I want to share how an indigenous understanding of the spiritual is integral to the salvation of Native American peoples, quite apart from the struggle towards liberation envisioned by many Latin American theologians. I would like to begin by drawing both some contrast and some affinity between third-world theology and what might define a fourth-world Native American theology.

Gustavo Gutiérrez, the foremost thinker on liberation theology, argues four important points. (1) Liberation theology should focus on the non-person rather than on the non-believer; (2) it is a historical project that sees God as revealed in history; (3) it makes a revolutionary socialist choice on behalf of the poor; and (4) it emerges out of the praxis of the people. The latter emphasis on praxis is perhaps the most enduring and pervasive gift of liberation theology. For reasons I hope to articulate clearly, however, a Native American theology must find the emphasis on the historical unsuitable for us and will begin with a much different understanding of Gutiérrez's category of the non-person. Moreover, Native American culture and spirituality will imply different political solutions from those currently imposed by any socialist paradigm. I trust that my critique will be received as a collegial attempt at constructive dialogue leading to mutual understanding and solidarity between third- and fourth-world peoples and an advance for the cause of genuine and holistic liberation. And perhaps we may be able to envision a new socialist paradigm that is less rooted in the pervasive modern notion of the nation state.

PERSONHOOD AND GENOCIDE

In an early *Concilium* essay, Gutiérrez describes the meaning of his category of the non-person in language that strongly distinguishes the concern of liberation theology from the rest of modern theology:

> Much contemporary theology seems to start from the challenge of the *non-believer*. He questions our *religious world* and faces it with a demand for profound purification and renewal. . . . This challenge in a continent like Latin America does not come primarily from the man who does not believe, but from the *man who is not a man*, who is not recognized as such by the existing social order: he is in the ranks of the poor, the exploited; he is the man who is systematically and legally despoiled of his being as a man, who scarcely knows that he is a man. His challenge is not aimed first at our religious world, but at our *economic, social, political and cultural world*; therefore it is an appeal for the revolutionary transformation; of the very bases of dehumanizing society. . . . What is implied in telling this man who is not a man that he is a son of God?[3]

This is a powerful statement naming the alienation of marginalized poor and oppressed peoples and the impetus for a liberative theological response to people in contexts of systematically imposed suffering. While these words frame the experience of oppression suffered by indigenous and third-world peoples alike, however, they fall short in naming the particularities of indigenous peoples' suffering of non-personhood. The very affirmation of third-world "non-persons" tends to continue what has been, in praxis, a disaffirmation of indigenous people for now five hundred years in the Americas. While he avoids the language of explicit political programmes, especially in a later essay,[4] Gutiérrez, like other Latin American theologians, explicitly and implicitly identifies the preferential option for the poor with socialist and even implied Marxist solutions that analyze the poor in terms of social class structure[5] and overlook the crucial point that indigenous peoples experience their very personhood in terms of their relationship to the land. The argument and the ensuing analysis are powerful and effective to a point. By reducing the non-person to a class of people that share certain universal attributes, however, other sometimes more telling attributes become nonfunctional and unimportant in the minds of those engaged in the analysis.[6]

Native American peoples resist categorization in terms of class structure. Instead, we insist on being recognized as "peoples," even nations with a claim to national sovereignty based on ancient title to their land. Whether we be classed as "working class" or "the poor," such classification continues the erosion of the group's cultural integrity and national agenda. As much as capitalist economic structures—including the church (missionaries) and the academy (e.g., anthropologists)—have reduced Native American peoples to non-personhood, so too the Marxist agenda fails finally to recognize our distinct personhood. Reducing our nationness to classness imposes upon us a particular culture of poverty and especially a culture of labor.[7] It begs the question as to whether indigenous peoples desire production in the modern economic sense in the first place. To put the means of production into the hands of the poor eventually makes the poor exploiters of indigenous peoples and their natural resources. Finally, it runs the serious risk of violating the very spiritual values that hold an indigenous cultural group together as a people. This is not intended to suggest a simple discarding of Marxist or any other tools of analysis. Rather it is intended as a constructive critique of them and a critique of the implicit hegemony they exercise in much of our midst in the third world.

This failure to recognize the distinct personhood of Native American peoples has a history as long as the history of European colonialism and missionary outreach in the Americas. In particular, it should be noted that it was the church's failure to recognize the personhood of Native Americans that proved to be the most devastating, from Mendieta to Eliot. While colonial armies engaged in direct genocidal destruction of American Indian tribes, the missionaries were from the beginning just as complicitous in acts of genocide. However well-intentioned, the missionaries were of a piece with the colonial conquest. Less direct than the military (yet always accompanied by them), the missionaries consistently confused the gospel of Jesus Christ with the gospel of European cultural values and social structures. As a result, they engaged in what can only be called the cultural genocide of Indian peoples, all in the service of conquest and the expansion of capitalist economies.

Even those missionary heroes who are most revered in modern memory, from Las Casas in the south to Eliot in the north, conspired with the political power of the colonial oppressors to deprive Indian peoples of their cultures, to destroy native economies, and to reduce culturally integrous communities to subservient dependence—all for the sake of the "gospel" and with the best of intentions.[8] It was, after all, Las Casas who invented the *reduction* paradigm for missionary work among Indian peoples as a way of more gently exploiting Indian labor on behalf of the king. The consistent error of the missionaries of all denominations who came to evangelize our Native American tribes was precisely that they failed to notice, let alone acknowledge, our personhood. They saw our cultures and our social structures as inadequate and needing to be replaced with what they called a "Christian civilization." Even as they argued liberally for the humanity of Indian people, they denied our personhood.

Much of liberation theology and socialist movements in general can promise no better than the continued cultural genocide of indigenous peoples. From an American Indian perspective, the problem with modern liberation theology, as with Marxist political movements, is that class analysis gets in the way of recognizing cultural discreetness and even peopleness. Small but culturally integrous communities stand to be swallowed up by the vision of a classless society, of an international workers' movement or of a burgeoning majority of third-world urban poor. That too is cultural genocide and signifies that we are yet non-persons, even in the light of the gospel of liberation.

GOD AND HISTORY

In *The Power of the Poor in History* Gutiérrez begins by expounding on God's revelation and proclamation in history, arguing that God reveals God's self in history.[9] I want to argue that this is not only not a self-evident truth, but that a culturally integrous Native American theology, rooted in our indigenous spiritual traditions, must begin with a confession that is both dramatically disparate from and exclusive of Gutiérrez's starting point. Essentially, a Native American theology must argue out of Native American spiritual experience and praxis that God reveals God's self in creation, in space or place and not in time. The Western (nineteenth-century European) sense of history as a linear temporal process means that those who heard the gospel first have and always maintain a critical advantage over those of us who hear it later and have to rely on those who heard it first to give us a full interpretation. In a historical structure of existence, certain people carry the message and hold all the wisdom. They know better and more than later converts.[10] For better or worse, this has been our consistent experience with the gospel as it has been preached to us by the missionaries of all the denominations, just as it has been our experience with the political visions proclaimed to us by the revolutionaries.[11]

The problem, from Las Casas to Marx, is the assumption of the hegemonic trajectory through history which fails to recognize cultural discreteness. Even with the best of intentions, solutions to the suffering of oppressed peoples are proposed as exclusive programmes not allowing for a diversity of possibilities. We must never forget that Las Casas, the hero of the 1992 quincentenary, was just as much given over to the conquest of Native Americans as were Cortez and Pizarro. He only hoped to do it more gently and less violently. He accomplished much of his goal in his creation of the so-called reduction missionary system, used so effectively—and destructively—by later generations of European Jesuits, Franciscans, and also Protestants in both the northern and southern hemispheres. The missionaries of all denominations consistently expressed their historical commitments to the progressive conquest of Christianity and what they identified as the culture of Christianity.

Whatever the conqueror's commitment, to evangelization and conversion or to military subjugation and destruction, it was necessary to make the conquest decisive—at military, political, economic, social, legal and religious levels.[12] Just as the conquest had to be decisive, so too must the revolution be divisive. There can be no room for peoples who consider themselves distinct—economically, politically, socially and culturally—to find their own revolution or liberation. A prime example of this was the situation of the Miskito Indians in Nicaragua during the Sandinista revolution. Summarily relocated from their coastal territories, where they had self-sustaining local economics, to high-altitude communal coffee plantations, Miskito peoples were forced to labor as culturally amorphous workers with no regard to the abject cultural dislocation they had suffered. Once they had been a people; then they were reduced to a class whose peopleness could not be a factor. In order to ensure the decisiveness of the socialist conquest over cultural autonomy, the Sandinistas proceeded to colonize the Atlantic coast region of the Miskitos with Hispano families from the western regions of Nicaragua. The ultimate irony is that the Sandinista revolution used ancient strategies of European colonialism that have been so roundly criticized by leftist thinkers in the rest of Latin America in order to attempt to consolidate their power and the hegemony of Hispano socialism over other cultures in Nicaragua. It was a conscious attempt to disrupt and destroy the cultural solidarity of Indian peoples in order to impose the revolution and its social control. The result was to reduce the Indian majority of the Atlantic coast to a minority population and further dilute any hope for the self-determining autonomy of a people, and thus reduce Indian people to a part of the general class structure of Nicaragua. Even now under the Chamorro regime, the damage is done and Miskito survival as a people will take a long and protracted struggle. The predetermined trajectory of historical dialectic allows no culturally disparate options, at least not cultural options that are decidedly disparate.[13]

Whether in its capitalist or socialist guise, then, history and temporality reign supreme in the West. On the other hand, Native American spirituality, values, social and political structures, even ethics are rooted not in some temporal notion of history but in spatiality. This is perhaps the most dramatic (and largely unnoticed) cultural difference between Native American thought processes and the Western intellectual tradition. The Western intellectual tradition is firmly rooted in the priority of temporal metaphors and thought processes. Native Americans think inherently spatially and not temporally.[14] The question is not whether time or space is missing in one culture or the other, but which metaphoric base functions as the ordinary and which is the subordinate. Of course Native Americans have a temporal awareness, but it is subordinate to our sense of spatiality. Likewise, the Western tradition has a spatial awareness, but that lacks the priority of the temporal. Hence, progress, history, development, evolution and process become key notions that invade all academic discourse in the West, from science and economics to philosophy and theology. History, thus, becomes the quintessential Western intellectual device and gives rise to structures of cognition and modes of discourse that pay dutiful homage to temporality.

If Marxist thinking and the notion of a historical dialectic were finally proven correct, then American Indian people and all indigenous peoples would be surely doomed. Our cultures and value systems, our spirituality, and even our social structures must soon give way to an emergent socialist structure that would impose a notion of the good on all people regardless of ethnicity or culture.

CULTURE, DISCOURSE, AND SPIRITUALITY

All of this has much to do with my assigned topic of spirituality. Without understanding the spatiality of Native American existence, one cannot understand Native American spiritual traditions. Spatiality and spiritual traditions are key to understanding the continuing threat to Indian personhood and the spectre of cultural genocide (economic, political, intellectual and religious) that constantly hovers over our heads.

One could argue with Native American peoples that we must learn to compromise with the "real world," that to pursue our own cultural affectations is to swim upstream against the current of the modern socio-economic world system. When rightists or capitalists of any shade make the argument, I am clear that they are arguing the self-interest or prerogatives of those who own the system. When third- or fourth-world peoples make the argument, I am curious at how readily some of us concede the primacy of Western categories of discourse. How easily we internalize the assumption that Western,

Euro-American philosophical, theological, economic, social, spiritual and political systems are necessarily definitive of any and all conceivable "real" worlds! We Native Americans are just arrogant enough, in the midst of our oppression and poverty, to think that our perception of the world is just as adequate, and perhaps more satisfying and certainly more egalitarian than the West's. In order to sense something of the power of our culturally integrated structures of cognition, a beginning understanding of Native American spirituality is a necessary starting point, for all of existence is spiritual for us. That is our universal starting point, even though we represent a multitude of related cultures in actuality, with a great variety of tribal ceremonial structures expressing that sense of spirituality.

If the primary metaphor of existence for Native Americans is spatial and not temporal, this goes a long way towards explaining what nearly everyone already knows, that American Indian spirituality and American Indian existence in general is deeply rooted in the land. It explains why the history of our conquest and removal from our lands was so culturally and genocidally destructive to our tribes. There is, however, a more subtle level to this sense of spatiality and land rootedness. It shows up in nearly all aspects of our existence, in our ceremonial structures, our symbols, our architecture, and in the symbolic parameters of a tribe's universe. In my own tribe, for instance, the old villages were always laid out in two halves, dividing the peoples into Hunka and Tzi Sho, an Earth Division and a Sky Division. This reflected the fundamental manifestation (revelation?) of Wakonta, the Sacred Mystery, Creator, God(?) to the people. Since Wakonta is an unknowable Mystery, Wakonta had to make itself known to people. It did so as a duality, as Wakonta Above and Wakonta Below (Wakonta Monshita and Wakonta Udsetta), as Grandfather (Itsiko) and Grandmother (Iko), as Sky and Earth. We should not think here of the oppositional dualism of good and evil that we have learned to identify as typical Western (Eastern) dualism. American Indian duality is a necessary reciprocity, not oppositional. They are different manifestations of the *same Wakonta*, not of two Wakontas even though they carry personality specificity just as traditional Christian Trinitarian doctrine would assert. While they are manifestations of the same Wakonta, they are different manifestations, both of which are necessary in order to have some balanced understanding of the Otherness that is the Sacred Mystery. Indeed Wakonta has manifested itself in a great many other ways, all of which help our people to better understand the Mystery, our world, ourselves and our place in the world.

The architectural geography of our spirituality was played out even further in a variety of ways. Most significantly, we were what anthropologists call an exogamous kinship system. Individuals were required by social mores to marry outside of their own division, meaning that every child—and every person—is both Hunka and Tzi Sho, even though she or he belongs structurally to only one division. While this functions politically to give the village group cohesion, it functions at a much more deeply spiritual level that still pertains for a great many Indian people today. Namely, each individual recognizes herself or himself as a combination of qualities that reflect both sky and earth, spirit and matter, peace and war, male and female, and we struggle individually and communally to hold those qualities in balance with each other.

This is not the only spatial symbolic paradigm of existence that determines Native American individuality and community. The fundamental symbol of plains Indian existence is the circle, a polyvalent symbol signifying the family, the clan, the tribe, and eventually all of creation. As a creation symbol, the importance of the circle is its genuine egalitarianness. There is no way to make the circle hierarchical. Because it has no beginning and no end, all in the circle are of equal value. No relative is valued more than any other. A chief is not valued above the people; nor are the Two-legged valued above the animal nations, birds, or even trees and rocks. In its form as a medicine wheel, with two lines forming a cross inscribed vertically and horizontally across its whole, the circle can symbolize the four directions of the earth and, more importantly, the four manifestations of Wakonta that come to us from those directions. At the same time, those four directions symbolize the four cardinal virtues of a tribe, the four sacred colors of ceremonial life, the sacred powers of four animal nations, and the four nations of Two-leggeds that walk the earth (Black, Red, Yellow and White). That is, in our conception of the universe, all human beings walk ideally in egalitarian balance. Moreover, Native American egalitarian proclivities are worked out in this spatial symbol in ways that go far beyond the classless egalitarianness of socialism. In one of the polyvalent layers of meaning, those four directions hold together in the same egalitarian balance the four nations of Two-leggeds, Four-leggeds, Wingeds, and Living-moving Things. In this rendition human beings lose their status of primacy and "dominion." Implicitly and explicitly, American Indians are driven by their culture and spirituality to recognize the personhood of all "things" in creation. If temporality and historicity lend themselves implicitly to hierarchical structures because someone with a greater investment of time may know more of the body of temporally codified knowledge, spatiality lends itself to the egalitarian. All have relatively similar access to the immediacy of the spatially present.

This sense of the egalitarian plays itself out in Native American life precisely where one might expect Indian culture to be challenged; namely, in ceremonial aspects around hunting and harvest. The key to understanding hunting and harvest practices is the principle of reciprocity, whereby the hunter or harvester engages in some action reciprocal to the act of harvest itself. Native American tribes, as is well known, had and many still have extensive hunting ceremonies, ceremonies that begin before the hunters leave the village, continue on the hunt itself, reach a climactic point when the animal is killed and do not conclude until the hunters all undergo purification rites prior to re-entry into the village with their hard-earned cache of meat and hides. While these ceremonies include aspects of prayer for a successful hunt, the more dominant theme is the one of reciprocity. Namely, the hunter is participating in a mythic activity which has its origin in mythological stories in which human beings were given permission by the animal nations to hunt themselves for food. The resulting covenant, however, calls on human beings to assume responsibilities over against the perpetration of violence among Four-legged relatives. Prayers for the animals must be offered, even prayers to the animals, asking their immediate permission to be taken for food. Moreover, some reciprocal offering is almost always made, as the hunter sprinkles tobacco around the slain animal or corn pollen on its closed eyelids, depending on tribal tradition. Agricultural harvest calls for similar ceremonial attention and reciprocity. Nothing is taken from the earth without prayer and offering. When the tree is cut down for the Sun Dance, for instance, something must be offered, returned to the spirit world, for the life of that tree. The people not only ask its permission but ask for its cooperation and help during the four days of the dance itself. These animals, crops, trees and medicines are relatives and must be treated with respect if they are to be genuinely efficacious for the people.

Lakota peoples, one of hundreds of distinct Native American peoples in North America, have a short prayer that captures the general cultural and spiritual sentiment of all Native Americans. *Mitakuye ouyasin*, they pray, "for all my relatives." In this prayer relatives are understood to include not just tribal members but all Two-leggeds, and not just Two-leggeds but indeed all the createds of the world: the Four-leggeds, the Wingeds, and all the Living, moving things, the trees and rocks, mountains and rivers, fish and snakes, etc. It is for this reason, then, that not even an animal or a tree is harmed without appropriate spiritual reciprocity in the American Indian world. In the act of hunting or in harvesting, ceremonial acts of reciprocity must be performed in order to maintain the balance and harmony of the world in the midst of perpetrating an act of violence. To act without such responsibility is to introduce imbalance and disharmony into the world. All the createds of the world are our relatives and command our respect as fellow createds.

This matrix of cultural responses to the world that we might call spirituality continues to have life today in North America among our various

Indian tribes. A great many Indian people have chosen to leave Christianity in favor of a more direct living out of these traditional ways. Yet these ways continue to be a vital part of all Indian existence, even for those who remain in the church and continue to call themselves Christian. What we call spirituality is, for us as it is for most indigenous peoples, a way of life more than a religion. It is a way of life that encompasses the whole of life. More and more frequently today, Indian Christians are laying claim to the old traditions as their way of life and claiming the freedom of the gospel to honor and practice them as integrous to their enculturated expression of Christianity. Today there can be no genuine American Indian theology that does not take our indigenous traditions seriously. This means, of course, that our reading of the gospel and our understanding of faithfulness will represent a radical disjuncture from the theologies and histories of the Western churches of Europe and America as we pay attention to our stories and memories instead of to theirs. This can only concern us, however, where we see the possibility that our interpretations can prove renewing, redeeming and salvific for Western theology and ecclesiology. More to the point, this inculturation to an indigenous theology is symbolic of American Indian resistance and struggle today. More than symbolic, it gives life to the people.

CREATION, JUSTICE, PEACE

With this axiom in mind, I want to suggest that a Native American theology coupled with a Native American reading of the gospel might provide the theological imagination to generate a more immediate and attainable vision of a just and peaceful world. What we lack yet today is a creative and powerful theological foundation for the justice we desire. All our churches take seriously to some extent the scriptural demands for justice, yet none of them has a persuasive and satisfying means for arguing or achieving those goals. While God revealing God's self in history holds out some promise for achieving justice and peace in some eventual future moment, the historical/temporal impetus must necessarily delay any full realization of the *basileia* (kingdom) of God.

As a world of discourse that is primarily spatial, a Native American Christian theology must begin with the native American traditional praxis of a spirituality that is rooted first of all in creation. I consistently argued that the WCC's "Justice, Peace and the Integrity of Creation" (JPIC) process should have been called "Creation, Justice, Peace." Such a theological prioritizing of creation on my part is far more than a prioritizing of environmental concerns. Rather, it functions to provide a spiritual and theological foundation for justice. Respect for creation must necessarily result in justice, just as genuine justice necessarily is the achievement of peace.

I start with a particular understanding of the *basileia tou theou*, the *basileia* (or kingdom) of God,[15] a concept so central to the preaching of Jesus in the gospels. While Euro-cultural scholars have offered consistently temporal interpretations of this metaphor, any American Indian interpretation must build on a spatial understanding rooted in creation. Western scholars consistently want to ask the question "when?" of the *basileia* and disallow any query about the where of the *basileia*. While Native Americans know little about either kings or kingdoms, only a spatial response to the question "where" begins to make any sense at all of the metaphor. Whatever the *basileia* is, it must be a place. Certainly, the verb *engizein* allows for and even predicates a primary meaning of spatial nearness, and in Luke 17:20 Jesus instructs the Pharisees that the *basileia* is "in your midst" (*entos humas*), that is, already spatially present.

My own interpretation treats the *basileia* as a metaphor for creation. Indeed, the metaphor is not used in the Old Testament at all, but the image of God as king occurs almost always in contexts that refer to God's act in creation. If the metaphor has to do with God's hegemony, where else is God actually to reign if not in the entirety of the place that God has created. To assume any less is to lapse again into a triumphalistic mode that permits human beings, the church or governments to decide who is and who is not privileged and to determine the process by which one might become so privileged.[16]

American Indian spirituality sees as its fundamental goal the achievement of harmony and balance in all of creation. We do see the hegemony of the Mystery (God?) in the whole of existence, but we see ourselves as participants in that whole, doing our part to help maintain harmony and balance. After all we see ourselves as merely a part of creation and not somehow apart from creation free to use it up at will, a mistake that was and is epidemic in both the first and second worlds, and has been recklessly imposed on the rest of us in the name of development. While our spirituality is enormously complex in this regard, maybe it is enough in this context to say that we are pressed by our spirituality to understand the *basileia* as the place that is all of the real world, creation. Thus no one can be left out of the *basileia*. In the spirit of the prayer *mitakuye ouyasin*, we all belong. The question is whether I will recognize God's hegemony over myself and all of creation. Will I live faithfully in relationship to God and creation?

In Mark 1:15, Jesus' first audience is told that because the *basileia* is near they are to "be repenting and be faithing in the gospel." If, as many scholars since Jeremias have argued, the Hebrew/Aramaic word *shub*, to turn or return, is the underlying notion that Mark has translated as repentance, then the call to repentance becomes a call to return to a proper relationship not only with the Creator but also with the rest of creation. The call to repentance I understand as a call to be liberated from our human perceived need to be God and instead to assume our rightful place in the world as humble Two-leggeds in the circle of creation with all the other created.

This understanding of *basileia* and repentance, I want to argue, can become a powerful impetus for justice first of all and finally for peace. What I am arguing is not some value-neutral creation theology of Matthew Fox, some new-age spirituality of feel-good individualism. Rather, it is an ultimate expression of a "theology of community" that must generate a consistent interest in justice and peace. Namely, if I image myself as a vital part of a community, indeed as a part of many communities, it becomes more difficult for me to act in ways that are destructive of the community.

If we image ourselves as fellow createds, mere participants in the whole of creation, functioning out of respect for and reciprocity with all of creation, then our relationships with each other as Two-leggeds must also be grounded in respect and reciprocity. As fellow createds, acknowledging God's hegemony over all, there can no longer be any rationale for exploitation and oppression. The desire for or even the perceived necessity for exerting social, political, economic or spiritual control over each other must give way to mutual respect, not just for individuals but for our culturally integrous communities.

This understanding of *basileia* would mandate new social and political structures, genuinely different from those created by either of the dominant Euro-cultural philosophical-political structures of capitalism or socialism. The competition generated by Western, Euro-cultural individualism, temporality and paradigms of history, progress and development must give way to the communal notion of inter-relatedness and reciprocity.

The pervasive nature of the social transformation that might be involved as a result of such a theology may become apparent in the singular challenge that it represents to the reified status of the "nation state" ideology of virtually all modern political theory. By what divine right does any immigrant political entity under the guise of a nation state assume explicit sovereignty over conquered and colonized indigenous populations? The challenge of indigenous peoples is a socio-economic and political challenge as much as it is a spiritual one.

In the wake of JPIC it should be clearly noted again that the theological priority of creation is not simply a priority for environmental concern, but rather, creation is a firm foundation for justice and a vision for peace. If we can begin with an affirmation of God as Creator and ourselves as created, then perhaps there is hope for a spiritual transformation that can bring us all closer to recognizing the kingdom of God in our midst (Luke 17:21). Then perhaps we can acknowledge our humanness in new and more significant ways, understanding that confession precedes return, and that both become the base for living in harmony and balance with God and all creation. Besides confession of our individual humanness, this means confessing the humanness of our churches, the humanness of our theologies, and the humanness of the world economic and political order in which we participate. Then it is possible to make our repentance, to return, to go back from whence we came, that is, to go back to the Creator in whom we like all of creation "live and move and have our being" (Acts 17:28). We must go back to a proper relationship with the Creator in which we confess our human inclination to put ourselves in the Creator's place and renew our understanding of ourselves and our institutions as mere creatures. We must go back to a recognition of ourselves as a part of and integrally related to all of creation.

The American Indian understanding of creation as sacred, of Grandmother, the earth, as the source of all life, goes far beyond the notion of such Western counter-institutions as the Sierra Club or Greenpeace. It embraces far more than concern for harp seals or a couple of ice-bound whales. It embraces all of life from trees and rocks to international relations. And this knowledge informs all of the community's activity, from hunting to dancing and even to writing grant proposals or administering government agencies. It especially concerns itself with the way we all live together. Perforce, it has to do with issues of justice and fairness and ultimately with peace. If we believe we are all relatives in this world, then we must live together differently than we have. Justice and peace, in this context, emerge almost naturally out of a self-imaging that sees the self only as part of the whole, as a part of an ever-expanding community that begins with family and tribe but is finally inclusive of all human beings and of all creation. All in this world are relatives, and we will live together out of respect for each other, working towards the good of each other. Respect for creation, for instance, must result in an ongoing concern for economic balance and resistance to economic injustices that leave many poor and oppressed while their white American or European relatives or even Japanese relatives live in wealth at the expense of others.

American Indian people have experienced and continue to experience endless oppression as a result of what some would call the barbaric invasion of America. On the other hand we certainly suspect that the oppression we have experienced is intimately linked to the way the immigrants pray and how they understand creation and their relationship to creation and Creator. Moreover, we suspect that the greed that motivated the displacement of all indigenous peoples from their lands of spiritual rootedness is the same greed that threatens the destruction of the earth and the continued oppression of so many people. Whether it is the stories the immigrants tell or the theologies they develop to interpret those stories, something appears wrong to Indian people. But not only do Indians continue to tell the stories, sing the songs, speak the prayers, and perform the ceremonies that root themselves deeply in Grandmother, the earth, they are actually audacious enough to think that their stories and their ways of reverencing creation will some day win over the immigrant conquerors and transform them. Optimism and enduring patience seem to run in the life blood of Native American peoples. Such is our spirit of hope that marks the American Indian struggle of resistance in the midst of a world of pain.

NOTES

1. See Ben Whitaker (ed.), *The Fourth World: Victims of Group Oppression*, eight reports from the field work of the minority rights group (New York: Schocken, 1972).

2. Julian Burger, *Report from the Frontier: the State of the World's Indigenous Peoples* (London: Zed Books, 1987).

3. "Liberation, Theology and Proclamation," in *The Mystical and Political Dimension of the Christian Faith. Concilium: Religion in the Seventies*, vol. 6, eds. Gustavo Gutiérrez & Claude Geffre (New York: Herder & Herder, 1974), p.69.

4. See Gutiérrez' essay "Theology and the Social Sciences," reprinted as appendix II in Paul E. Sigmund, *Liberation Theology at the Crossroads: Democracy or Revolution* (New York: Oxford, 1990), pp. 214–25.

5. See Gutiérrez, *Praxis de Liberación y Fé Cristiana* (San Antonio: Mexican American Culture Center, 1974), p.19. Cf. José Míguez Bónino, *Doing Theology in a Revolutionary Situation* (Philadelphia: Fortress, 1975), esp. pp. 85–97, 147ff.; Hugo Assmann, *Theology for a Nomad Church* (Maryknoll, NY: Orbis, 1976); and Juan Luis Segundo, *The Liberation of Theology* (Maryknoll, NY: Orbis, 1976), esp. p. 115. His later denials to the contrary, this Gutiérrez clearly says in his 1971 *A Theology of Liberation* (Maryknoll, NY: Orbis, 1973), pp.26ff.: "Attempts to bring about changes within the existing order have proven futile. This analysis of the situation is at the level of scientific rationality. Only a radical change from the status quo, that is, a profound transformation of the private property system, access to power of the exploited class and a social revolution that would break this dependence would allow for the change to a new society, a *socialist society*. . . . " (emphasis added).

6. Segundo is most explicit in this regard when he argues for the sacrifice of "minority" freedoms for the sake of improving the well-being of the "masses": ". . . minority aspects (e.g., freedom of thought, freedom of religion, freedom for Christian political actions) seem to be systematically overvalued in comparison with factors that are more revolutionary because they affect great human masses at one extreme of the process, e.g. in conditions of dire poverty, ignorance, disease and death" (*The Liberation of Theology*, p. 89).

Gutiérrez, for his part, in his recitation of dependency theory, argues to expand the analysis beyond that of a confrontation between nations to an analysis of class struggle. "But only a class analysis will enable us to see what is really involved in the opposition between oppressed countries and dominant peoples" (*Theology of Liberation*, p.87). Both levels of his analysis, however, begin with assumptions about the validity of the nation state. Moreover, class analysis has not yet been developed to analyze or significantly treat small culturally integrous communities except as part of a larger, more amorphous class grouping. Certainly, to devise strategies for such a level of analysis would require a different categorical nomenclature from that of class analysis.

7. The North American Catholic bishops fell into a similar pattern in their epistle on the economy, suggesting the right to have a job as an immediate basic human right. See G. Tinker, "Does All People Include Native Peoples?", in Charles Lutz, *God, Goods and the Common Good* (Minneapolis: Augsburg, 1987).

8. Leonardo Boff clearly and briefly details the cultural complicity of the early missionaries in the European conquest of the Americas: "All missionaries, even the most prophetic, like Pedro de Córdoba (author of *Christian Doctrine for the Instruction and Formation of the Indians, after the Manner of a History*, 1510) and Bartolomé de Las Casas (*The Sole Manner of Drawing all Peoples to the True Religion*, 1537) begin with the presupposition that Christianity is the only true religion: the Indians' religions are not only false, they are the work of satan. Method alone is open to discussion: whether to use violence and force (the common method, which went hand in hand with colonialism), or a 'delicate, soft and sweet' method (in the words of Las Casas). Either method was calculated to achieve the same effect, conversion. . . . All persons must be compelled to assimilate this religious order, which is also a cultural one." From *New Evangelization: Good News to the Poor* (Maryknoll, NY: Orbis, 1991), p.15. My own volume is also forthcoming: *Missionary Conquest and the Cultural Genocide of Native Americans: Case Studies in the Confusion of Gospel and Culture* (Minneapolis: Fortress, 1993).

9. *Power of the Poor in History*, trans. Robert R. Barr (Maryknoll, NY: Orbis, 1983), pp. 3ff.

10. Elizondo, in distinguishing between the "old" churches of the first world and the young churches of the third world, says of the old churches: "They are encumbered by centuries of traditions of seeing themselves as THE church and their missionaries carried their model of church to many parts of the world as if it were the one and only model of the church. This myopia was simply the product of the interiorized culture of the church seeing itself through the optic of the empire or the optic of the sociological model of the monarchy." Virgil Elizondo, "Conditions and Criteria for Authentic Inter-cultural Theological Dialogue," in *Concilium*, 171: *Different Theologies, Common Responsibility: Babel or Pentecost?*, eds. Claude Geffré, Gustavo Gutiérrez & Virgil Elizondo (Edinburgh: Clark, 1984), p.21.

11. This impetus, no doubt, is the reason the early Gutiérrez felt the need to trace the historical intellectual development of *all humankind* from Kant to Hegel, to Marx, to Freud and finally to Marcuse. *The Theology of Liberation*, pp. 30ff.

12. Robert Williams, *The American Indian in Western Legal Thought: The Discourses of Conquest* (New York: Oxford, 1990).

13. Glenn T. Morris & Ward Churchill, "Between a Rock and a Hard Place: Left-Wing Revolution, Right-Wing Reaction and the Destruction of Indigenous People," *Cultural Survival Quarterly*, 11, 1987, pp.17–24. They argue that the autonomy plan devised by a "repentant" Sandinista government was, in the final analysis, "little different in substance than the Indian Reorganization Act, used by the US government since 1934 to subordinate American Indian nations within its borders." See also K. Ohland & R. Schneider, *National Revolution and Indigenous Identity*, International Work Group for Indigenous Affairs [United Nations], Document 47, Copenhagen, IWGIA, 1983; and S.J. Anaya, *The CIA with the Honduran Army in the Mosquitia: Taking Freedom out of the Fight in the Name of Accountability*, report of the National Indian Youth Council, Albuquerque, NIYC, 1987.

14. See Vine Deloria, Jr., *God is Red* and *The Metaphysics of Modern Existence*; and Tinker, "American Indians and the Arts of the Land: Spatial Metaphors and Contemporary Existence," *Voices from the Third World: 1990* (Sri Lanka, EAT-WOT, 1991), pp. 170–93.

15. I use the Greek word *basileia* as a way of avoiding the unnecessarily sexist language of the usual English translation. Of course, the metaphor itself makes little sense to Native American peoples when it is literally translated. The praxis of our existence allows for no experiential knowledge about kings, queens or other monarchical rulers.

16. I use the word privilege here not only in an economic, social and political sense, but specifically in a soteriological sense. We dare not pretend that these two categories are unrelated in Western theology. Certainly they were thoroughly intertwined in the missionary evangelization of Native American peoples.

10

MARIE THERESE ARCHAMBAULT

NATIVE AMERICANS AND EVANGELIZATION

Marie Therese Archambault, OSF (Hunkpapa Lakota) is a Franciscan Sister and is originally from the Standing Rock Reservation in North Dakota. She holds several advanced degrees in theology, spirituality, and religious studies and has served in a variety of teaching and ministry positions throughout the United States. Archambault is currently the Native Urban Outreach Facilitator for the Tekakwitha Conference, a national organization serving native people in the Roman Catholic Church. She wrote this essay for *The People* (National Catholic Educational Association, 1992), a collaborative collection of reflections by native Catholics on the North American experience in light of the Columbus Quincentenary. Archambault's contribution focuses on the meaning of evangelization in contemporary native communities. She engages in historical analysis and personal reflection that together point to the need to "de-evangelize" native people in order to facilitate religious self-determination. Believing that enculturation represents a better approach to the formation of native Christian identities, she analyzes the important social and cultural factors that will affect this "praxis of evangelization." By highlighting the spiritual and psychological legacy of the colonization process, Archambault emphasizes the personal dimension of the liberation struggle.

When we, as Native American Catholics, reflect upon the meaning of evangelization for us, a flood of memories and ambivalent feelings is bound to arise.[1] It is difficult to sort out our experiences around this word, evangelization. But, in doing it, we must look at what we can become as Natives and not at what has happened to us as Indians.[2]

It is critically necessary to reflect upon what has happened to us, not only in the Catholic Church, but in Western history. Not to do this would be to deny our very selves and our memory. It would in effect make us hollow people with no identity. If we do not look at both the life and death aspects of our history, we will deprive ourselves of a means for coming to terms with it and of being healed from the psychological wounds it has left within us.

We must admit that our history, in general, has been wiped out of the public memory of the United States of America. We as a people have been trivialized or romanticized out of the conscious memory of most North American people. We must look carefully and long at what this has done to us, especially to our deep inner selves where the image of self is formed and where self-love/self-respect or hatred of self begins. Only after this will we be able to act out of a clear place within us.

The opposite alternative is to react to our history in pain and rage again and again, a normal reaction to such a background as ours. But, in the end, it is not life-giving to repeat this reaction endlessly. Let us choose a dignified way to respond to the memory of our oppression. If we choose otherwise, we risk becoming our own worst enemy, risk allowing the powerful history of our people not to be taken seriously by us and others, and thus to fade totally out of the American memory. We cannot allow this.

THE 1992 COMMEMORATION

The commemoration of Columbus's arrival in the Americas calls us to imagine our future in a new way and to take responsibility for what we can become as descendants of the people who dwelt here when he, by chance, landed on a Caribbean island and claimed it for the Spanish monarchs. We owe honor to the memory of our people, those who perished silently throughout the European invasion following 1492 and those who spoke out eloquently, pleading for the survival and honor of our people.[3] We must not let their voices go unheard or unanswered.

Who better than we can hear their pleas and answer them? Our memory of them contains the seed of what we can become, it points to our future. We should celebrate during this year, we should celebrate our survival and build a better future for our descendants. Despite centuries of the

European invasion and occupation, attempts to "civilize" us, and the misguided evangelization which accompanied it, we survived, we are still here. This is why the word *evangelization* raises ambivalent and confusing feelings within us. The time has come for us to look at these feelings.

To seek the meaning of the true evangelization of us, Natives of North America, we must take up these tasks. We must:

> Remember, relearn, and integrate our tribal histories and cultures *with compassion* and not seek vengeance upon those who helped to destroy them.
>
> Listen to the Gospel again with a loving self-respect and dignity.
>
> Take a fresh look at the tradition of the Roman Catholic Church.

OUR HISTORY, OUR IDENTITY

Ours is not only a history of oppression. No, it is the history of peoples who lived at least 13,000 years on this continent, by modest estimates, before Columbus arrived.[4] Our people created cultures based upon spiritual beliefs which bound them together in a life of simplicity and balance with each other and with the earth. These cultures were never static; they adapted and changed according to the needs of survival and spirit.

Theirs was not a life of perfection. We do not mean to remember our ancestors as though they were all saints or "noble savages" living in paradise. They were human beings prone to error as all humans yet they, like many indigenous people of the earth, founded and lived a balanced way of life. Many of them became persons of great character and dignity.

Recall the Arawak people who swam out and went in boats to welcome Columbus and his strange entourage as he sailed into their home waters. There is irony in this story of hospitality, for the Arawak unknowingly welcomed their own destruction.

The history of America has been taught in schools and universities as though it were only the history of the European colonies. Many have forgotten our story, but we cannot forget it. If this amnesiac view of North American history is to change, then we must first revive the memories of our people lying hidden within ourselves, for we are the same yet different from our ancestors.

One reason we are different is because we are literate and becoming more and more so. Yet our people, with rare exception, lived in a culture of primary orality.[5] Studies have shown the profound effect literacy has upon people; practically speaking, it reshapes them into different human beings. As literate people, we perceive and learn in ways other than our ancestors did. Given this profound change, we must reappropriate our tribal ways before they die, or before others appropriate them for their own purposes. We know that both of these things have already happened.[6] Studying and reclaiming our religious traditions must be our necessary task if we are to maintain our identity and survive spiritually.

This quincentennial can be the occasion to draw upon the vast energy which lies dormant in this memory of our ancestors rooted within us and in the land of North America. Only we can respond in a way yet unknown on this continent.

THE GOSPEL: AN ENCOUNTER WITH JESUS

When we read the Gospel, we must read it as *Native people*, for this is who we are. We can no longer try to be what we think the dominant society wants us to be. As Native Catholic people, we must set out with open minds and hearts; then we will encounter Jesus Christ. We must learn to subtract the chauvinism and the cultural superiority with which this Gospel was often presented to our people. We must, as one author says, "de-colonize"[7] this Gospel, which said we must become European in order to be Christian. We have to go beyond the *white gospel* in order to perceive its truth.

When we do this, we shall meet Jesus as our brother and recognize him as one who has been with us all along as the quiet servant, the one who has strengthened us through these centuries. Then we will know that the cry of Jesus Christ from the cross was the cry of our people at Wounded Knee, Sand Creek and other places of the mass death of our people. He was our companion during these years of our invisibility in this society. This same Jesus is the one who challenges us to grow beyond ourselves. This is the challenge of evangelization. If we take up the challenge, we shall sense that he is with us and be glad. This is the heart and core meaning of the Gospel.

THE TRADITION OF THE CATHOLIC CHURCH

The Catholic Church has an enormously long and varied history of approximately 2000 years. Yet, many of us know nothing of this history beyond what we picked up at mission school or in release-time classes. Frequently, our ancestors were never given a chance to actually choose to be Catholic. Thus, estrangement from the church is common for many of us in our adulthood, we know this all too well. Consequently, as we approach the quincentennial commemorative year, we find we are ignorant of the meaning of the Catholic Church for us, even as we claim to be Catholic.

Furthermore, we have to admit that some of the church's teaching is advanced by humans and, therefore, prone to faults and historical limitations.

For example, during the centuries following Columbus's arrival in the Americas, many church leaders did not believe that the "Indians" were human. A Dominican priest named Bartolome De Las Casas taught that the Indians of the Americans were human beings with souls and spiritual capacities.[8] For years, his teaching was banned and considered mistaken.

In recent times the teachings of the great gathering called Vatican Council II (1963–65) were unprecedented for us and for all human beings. In that Council, the Catholic Church opened it doors, its windows, its very self to all cultures and called them to the destiny of Jesus Christ.[9] The Catholic tradition deserves scrutiny by us. Unlike many of our ancestors,[10] we are allowed to freely choose the Catholic faith. Whether our particular tribe chose freely or not, we are called to make that choice anew today. This also is a fresh call to the process of evangelization.

The tasks described above are unsettling ones. If we take up these tasks of looking at our history and traditions, reading the Gospel anew and looking again at the history of the Catholic Church, it will change us. It will call us to be *awake*, not lulled by the comfortable paths of least resistance and safe peace. It will call us to remember and name ourselves in a new way and to reclaim our traditional ways together with the Catholic faith as the real way to spiritual healing and power.

A PERSONAL EXPERIENCE

I must clarify my own perspective a little and describe some events which have brought me to this writing. My experience is much like the experience of many Native Catholics. I was born in the Standing Rock Reservation in Fort Yates, North Dakota before Vatican II. My family were nominal Catholics who never practiced the Catholic faith seriously. My brothers, sister and myself attended Catholic mission boarding schools in the Dakotas for our elementary and secondary education because, like so many of our classmates, our parent(s) could not afford to keep us at home.[11] Attending a mission boarding school before Vatican II meant daily Mass and frequent catechism lessons in the Catholic faith.

At an early age I felt called to a contemplative lifestyle and joined the Franciscan sisterhood after high school. I have remained there since. In this life, I have been evangelized in the best ways that the Catholic tradition offers and have acted as evangelizer for others, Native and non-Native.

However, there are two moments of insight which touched me *as an Indian woman* and remain in me as healing memories.

> In the late 1970s, I attended a meeting of the ANCR, the Association of Native Clergy and Religious. A young Native priest dressed casually in

jeans, tee-shirt and with long hair pulled back in a ponytail, also attended. The sight of him brought a new consciousness to me. For the first time it occurred to me that the Catholic Church belonged to us as well. The Catholic Church could take on the look of us, Native people.

Another key event of evangelization centered around the reading of *The Sacred Pipe*[12] and *Black Elk Speaks*.[13] Through this encounter with Nicholas Black Elk, I was deeply evangelized by a sense of the sacred which came through his life as a holy man and as a Catholic catechist. Especially powerful was his account of the Wanekia vision.[14] For me it was a vision of Jesus Christ as a Lakota man. Something was transformed within me at that moment; it touched me and I wept for my people many times.

I marvel even today that my sense of self as a Native woman was hidden from me. I never even imagined my Native identity and reality as identical with the *Catholic* reality taught me in the mission boarding schools and in convent life. Suddenly, in each instance, upon seeing this young man dressed as my brothers would dress, and upon reading the description of Jesus Christ as an Indian man, these two worlds—Catholic and Native—came together within me. These were moments of evangelization.

It never occurred to me before then that nowhere in my specifically Native world was my Catholic experience embodied. Since that time, I have striven, through prayer and study, to bring these two worlds together within myself even more. Now I am aware that many other Indian people, my classmates and others, share the same experience of separation between these identities.

EVANGELIZATION AND ENCULTURATION

We can no longer speak of evangelization of Native Americans[15] without simultaneously speaking of enculturation.[16] Our Catholic faith and our Native culture must find a place together. Paul VI has opened and led the way in his teaching *Evangelii Nuntiandi*.[17] For him, evangelization is a call to experience, or to experience anew, the reality of Christ Jesus in the present moment of history, so that the Gospel carries the capacity to be ever new. Evangelization is the witness and proclamation of the presence of Jesus Christ by his followers, based upon their own encounter with him and the inner conviction that only this experience can give. It is only through the evidence of their following the Gospel in such an *outward* way that Christ's way becomes clear, so clear for those who experience this witness of life that they are able to choose or reject the values of the Gospel which he taught.

When the followers of Christ live in a way that reflects his life, they also evangelize all who contact them, no matter where they are. As Paul VI states:

For the Church, evangelization means bringing the good news into all the strata of humanity, and through its influence transforming humanity from within and making it new. . . . The purpose of evangelization is therefore precisely this interior change, and if it had to be expressed in one sentence the best way of stating it would be to say that the Church evangelizes when she seeks to convert . . . both the personal and collective consciences of people, the activities in which they engage, and the lives and concrete milieu which are theirs.[18]

It is important to reflect upon the words "transforming humanity from within and making it new." When Paul VI writes the word *within*, he, in the name of the church, calls its "evangelizers" to view the world from *inside* the people it sets out to evangelize. Only at this place inside will the evangelizers know how to call a person within that culture to an interior change. The evangelizers must take seriously the deepest, most dear values, the cultural structures, and ways of those being evangelized. They must see from within the world of the people. As John Hatcher, a missionary from South Dakota says:

The Gospel cannot be preached in a vacuum. The people who hear the Gospel have rich cultural and religious traditions which have been handed down for centuries. They have a unique language, value system and way of looking at the world. They have developed customs and laws and distinct ways of interacting. The purpose of the gospel proclamation is not to destroy this heritage. Rather it is to transform it. When a people accepts the gospel proclamation their culture is enhanced. The Gospel gives new vitality to a culture.[19]

Thus, the followers of Christ must seek to enter the reality of those to whom they are sent. When Christ is taught with their inner reality in mind, the Gospel has a chance of making sense to those who hear it. It is Jesus Christ who stands as the center and is the source of every evangelical action or word. The church sets out upon a profound inner journey when it sets out to evangelize.

But evangelization is not only an interior experience of the "consciences of people." When it is genuinely proclaimed and accepted, it will manifest its reality in the "activities, the lives and the social milieu" of the people who interiorize it. Evangelization begins a transformation of the historical reality of the people into a way of life that is compatible with the Gospel and with the best of their own culture. Hatcher, speaking of the exhortation of Paul VI, writes:

The exhortation instructs missionaries to proclaim the Gospel in a way that does not put pressure on people to receive it. The Gospel is to be presented in a gentle, loving way. Missionaries are to respect the cultural values of the people and respect the pace at which the people can assimilate the message.[20]

It is critical to keep focused on Jesus Christ. By his words and deeds he proclaimed a kingdom of liberating salvation meant to be experienced within a given historical reality. For Natives this is important because even though "he is inseparable from the Church,"[21] sometimes his face is obscured for us by church bureaucracy and its plethora of rules and regulations. This is experienced much like the Bureau of Indian Affairs, as a huge impersonal complex. One can miss the welcoming presence of Jesus within the institutional structures. The vision of the kingdom preached by Jesus and its liberating salvation has in the past often been hidden from Native people due to this particular face and style of the church.

NEED TO "DE-EVANGELIZE"

In the past the church has obscured the face of Christ through ignorance of or outright dismissal of Native cultures. It has attempted to enter the reality of Native people at superficial levels, almost always from the European viewpoint and perspective. And although archives show that the church missionaries were often far more humane than government representatives when it came to dealing with Native people, what they did was also misguided. Consequently, Native cultures were devalued and rejected by the church's missionaries.

Through this manner of teaching, many Indian people were placed in the profoundly impossible situation of accepting the Gospel for their own good on the one hand while, on the other, having to devalue their culture and thus themselves. It is no wonder that many Native people mistrust all Christian churches and frequently appear outwardly "religionless" in this land. Now, we must undo this attitude and do all we can to reveal the face of Christ, who goes beyond all cultures. This means we must "de-evangelize" Native people. Bishop Pedro Casaldaliga writes:

> De-evangelizing would mean decolonizing evangelization. The gospel came to Latin America wrapped, borne, and served by a culture at the service of an empire, initially the Iberian Empire. Rather than a pure, supracultural, liberating gospel message, what came was a message that was a cultural import, which for five hundred years has prevented a really indigenous church from developing in Latin America.[22]

Although Casaldaliga speaks from a South American perspective, there is little doubt that, practically speaking, this same process happened in North America. It is clear that no real indigenous church has developed here either. To Native people, the Gospel is often seen as co-opted by the European-rooted, American style.

Yet, this was not the intent of Jesus, as Schillebeeckx attempts to describe in speaking of the early "messianic communities."

> For Jesus the kingdom is to be found where human life becomes "whole," where "salvation" is realized for men and women, where righteousness and love begin to prevail, and enslaving conditions come to an end. Jesus makes the reality of God imaginable in terms of a common participation in a festive and splendid banquet the poor and the social outcasts can share.[23]

In the gospel accounts Jesus finds the ordinary people, even the poor and the outcasts of society, spends time with them, treats them as equals and directs his message to both women and men. This way of acting did not come totally into being once and for all, but whenever it appeared it was something new. Schillebeeckx says:

> The kingdom of God is a new world in which suffering is done away with, a world of completely whole or healed people in a society no longer dominated by master-servant relationships, quite different from that under Roman rule. For this very reason Jesus turns especially to the poor. "Salvation is preached to the poor." To a great degree Jesus' action consisted in establishing social community, opening up communication, above all where "excommunication" and rejection were officially in force: in respect to public sinners, publicans making themselves rich from the poor, lepers and others, whoever and whatever were "unclean." These are the ones he seeks out, the ones with whom he eats.[24]

Jesus, the first evangelizer, through the power of the Holy Spirit and in this moment of history, continues to evangelize and to call Native men and women to experience his kingdom and then to join in proclaiming the reign. This calls for the church's representatives to learn this history for themselves and to teach the Gospel with a renewed understanding of its truth in our context. The Gospel does go beyond the politics of those who preach it. It must be communicated as hospitable and welcoming to all people and their cultures. When this is done, the Gospel casts light upon those cultures and challenges them to a greater destiny, to transcend themselves to become who they really are.

CATHOLIC TEACHING TODAY

Most recently Popes Paul VI and John Paul II, in their worldwide journeys and in their writing and speeches, have spoken clearly about the centrality of evangelizing cultures "in depth and to their very roots."[25] The activity of these two contemporary Popes and their words is itself evangelizing.

Pope John Paul II addressed Native Americans in Phoenix during his 1987 visit to North America. In that speech and in later ones, he clearly stated the value of Native cultures. He acknowledged the mistakes made in the past by church representatives and called all Native Americans themselves to participate in a new evangelization.

> Your encounter with the Gospel has not only enriched you; it has enriched the church. We are well aware that this has not taken place without its difficulties and, occasionally, its blunders. However you are experiencing this today, the Gospel does not destroy what is best in you. On the contrary, it enriches, as it were, from within the spiritual qualities and gifts that are distinctive of your cultures.[26]

"The Gospel does not destroy what is best in you." When we reflect upon these words, we can begin to realize that we are called to become *precisely* Native within the Catholic Church. We are not to model ourselves after something or someone which we are not, either in religious response, in prayer-style or worship! We must draw deeply from the inner being given us at our creation. It is only by drawing from our own depths where the Great Holy Spirit, the "creative, living source" dwells within us, that we can hope to find our way into the future.

GENUINE EVANGELIZATION

We know that at least one of our ancestors did not identify Jesus Christ as an oppressor. History has revealed that some early missionaries taught in such a way that Nicholas Black Elk accepted Jesus Christ as Savior.[27] The story of Jesus appealed to his imagination for there is much about Jesus which resounds in Native ways: his humility and bravery in facing death, his love and service of the people. This identification can be seen in the great Black Elk's vision of Jesus during his Ghost dance experience:

> Then they led me to the center of the circle where once more I saw the holy tree all full of leaves and blooming . . . Against the tree there was a man standing with arms held wide in front of him. I looked hard at him, and I could not tell what people he came from. He was not a Wasichu and he was not an Indian. His hair was long and hanging

loose, and on the left side of his head he wore an eagle feather. His body was strong and good to see, and it was painted red . . . He was a very fine looking man. While I was staring hard at him, his body began to change and became very beautiful with all colors of light, and around him there was light. He spoke like singing: "My life is such that all earthly beings and growing things belong to me. Your father, the Great Spirit, has said this, You too must say this."[28]

With this vision of the Wanekia, standing at the center of the Sundance circle, we see Jesus Christ among Native people, as one of us. His presence made the tree at the center bloom. He was surrounded by light. This was the Christ who caught the imagination of Black Elk. It does not matter whether this vision came at the beginning or at the end of Black Elk's life as a catechist. It points to his own encounter with Jesus Christ.

In conclusion, we emphasize the church's recent teaching about respect for cultures. It is unmistakable in the teaching of Paul VI, and even today, his teaching is still fresh and challenging:

> All this could be expressed in the following words: what matters is to evangelize man's culture and cultures (not in a purely decorative way, but in a vital way, in depth and right to their very roots), in the wide and rich sense which these terms have in *Gaudium et Spes*, always taking the person as one's starting-point and always coming back to the relationships of people among themselves and God . . . Therefore every effort must be made to ensure a full evangelization of culture, or more correctly of cultures. They have to be regenerated by an encounter with the Gospel. But this encounter will not take place if the Gospel is not proclaimed.[29]

We as Catholic Native people are ourselves called to be the proclaimers of this faith in Jesus Christ, with a true sense of our own Native traditions and within the great Catholic tradition. In the next section we will look at cultural ways of Native people which open the way for the Gospel and make its entry smooth.

WAYS TO THE SACRED

What makes it easier for Native people to hear the Gospel? What is it in native cultures that clears the path for the Gospel to be embodied among us? There are many ways and we need to reflect frequently on what they are.

"ALL MY RELATIVES"

We are people who always sense ourselves in relationship. Our identity has been passed on from within our family groups and clans. Our people formed cultures marked by deep interrelationship within themselves and outwardly with the earth. Living within community and acting with a primary community mentality comes easy for us. Because of this, we have the potential to easily form circles and communities in which to pray, to play, and to support each other.

When Jesus Christ joins the circle of life, church begins. When we look to Christ among us as our life-giver, our strength and light, and seek to embody this goodness among us, church is formed. When we do this, we enter upon an inner and outer journey which will change our lives.

We must be open to the formation of the life-giving community called into being by Jesus Christ by building upon this strong inner cultural quality of being a relative. Then our natural tendency to be within family groups and clans will be enhanced by the richness of Christ's outlook. We will be strengthened to forgive each other more, to help heal each other, to call each other to service. This is what our culture, in union with the church, as it exists among us, can do to lead us further into the sacred.

SENSE OF HUMOR

We love to laugh. Through these 500 years we have survived by spotting the humor of human foibles, those of ourselves and those of others. Funny stories abound when our families gather. Furthermore, the traditions of the clowns and jesters is rooted in our community consciousness. Among the Lakota, the Heyoka clown figure is sacred. The one representing Heyoka has been called upon in prayer and visions to do everything backwards so that people will laugh and not take themselves so seriously. This ability to find joy even in hardship and suffering opens us to the gospel life. The sign that the Gospel of Christ is among us will result in a deeper sense of joy.

GENEROSITY

Generosity is a deeply formed quality of our people. It manifested itself in many ways and aspects of our life in the past and does so today in contemporary America. When we visit our city or reservation relatives, or when we go to see an old friend after many years, or when we meet relatives of a friend for the first time, we instinctively want to give them gifts.

Years ago when my mother attended the graduation of my youngest brother from a reservation school, she met there the family of his best friend. That family invited her to their home where they treated her as an honored guest. They gave her simple gifts of all kinds, whatever they considered valuable or thought she might enjoy or need: a tire, some quilting material, a few dollars. She knew instinctively to accept these gifts in a spirit of humility. This is the Lakota way.

The Giveaway is a ceremony which continues to exist, although it stands as totally different from the "white" way. It is diametrically opposed to the views of the smart consumer, so upheld in the dominant wealthy modern-day culture. Yet, the experience of gift-giving comes closest to the meaning of the unconditional love of God for us. This doctrine of the church can best be experienced in a Giveaway ceremony.

SHARING

There is another way of being which is almost second nature to us and this is sharing. Sometimes it even goes to the point of doing without so much in order to share with our relatives who need. When we were growing up in mission schools, we always shared what we had. If one of us happened upon a candy bar, it would be shared with friends, even if each received only one bite! We shared buns and bread which we got in whatever manner. It seemed we were always hungry. We learned from our families that sharing equally was our way of life and practiced it without question. This is not to intimate that our boarding school experience was paradise, far from it. But it is good to remember that even in that strange boarding school environment, we behaved according to the ways we had learned in our homes.

The qualities of generosity and sharing are ways which reveal the generosity of God to us. They help us to see God in each other. One of the most profound moments of evangelization for me was when I received a beautiful blanket at my cousin's Giveaway ceremony. He had been given a great honor in his home state for achievements in Native education. To show gratitude, his family held a Giveaway and Honoring ceremony. When my name was called and a beautiful blanket was given to me, it brought with it a sense of the goodness of this family, my own worthiness and the goodness of life. This experience revealed a sense of the sacred to me.

Such a ceremony could act as a bridge leading one into a deeper understanding of the sacred and of the divine mystery. When we become aware that Jesus Christ is a bridge leading us into a sense of the sacred, a sense that is much greater than we can imagine, then we know the meaning of evangelization.

Other qualities such as hospitality, story-telling, honor, respect and humility have been passed on to us. We must explore these as well and let the memory of these qualities form us today. Those described above are very widespread among Native peoples regardless of tribe and so are emphasized.

These qualities—a sense of relationship and humor, generosity and sharing—"make the way straight" for the Gospel to enter and take root among us.

OBSTACLES TO EVANGELIZATION
NATIVE CODEPENDENCY

The devastation of drug and alcohol abuse among our people is still evident and stands as a towering obstacle to every aspect of our health. It certainly puts a stop to genuine evangelization. Coping with these forms of abuse saps our strength and puts chaos and negative energy into the interior space needed for the spiritual change and conversion to which evangelization invites us.

There have been courageous moves among Natives all over North American not just to "sober up" but to address the social destruction that generations of drunkenness have wrought among us.[30] Perhaps one of the most pervasive effects of addictive behavior is what we have lately named codependency. This word is variously defined by experts. The following definition is from a professor of counselor education at Ohio University:

> Codependence is preoccupation and extreme dependence (emotionally, socially, and sometimes physically) on a person or object. Eventually, this dependence on another person becomes a pathological condition that effects the codependent in all other relationships. . . . [this] ill health, maladaptive or problematic behavior that is associated with living with, working with or otherwise being close to a person with alcoholism . . . affects not only individuals, but families, communities, businesses or other institutions, and even whole societies.[31]

This passage describes well the Native situation in regard to alcoholism and drug abuse. The addictive substance preoccupies the addicted one, which then causes preoccupation by worried family members. In a sense, we all become preoccupied by the addictive substance whether we are physically addicted or not. Furthermore, the phenomenon of codependency is so widespread in our addictive American society[32] that its detection and remedy among us is hindered because it is condoned in the dominant culture. It is not a generalization to state this: Codependency/addiction and Native American are not only words, but also co-existent realities in Native memory and awareness which endure even into our contemporary world. We cannot deny that some Native families have escaped this suffering, but not too many.

In the scenario of codependency and addiction, the reality of evangelization is far removed. Yet, the evangelists quickly learn that they step into a pervasive culture of alcoholism in which at least two generations have learned codependent behaviors. Many of these behaviors have become habitual in Native society, so much so that many Native people respond to reality through these learned behaviors. This complicates the situation for a well-meaning Christian minister who comes to serve Native people.

At first, the codependent behavior makes sense to those acting it out because it helps them to survive within an anguished family situation. But what was initially a survival mechanism later becomes socialized into behavior which helps neither the drinking person nor the sober relative. Soon the entire family grows so accustomed to the addictive behavior that habitual tolerance develops which, in the end, enables the drinking. This attitude of enablement becomes a mind-set which affects the clan, the village and Native society.

Codependent persons try not to cause trouble in an already troubled situation. Codependent persons think: Why challenge the drinking relative when she has stopped drinking for the day? Why bother and upset him when he is at work today? I cannot hurt my father, he has already suffered enough.

They become unable to judge what is tolerance and what is enablement. Soon, they act only to survive. For many Native people desperately seeking to hold a family or clan together in a society that is unfriendly to them, codependent behaviors seem like an easier solution. These behaviors become intertwined with the need to survive. This is particularly true of those who live in urban settings.

Widespread studies have shown that the effects of addiction and codependency in a family are profoundly disfiguring, especially to the self-esteem of individuals. Frequently, this lack of self-esteem takes the form of inaction or inability to act for the good of the family or group. It acts as misdirected frustration, anger and rage, which show up in petty fighting and mistrust of family and group members. There also is a learned, pacifying behavior which transfers over to other situations and takes on the look of tolerance and even long-suffering.

Within church communities, it shows itself as group inability to accept challenges and prophetic voices. These effects spread out to the clan, the village and the Native society. Thus, we cannot exaggerate the reality of codependency in Native life today. In the video *Honor for One, Honor for All*, this societal addiction is graphically portrayed, along with steps for its cure.[33]

Evangelization or any other attempt to bring health is stopped short by codependency because Native people frequently are not acting from a place of health within themselves. They are responding to church workers and activities as people profoundly formed by addictive situations and families formed by codependency. They may appear to be tolerant, forgiving and long-suffering, but one look at the stagnant local church situation says something else.

Natives in this state of mind do not possess the inner strength to take on leadership roles or to allow other Native people to grow in leadership roles. How often have we experienced the "disappearance" of said appointed leader? How often have our groups disintegrated because of conflict? Church representatives can be co-opted into this syndrome. It takes a perceptive and courageous minister, one who has faced his/her own leanings to codependency, to challenge such a situation in a compassionate spirit.

The Gospel sheds light on codependency. Jesus never took the easy way out or ran away from speaking the truth even when it was difficult. In the encounter with the risen power of Christ among us, we can find strength to face this situation and act to change it for the better. As Native men and women, we also must courageously examine our own codependent behaviors, such as excessive timidity due to low self-esteem, fear of leadership, lack of self-confidence, jealousy at another's leadership. We must allow ourselves to see how these behaviors hinder the Gospel from taking root among us. We must ask ourselves if these behaviors keep us from challenging our own church and family members to greater growth.

PATERNALISM

One area of church life blends quite easily with Native codependency. This is the area of *paternalism*. At first, most Indian people appreciated the kindness of the missionaries. They wanted to help in whatever way possible and frequently did with great personal sacrifice. Any diary or notebook of an early missionary reveals the enormous efforts made to help our people for the sake of the Gospel. But we know now that frequently enough their idea of *to help* became *to do for*.

Paternalism is frequently an interior structure of codependency deeply internalized by non-Natives and Natives involved in the missionary endeavor. Unfortunately, it describes a relationship which has grown into existence historically between church representatives and the Native people in many places. It also delineates the self-images of both groups and from these images it flows into certain roles played by each. The structure is basically either dominator versus the one dominated or the power-possessor versus client-recipient in need.

Usually, the client-recipient is in need of the "goods" or "power" (material or spiritual) of the possessor in order to survive and therefore must remain in the relationship in order to receive them. This is the relationship of parent and child. One plays the knower and the other plays the ignorant and needy member. The giver easily dominates the receiver.

This becomes *externalized* in the behavior of the Native society. As these behaviors become deeply internalized by both sides and acted out over a long period of time, they slowly become jelled into social structures. The structures endure in time because they result in rewards for both sides. Gradually, this way of relating becomes habitual and comfortable because the relationship fills a perceived need of each. Unfortunately, too often this relationship describes the relationship of the church and Native Catholics.

What began within Native people as a sense of insecurity in a strange religion later led to deepening dependency on the church leaders. The behavior of the leaders did not call forth creative response from our people, instead it made us passive.[34] It did not allow us to perceive ourselves as leaders and dynamic participants in the church.

Hatcher calls paternalism "the greatest obstacle to the development of native leadership." He goes on:

> Paternalism is an insidious disease which militates against the formation of a local Church. . . . It is fair to say that most missionaries today try to avoid the glaring mistakes of the past. However, a new form of paternalism abounds in today's mission field. Missionaries want to protect Indian people from making mistakes and taking risks. They often see themselves as taking care of the Indian people. They want to be sure that the people make the "right" choices when they enculturate the liturgy and develop the "right" spirituality.[35]

CODEPENDENT KINDNESS

Although paternalism is a problem in itself, it becomes complex when it blends with the substance codependency of Native people. It becomes even more complex when it is done with great kindness. When this happens, Native people depend even more profoundly upon the church representative and even become addicted to the rewards which their behavior gives. Finally, they believe less and less in their own goodness. At this point, the process of evangelization is totally stopped.

Before evangelization can even be addressed, the church must look into the ways that the Native people of a particular church community have been formed in the paternalistic mind-set and how this, along with codependency, has affected both their ability to really own their own capacities for leadership or allow each other to be leaders within it.

A story by an unknown author illustrates this point:

> A French anthropologist working in Chiapas, Mexico, compared the Indian people (80% of that diocese) to a horse that was feeble, so thin

his ribs showed, and was dispirited. People noted that over the passage of time his condition only worsened. Veterinarians were brought in who prescribed medicines and treatments, but the horse was not healed. Finally, a wise old woman came and looked at the ailing animal. "Untie his hooves," she said, for they were securely bound. So they were untied, and soon the horse was youthful, strong and galloping free.

What may appear as kindness within the paternalistic relationship is really what keeps the "horse's hooves tied," it keeps the people from standing and walking on the strength of their own faith and self-confidence or of allowing others among them to do it.

IN THE GOSPEL'S LIGHT

It bears repeating that a paternalistic relationship has nothing to do with evangelization. Christ approaches all persons as brothers, sisters, as equals. The possessor and the clients are both acting out of a distorted view of themselves. Neither is acting as an adult or as a true follower of Christ. By not calling each other to take equal responsibility in the relationship, the participants remain either as benevolent, incompetent parents or as adult-children. Challenging the other in the spirit of the Gospel and sharing the truth in a mutual way would gradually but surely break this profoundly unhealthy way of relating. Until this break comes, Natives and non-Natives who are involved in this codependent, paternalistic behavior will never experience the reality of an indigenous church.

This style of relating stands in stark contrast to the word of God revealed through the Gospel. This word calls us to a freedom from and far beyond codependency. The church representative should begin gently to root out this form of codependency, first within herself or himself, then look to the community. This is the true call of the church. As Ekstrom and Roberts note:

> The Church seeks to upset the criteria of judgment, prevailing values, points of interest, lines of thought, sources of inspiration and models in life which are in *contrast with the Word of God and the plan of salvation.* With the human person as the starting point and always coming back to the relationships of people among themselves and with God, every effort must be made to ensure the full evangelization of culture, or more correct, of cultures. They have to be regenerated by the encounter with the Gospel. But this encounter will not take place if the Gospel is not proclaimed.[36] (italics mine)

As we Native people begin to sense the strength of our Native heritage within us, the Catholic heritage will find its place and many more will be called to evangelize our own people. This cannot be done until the effects of our addictive society, its widespread codependency and its interlocking paternalism is acknowledged, first within ourselves and then within Native society. Church leaders also have an obligation to allow the Gospel to enlighten and question their decisions regarding Native communities and paternalism.

PRAXIS FOR EVANGELIZATION

Praxis is a theological term which means "practice" or "work." It will take work to grow beyond where we are now and to become someone more, i.e., who we are in the church. The following process is a suggested way to begin.

In order for Catholic Native people to experience the fruit of evangelization and take their place as participants in the Catholic Church, the healing of memories must take place. When this begins, the process itself will evangelize, because it begins and ends in the living memory of Jesus Christ among the people. This process-work is a ministry which must be done in small communities, or circles. Every person in the group must be on an equal basis and have equal time to speak; it is important that each be heard. Native leaders must come forward for training so that they can learn to facilitate this process themselves. Such leadership demands that the person already has begun a spiritual journey of sobriety and has training in the skills needed. The process involves the following components:

Prayer based on Native ceremonies and Catholic ritual.

Revival of the memory of who we were as a people before the coming of Western culture, before the devaluation and the distortion of our self-image. This can be done through appropriate readings, films, prayer, stories, personal memories.

Grieving for what was lost, so that we can move on. Discerning leadership is needed to know when to move on. It involves facilitating the ministry of retelling our stories and revisiting our history, much as was done in the movie "Dances with Wolves." Speakers and listeners are necessary for this healing to begin. This process will take time, and it will result in the gradual healing of negative self-images such as the following:

Indian self-image: wooden Indian, drunken Indian; cultural shame which is learned and resides on an unconscious level.

Non-Indian images: a sense of non-forgiveness, feeling badly about being the "ugly American" or the unjust aggressor. There is a need to forgive what was done to our ancestors and to seek healing in the relationship with non-Native people.

Celebrating the new awarenesses that comes with healing.

Naming the way of the future through reflecting: What have we become and what way shall we walk in the future?

CONCLUSION

The memory of Jesus Christ as friend, as companion in suffering, as our relative risen and among us, as pilgrim walking and dancing with all of us, will heal us. But not only this. Healing will only take place within the setting of our Native ways and Native memories. From this viewpoint, we will begin to perceive ourselves and Christ in a different way: He will be one of us, he will have a Native face. As these memories intersect, we will experience ourselves, our life, our life-giving stories and ceremonies as forming a new and honorable tradition in the Catholic Church of the future. Only after following such a process will we act from this healed place within and be ready to grow into the future as Native Catholics.

In conclusion, we look to an elder for guidance through the tasks which lie ahead. The simple words of Alfretta Antone as she addressed Pope John Paul II during his 1987 visit to Phoenix express our best motivations.

> We choose not only to survive, but to live fully. We want to live in harmony with all people and all creation. We choose to keep alive for all generations the ways of living carved in the stones and bones of our ancestors. We are open to share and receive whatever is good for the life of the human family with all people of good will. . . . As Catholic Natives, we have come to know Jesus as the Son of God who loves us and lives with us. The Holy Spirit works in many ways through our people.[37]

By allowing the Holy Spirit to move among us, we shall know who we are called to become as Native people and as Native Catholics.

NOTES

1. For the quincentennial year many articles and books discussing the result of Columbus's arrival have been printed. For the Catholic viewpoint, see: Leonardo Boff, "1492–1992 Celebration of Penance, Celebration of Resistance," *Creation Spirituality*, Sept.-Oct. 1992, in which he says: "For Native Americans, the Quincentennial is a commemoration of five centuries of suffering and betrayal."

2. *Native* expresses a renewed understanding of ourselves and our history. Indian expresses that we were misnamed, along with the shame, the self-devaluation and self-hatred, and ambivalence toward ourselves that was internalized with this name for five centuries. For contemporary Native experience, see: Ted Zuern, *Bread and Freedom* (Chamberlain, SD: St. Joseph Indian School, 1991).

3. W. C. Vanderwerth, compiler, *Indian Oratory: Speeches by Noted Indian Chieftains* (New York: Ballantine Books, 1972).

4. Henry Warner Bowden, *The American Indians and Christian Missions: Studies in Cultural Conflict* (Chicago: University of Chicago Press, 1981).

5. See Walter J. Ong, S.J., *Orality and Literacy: The Technologizing of the Word* (London and New York: Methuen, 1982). Stresses the vast change within a human being which comes with literacy.

6. Jon Magnuson "Selling of the Native Soul," *Christian Century* 106 (November 22, 1989), 1084–1087.

7. Bishop Pedro Casaldaliga, *In Pursuit of the Kingdom, Writings 1968–1988* (Maryknoll, NY: Orbis Press, 1990), pp. 2–3.

8. Markus Gilbert, O.P., *Bartolome De Las Casas: The Gospel of Liberation*, Citadel Series (Dublin and Athlone: Verilas and St. Paul Publications, 1988).

9. Vatican Council II, *Declaration on the Relationship of the Church to Non-Christian Religions (Notra Aetate)*, 1965.

10. Bowden, op. cit. In Grant's Peace Policy, Indian territories were divided between thirteen Christian denominations as part of Grant's policy to civilize Indians as well as to bring the Indian wars to a peaceful end.

11. Canadian Natives have done a considerable amount of reflection on this widespread Native experience of the "residential/board school." See: "Residential Schools: A New Kind of Remembering," *Catholic New Times*, March 31, 1991, pp. 9–13, and the video "Where the Spirit Lives," Anglican Board of Canada.

12. Joseph Epes Brown, *The Sacred Pipe: The Sacred Rituals of the Sioux* (Bloomington, IN, University of Indiana Press), 1971.

13. John G. Neihardt, *Black Elk Speaks: Being the Life Story of a Holy Man of the Oglala Sioux*, A Bison Book (Lincoln, NE: University of Nebraska Press, 1961).

14. *Ibid.* A footnote defines Wanekia as "One Who Makes Live," p. 137.

15. A recent search of theology library computer files under the title "evangelization" revealed not one of 433 items dealt with evangelization of Native/American Indian people of North America, although one of Columbus's intentions in 1492 was to claim these "indians" for Christ.

16. See *Effective Inculturation and Ethnic Identity: Inculturation*, working papers on Living Faith and Cultures by Maria De La Cruz Aymes, S.H., Francis J. Buckley, S.J., Charles Nyamiti, William E. Biernatiski, S.J., George A. DeNapoli and Eugenio Maurer, Rome, Pontifical Gregorian University, 1987.

17. Pope Paul VI, *On Evangelization in the Modern World (Evangelii Nuntiandi)*, Washington, DC, United States Catholic Conference, 1976.

18. *Ibid.*

19. John Edward Hatcher, S.J., *Paul VI's "Evangelization in the Modern World" and the*

Mission to the Sioux Indians of South Dakota: Theory and Practice, unpublished thesis, Regis College, Ontario, Canada, 1987, p. 12.

20. *Ibid.*, p. 21.
21. *Evangelii Nuntiandi*, op. cit., p. 20.
22. Bishop Pedro Casaldaliga, op. cit.
23. Edward Schillebeeckx, *The Church with a Human Face* (New York: Crossroad Publishing Company, 1985), p. 20.
24. *Ibid.*, p. 21.
25. *Evangelii Nuntiandi*, op. cit.
26. John Paul II, "Address to Native Americans," *Origins*, NC Documentary Service, October 1987, vol. 17, no. 17, p. 295.
27. Bowden, op. cit.
28. Neihardt, op. cit., p. 249.
29. *Evangelii Nuntiandi*, op. cit.
30. The powerful story of the recovery of the Natives from Alkali Lake in British Columbia, Canada, can be seen in the video *Honor for One, Honor for All*.
31. Patricia Beamish, "Codependency and Individuation," a talk at the American Association for Counseling and Development Annual Convention at Reno, NV, April, 1991. Taken from her handout.
32. *The Addictive Society*; Diane Fassel, *The Addictive Organization*; Craig Nakken, *The Addictive Personality: Understanding Compulsion in Our Lives*, A Harper Hazelden Book, 1988.
33. *Honor For One, Honor For All*, op. cit.
34. This passivity is not evident in a Native ceremony where Native people prepare, plan and carry out all aspects of the ceremony.
35. Hatcher, op. cit., p. 93.
36. Ekstrom and Roberto, eds., *Access Guide to Evangelization* (New Rochelle, NY: Don Bosco/Multimedia Press, 1990).
37. Address by Alfretta Antone, *Origins*, Oct. 1987, vol. 17, no. 17, p. 296.

. . 3 . . . .

TRADITION
AND COMMUNITY

. . . .

11

KIM MAMMEDATY

REMEMBER THE SABBATH DAY

Kim Mammedaty (Kiowa) graduated from Colgate Rochester Divinity School in 1985 and has served as pastor of First American Baptist Church of Hobart, Oklahoma, and campus pastor of Bacone College in Muskogee, Oklahoma. She is currently studying Indian law at the University of Minnesota law school in order to continue her work on issues of social justice affecting native people in institutional contexts. Mammedaty wrote this essay for *And Blessed Is She* (Harper and Row, 1990), an anthology of sermons by women; it grew out of her concern that native Christians stop accepting the teachings of missionaries uncritically and instead develop their own interpretations of biblical stories. She locates the tradition of preaching within the specific context of a native Christian community. Mammedaty emphasizes the importance of personal and collective stories in the life of this community, especially as they work to affirm the community's own distinctive culture and history.

"Remember the Sabbath Day" was preached during the morning worship service at the First American Baptist Church of Hobart, Oklahoma. The congregation is unique because it is ninety-eight percent Indian. Most of the congregation comes from the Kiowa tribe although other tribal groups are represented. For example, the Comanche, Navaho, and Creek tribes are represented. The history of these peoples is rich and colorful, at times making one want to sing and dance. At other times, the history will move one to adorn sack cloth and ashes. Members of this congregation are direct descendants of great war chiefs. There is pride in carrying on the family name. Others are leaders in various warrior societies that give life to our culture in the now.

Another living historical reality that becomes a part of our community is governmental and religious paternalism. When conversion stories are shared in our church, we are reminded that our ancestors gave up all Indian ways to follow the Jesus way. These early converts are honored for the great sacrifices they made in order to embrace the Christian faith. Their stories are alive in the now.

It is understood that in spite of this paternalistic oppression and in spite of attempts to smother Indian expressions of self-identity, the cultural heritage remains alive and is the pulse of this congregation. The Kiowa language is spoken by the older members of our church. We have native speakers from both the Navaho and Comanche tribes. Kiowa Christian hymns are a part of every worship and frequently we include hymns from other tribes. It is important then to understand that the language, the songs, and the history are rooted in a spirituality of a great people who have known both triumphant victory and painful loss.

It becomes evident here that the preaching of the Word needs to be informed by the specific context of this community. If I were to say that the sermon must be *simple*, this could be misunderstood. Out of another context, this word might lead to assumptions regarding the intellectual abilities of the listeners. The assumption might lead to the notion that this congregation is limited intellectually. This is far from the truth. In this congregation, knowledge is gained from a world experience very different from that of the dominant culture. In this community, those most respected for their wisdom are those who have lived the longest, the elders. The elders know the language, the stories, and the complex extended family tree. They know the people, the lifestyle, and the culture. The sermon, then, is not "simple" or "primitive" in a pejorative sense. It moves out of the lived experience of this particular community.

The Word must be shared in a manner that bridges language barriers. There are members in this congregation for whom English is a second language. While English is the common language, Kiowa is used in hymns, prayers, and personal testimonies. In another sense, our thoughts are to a great extent organized by our language and experience.

One final note on context: The people of this community appreciate humor. Laughter and teasing are frequently a part of the whole worship experience. Perhaps it would be sufficient to say that laughter communicates a measure of love and understanding in situations where "logic" is impossible!

THE SERMON

> Remember the sabbath day, to keep it holy. Six days you shall labor, and do all your work; but the seventh day is a sabbath to the Lord your God; in it you shall not do any work, you, or your son, or your daughter, your manservant, or your maidservant, or your cattle, or the sojourner who is within your gates; for in six days the Lord made heaven and earth, the sea, and all that is in them, and rested the seventh day; therefore the Lord blessed the sabbath day and hallowed it.
>
> —Exodus 20:8–11

For many of us "remembering the sabbath day" carries with it a connotation of legalism; it is one of those "laws" that has become obsolete for our day. After all, Christ himself healed on the sabbath.

When we hear this commandment, we ask ourselves the question, "Does this mean I can't do *anything* on the sabbath?" We may also recall a familiar statement from childhood. "You must attend church every Sunday. The Lord commanded that we keep the sabbath day holy."

Very simply, sabbath means to desist, to abstain; for the Hebrews it became a special day to worship God; a time for both the community and the land to rest, gain renewed strength and refreshment.

Today I'm wondering how many of us take a sabbath day . . . and remember to keep it holy. How many of us take a day to stop . . . rest . . . reflect . . . to be peaceful . . . ?

The trouble with taking a sabbath is that for many of us, it requires work. We don't know how to be *still*. We don't know how to *rest*. Our world wants us to *work*; our culture *demands* that we keep moving and working.

Even our play becomes *work*. We must work in order to buy the best equipment for hunting, fishing, golfing, climbing, running, camping. . . . Then we must strive to be the best at our choice of recreation.

In our lives, there are so many things to *get done*, that if we stop doing— we begin to feel lazy or guilty. Modern technology has given us the ability to turn night into an eternal day—simply by flipping a switch. We even say to one another, "There aren't enough hours in a day!"

We may not have an 8–to–5 job, and yet we are busy. We may ask someone, "What have you been doing this week?" The response is, "I don't know, but I've been really busy!"

We have a very difficult time just *being*—resting, reflecting, playing, taking leisure. I read a meditation that said, "My life will not bear fruit unless I learn the art of lying fallow—the art of wasting time creatively."

My elders tell a story of an early missionary to the Kiowas of the Saddle Mountain area. These people knew how to take a sabbath. It was within their culture to live as part of the natural cycle of creation: hunting, feasting, resting, playing, telling stories, moving camp. The way was good—life giving.

As the story goes, the missionary wanted the Kiowas to work the land; in this way, they would be allowed to own it, and the land would not be taken away. But the Kiowas were not accustomed to working from sunup to sundown. They came in from the field one day and refused to go back to work. They didn't understand why they had to work so hard every day. In response to the "strike" the missionary told them all to open their mouths; they were each to receive a heaping teaspoon of baking powder—because the baking powder would make them "rise up" to work!

Why is it so hard for us to truly observe a sabbath day?

My guess is that it has to do with fear. Fear of silence, fear of stillness, fear of God's revelation. In our faith journey, it is necessary to take a sabbath day and set it apart from all other days.

It is necessary because powerful things happen in the stillness. We begin to see ourselves as we really are; our ugliness as well as our beauty. We learn that we have made ourselves much bigger than we really are; we learn that we take much more than we really need. We hear the voice of God.

It is necessary to take a sabbath because without it, our wellspring of the Spirit runs dry.

Remember the sabbath day, to keep it holy. Amen.

THE PREACHER REFLECTS

The story, as told to me by my parents, says that I was born on Thanksgiving Day. As a child this was a bit confusing as the calendar said that Thanksgiving was on one day and my birthday another. At any rate, the story of my birth and the sixty-mile trip home was told and retold in a variety of ways, depending on which relatives were present. I suppose that my birth was an occasion for the making of a good story as I was the youngest of eleven children to which my mother gave birth.

As I grew older, this birth story became less a story about me and more a story about us, my family, my people—the Kiowas. When the telling of the story began, it was time to stop all else—and listen. It was much later when I realized more completely, the sacredness of those moments; the sacredness of that history.

Since that time as a young girl, I've heard many stories. They become animate in the moment. They soak up the context, the people, the place, the air of the now. They are (at once) connected to yesterday and tomorrow. The stories come to my ears from different directions with varying degrees of depth. As my life changes, the stories move to meet me where I am.

In 1978, I left my Indian environment. I crossed an important boundary. The telling of my story is recounted in years rather than in a community's retelling of a story. My community changed. I was changed. I entered Eastern College, in St. Davids, Pennsylvania, where I studied to receive a degree in psychology.

I grew both spiritually and intellectually. I learned a great deal, Emotionally, this was a painfully difficult time for me. I missed my Kiowa community. I was lonely. In my heart, I stayed connected to my people by running, praying, and walking. Outside, in the wind, I could feel the presence of my people. I knew the comfort of our God.

After graduating from Eastern, I continued my education at Colgate Rochester Divinity School in Rochester, New York. The distance and time away from my people grew. My knowledge and experience became more diverse. The loneliness of separation remained as it was. It was a reality that I coped with and moved through as God added depth and direction to my faith.

I did my field work in seminary at the Tuscarora Mission near Lockport, New York. It was within this Indian community that I preached my first sermon. Here, in this community, I grew in understanding that God was meeting me where I was as a Kiowa woman in the midst of a living gospel story. The stories of the Tuscarora community and the stories of the Kiowa community shaped my understanding of the world, of God's activity in the world. Finally, the stories of Indian people have a prominent place in the preaching of the Word.

THEOLOGICAL AND HOMILETICAL CONCERNS

"Remember the Sabbath Day" was preached as one sermon in a series on the Commandments. This series was developed as a means of addressing what I thought to be a problem in our faith community. The people have been taught to use the Ten Commandments as a kind of "measuring stick" for their faith. Christianity then becomes a religion with a set of rules that can be followed on a day to day basis. Therefore, the attitudes prevail: "I am not good enough," "I am not acceptable." These attitudes perpetuate the notion that there are "cut and dry," "either-or" answers to very complicated issues and life experiences.

In taking a deeper look at the text in Exodus, we learn that the Ten Commandments also arose out of a historical context that needs to be explored before their significance for the Israelites can be understood. My concern is that the text be heard in a way that teaches my community about the context of the Jewish community. Then, I have given them an opportunity to decide for themselves whether or not the Commandments are to be used as "measuring sticks" and I have clarified the difference between Jewish values and the values of the dominant culture.

A central theological concern is that of liberation—liberation for the Indian community from paternalistic notions disguised in the rhetoric of the Christian faith, liberation from oppressive structures that perpetuate the idea that values from the dominant culture are a "measuring stick" for our faith. God's Word is a liberating word. It carries a message of freedom and hope rather than bondage and oppression. It is a message for the whole of God's people connecting tribe to tribe and culture to culture through inclusiveness rather than exclusiveness.

One way that liberation can happen is through empowerment and affirmation of Indian values. One example of this type of affirmation is found in this sermon. Work and leisure ethics are radically different in the Indian and dominant cultures. Indian people do not share the notions of working to "get ahead," working to rest, and using leisure activities for social prestige. Therefore, inherent in that particular example is an affirmation of how Indian people follow a more rational pattern of work and rest. The hope is that this congregation will experience affirmation from the expressed notions of a divine order in creation. The daylight for work and the night for resting. Also, the day set aside as a sabbath is named a sacred day. Indian people are well acquainted with sacred days and the necessity for periods of reflection.

The ideas of sacred days and divine order or creation are a part of Indian thinking. A choice to affirm these realities in our shared Christian story affirms these realities in Indian culture as well. The sermon seeks to affirm and empower the congregation.

Finally, the story of the early missionary works toward meeting three specific sermon goals. The first is to acknowledge the "saints" in our own history. It serves to honor the first converts and reaffirm their place in our present community. Second, it serves to say boldly our Indian history is alive and real. We have our own story. Finally, the use of humor adds to the cultural context and gives the congregation permission to be themselves.

When I reflect on the occasion and context of this specific sermon, I am reminded again of my own movement between two worlds, two cultures, two distinct "ways of thinking." It has been my goal to provide a few "simple" examples of how this sermon comes to life in our community. I am in the midst of the story myself so that I find myself trusting both God and you, the reader, to make connections with your stories in places where I might have been remiss.

12

ALBERTA PUALANI HOPKINS

THE CHALLENGE OF THE FUTURE
CREATING A PLACE CALLED HOME

Pua Hopkins (Native Hawaiian) is Acting Dean of Students and Associate Professor of Hawaiian Language at the University of Hawaii, Manoa. She is the author of *Ka Lei Ha'aheo* (University of Hawaii, 1992), an Hawaiian language textbook used in many universities, colleges, and high schools, as well as other publications on Hawaiian language and culture. As a popular speaker on the theory and practice of multicultural education, she is also actively involved in cross-cultural ministry development within the Episcopal Church; she is a member of the Commission on Native Hawaiian Ministry, which recently developed an alternative ordination process for native Hawaiian clergy. Hopkins originally presented this essay at "The Challenges of the Past, the Challenges of the Future," a symposium on mission in light of the Columbus Quincentenary held at the Church Divinity School of the Pacific in Berkeley, California. She presents a compelling example of how contemporary church hierarchies still suppress the cultural traditions of native communities, and how this affects the ability of native Christians to feel at home in the church. In calling for institutional change, Hopkins describes the cultural conflict that is invoked by the conventions of the ordination process and the impact this conflict has on native Christian leadership.

I maika'i ka 'olelo o ko'u waha, a me ka mana'o o ko'u na'au,
I mua o kou alo, e'Iehova, e ko'u ikaika ame ko'u Ho'ola.
Aloha auinala kakou.

My name is Pua Hopkins and I am a native Hawaiian and, at the moment, a practicing Episcopalian. This has not always been true, and it may not remain true. For me, and many others like me, the challenge of the future to the Christian church, and particularly to the Episcopal Church, is to create a nurturing and accepting environment that allows me to belong to the church without having to check my cultural identity at the door of the cathedral before entering. The challenge is to create a place that people like me can call home.

Any discussion of mission and the challenge of the future can only be meaningful in the context of a critique of the present and a remembrance of the past. As George Santayana has said, "Those who cannot remember the past are condemned to repeat it." And while we can celebrate what has been good, we must change what was not.

Since the beginning of evangelism and mission in Hawaii 173 years ago, becoming a Christian has involved the denial of our own heritage and the denigration of values basic to our culture.

Let me give you a recent example of what I mean. This year, 1993, marks the centennial of the overthrow of the Hawaiian Kingdom by a handful of American businessmen with the aid of the United States Marines. Overnight, Hawaiians became foreigners in our own land. For all practical purposes this has never changed. By every common socio-economic measure my people remain at the bottom of the ladder, stripped of our lands and our language and struggling to regain them, and looking to the United States government for some form of self-determination similar to that extended to Native American tribes. So far we have met with no success, because the United States reminds us that it signed no treaty with us. That is true; it signed no treaty with the Hawaiian nation because it annexed Hawaii as a territory through an agreement with a group of traitors who had overthrown the legitimate government.

I offer this brief lesson in Hawaiian history to provide the context in which the commemorative events of this year are taking place. This is a time of great pain and anger for many of us. It is a time when we are looking to the past and to the future and searching for ways to use the commemoration as a window of opportunity to provide healing and hope.

It was for that purpose that the Diocesan and Provincial Commission on Hawaiian Ministry, along with St. Andrew's Cathedral, planned a commemorative mass on January 2 of this year. The cathedral, by the way, was built by King Kamehameha IV and Queen Emma, who were personally responsible for inviting the Anglican Church to establish a presence in their Kingdom. The mass was to be celebrated in the Hawaiian language, and we planned to use poi, our staple food, and coconut water as the eucharistic elements, as we had last May during a meeting of the Synod of the Episcopal Church's Province VIII in Honolulu. Three days before the event our bishop called the priest who would be presiding into his office and announced his decision that we would have to use bread and wine. He provided no opportunity for discussion, either then or since that time. He made no theological case for his decision; it was based on concerns raised by unnamed individuals and the fact that bread and wine were "traditional" and what people expected when they came to an Episcopal service.

I don't know if the bishop understood the irony of his decision in the context of a service meant to heal the alienation of an entire people in the place of their birth. I only know that at a moment when I was dealing with the hurt of an act one hundred years ago that made my ancestors instant foreigners in the only place they had to call home, my bishop had made me a foreigner in the church I had considered my spiritual home. I can only tell you of the pain of refusing the sacraments at that service because I could not overcome my alienation and come to the table in good conscience. I can only tell you of my husband's pain and frustration, because he was the Native Hawaiian priest who had to obey his bishop's ruling and celebrate that mass using the "traditional" bread and wine. And I can only repeat what I said at the beginning: on that day in order to be an Episcopalian I had to check my identity as a Hawaiian outside the door of the cathedral that my king and queen had founded.

The issue, of course, is not the bread and wine; no Hawaiian Christian denies that it is what Jesus used, and we consume those elements every Sunday with thanksgiving. The issue is that Jesus was born in a particular time and place, and bread and wine were indeed traditional in that context and we recognize the need to keep the historical connection. Nevertheless, the good news is that the Christ was born for all people in all times and places and that he sanctified the common food and drink of us all by the sacrifice of his Body and Blood. The issue is that as Hawaiians and Christians, we should be able to take what is basic to our everyday lives and incorporate it into our celebration of God's great gift to us. And, clearly, this issue is relevant to all cultures that are not linked with that of the historical Jesus. The Rt. Rev. William Wantland, a Seminole and Bishop of Eau Claire, has written, "Various Indian cultures have ways of expressing theological concepts which are compatible with Christian understanding, and hence excellent teaching tools for the church. . . . There are many cultural ways various Indian peoples might use their own symbols to express Christian truth."[1]

Because of the occasion, the prohibition on the use of our native food for the elements was particularly poignant and painful. But this is not an isolated incident; cultural imperialism within the institutions that seek to promote and perpetuate Christianity has been a reality since the beginning of evangelism and mission throughout the Americas. This has certainly been true in Hawaii. The first missionaries were Congregationalists, now part of the United Church of Christ. While I do not question the purity of their intentions, there is no doubt that their presence had many negative consequences for the Hawaiian people, not the least of which was the participation of some of their descendants in the overthrow of the Hawaiian Kingdom. A month ago, as part of the commemoration of that event, the President of the General Synod of the United Church of Christ came to Hawaii to extend a formal apology to the Hawaiian people. It can serve as a model for all churches as a first step towards a new future for mission in partnership with cultures of color. Speaking of the missionaries he said:

> Some of these men and women, however, sometimes confused the ways of the West with the ways of the Christ. Assumptions of cultural and racial superiority and alien economic understanding led some of them and those who followed them to discount or undervalue the strengths of the mature society they encountered. Therefore, the rich indigenous values of the Hawaiian people, their language, their spirituality, and their regard for the land, were denigrated. The resulting social, political, and economic implications of these harmful attitudes contributed to the suffering of the people in that time and into the present. Justice will be pursued and reconciliation achieved as, together we recognize both the strengths and the weaknesses of those who preceded us, as we celebrate that which is good, and as we make right that which is wrong. . . . Justice and mercy demand rectification of these wrongs, so that we may be reconciled with each other and walk, together, toward a common future.[2]

The first step, then, toward making a place in the church for Hawaiians and others who have experienced similar treatment, is for the church to examine its past and present behavior and to acknowledge the western ethnocentrism that pervades it, the implicit assumptions of that perspective, and the devaluing of other cultures and peoples that results.

The second step is for the church to do something about it, to institute changes that respond to the insights gained from self-examination in partnership with its marginalized members. Too often the church equates *acknowledging* a problem with *solving* it. For instance it says, "Yes, we see that there are instances of institutional racism in the church; this is not a good thing; may we have the next problem please!" The church must do something beyond beating its breast, and crying, "Mea culpa, mea culpa!"

One place to start is to look closely at the process whereby we identify individuals for ordination. We are currently facing a dearth of ordained Hawaiians. There are only three active Hawaiian priests in the Diocese of Hawaii of a total active clergy of about seventy-five, even though Hawaiians constitute twenty percent of the state's population. I suspect we would find similar statistics for other ethnic minorities in the Episcopal Church. Let me suggest one reason why that is so, as well as a solution.

Although the church's espoused ideal is for a congregation or community to recognize a call to ordination in one of its members and to put that person forward for consideration and training for ordination, the reality is that most candidates for ordination put themselves forward, albeit with the support of their parishes. That process eliminates many possible candidates of color because in affiliation-oriented cultures like ours, self-nomination is unacceptable and self-defeating. People presumptuous enough to seek ordination on their own are, by the values of the culture, automatically unsuitable. Put simply, our culture prohibits us from volunteering ourselves. Given that reality, the church, through one or another of its agencies, must sound a clear call to promising candidates so that they will be perceived by their communities as *responding* to a legitimate recognition of their particular gifts for ministry, rather than *initiating* a self-aggrandizing quest for ordination.

Once they are identified and called, how will the church of the future prepare such candidates for ordination? How will Commissions on Ministry interview people who have been ingrained with modesty and reticence as a primary virtue? What are the costs of attending a western-oriented seminary? Are the candidates necessarily people with undergraduate degrees who can qualify for entrance? Can they and the economically-depressed communities that call them afford seven years of education beyond high school before they are ordained? Is the curriculum culturally relevant? Does it keep in mind what they have been called to do? Is training theologians synonymous with training priests? Is the environment supportive of diversity? Is it supportive of individuals who are used to living in nurturing extended families? Are there alternative training tracks that will meet the actual needs of the situations to which they will be called and take into account their personal obligations? Can we design and implement them without creating a second-class priesthood? There are no simple answers to these questions, but the church must grapple with them if it is to deal with the emerging demographical reality that surrounds it, and it must include those of us who are most vitally involved in its deliberations and decision-making.

The church is also challenged to change the process by which it chooses its leadership and the way it structures its decision-making process. The western democratic bias toward self-nominating leadership and the rule of the majority excludes participation by people who look toward peer recognition and nomination and who value time-consuming decision-making processes by consensus that nurture long-term relationships and the well-being of the community over time-saving votes by voice or show-of-hand or secret ballot. As presently constituted and organized, the "normal" vestry or Standing Committee or Diocesan Council or Commission on Ministry makes no concession to these different values and operational styles. Until it does, the church's organizational structure, and therefore its power base, will be dominated by those who know the rules of the game and are comfortable with them, and affiliation-oriented people of color will continue to be voiceless and faceless.

Another issue to be addressed is the cultural bias of mainstream theology. The western understanding of the human person in dualistic terms that separate thought from feeling and mind from body does violence to the holistic view of the human person that Hawaiians and many other affiliation-oriented cultures have. According to Gonzalo Castillo Cardenas, it results in a theology based on the divinization of reason, logic, and conceptual rationality. At the same time it is suspicious of and downgrades emotions and feelings, metaphors and symbols, vision and dreams.[3] The Rev. Jill Martinez has said:

> The Hispanic understands and lives the deep emotions of the heart. This is one of our strengths, not a weakness. Our heart makes us courageous and we are filled with power to love, care and risk. . . . Even so, we can say we stand in the presence of God with our mind in our heart. Prayer for us is not just an intelligent exercise of our mind. . . . Neither are we dependent on having only good feelings.[4]

So the church must reconnect its head with its heart, and develop a theological perspective that is holistic and accepting of the complete person that God created. Everyone will benefit from such a central transformation.

Finally, to return to the starting point of this discussion, the church must make room for aspects of native spirituality that are consonant with Christianity. Form and ritual have always been at the heart of Hawaiian culture and are part of the attraction the Episcopal Church holds for us. But we must be allowed to incorporate what has meaning for us as a people, as long as it does not become a token substitute for dealing with the other issues I have raised or run counter to Christ's teaching. Let me be clear that the church's teachings are not necessarily the same as Christ's teaching, and my concern is that our celebrations are true to him. In that light, our traditional call to worship by blowing a shell is no less valid than a tolling bell, our drums no less authentic than a pipe organ, our poi and coconut water no less a meal than bread and wine. We are as God made us; and God loves us as we are. Will the church do the same, so that going to church can be synonymous with going home? Or will it be one more place where we will be foreigners? That, as I see it, is the challenge of the future.

NOTES

1. William C. Wantland, "Our Mother, the Earth." *The Living Church* (July 5, 1992), 12.

2. "An Apology to Na Kanaka Maoli (The Indigenous Hawaiian People)," January 17, 1993.

3. Gonzalo Castillo Cardenas, "Theological Education Before the Altar." *Church and Society: Authenticity before the Altar*, LXXVI, 4 (Program Agency, Presbyterian Church U.S.A., 1986), 62.

4. Jill Martinez, "Worship and the Search for Community in the Presbyterian Church U.S.A.: The Hispanic Experience." *Church and Society: Authenticity before the Altar*, LXXVI, 4, (Program Agency, Presbyterian Church U.S.A., 1986), 44.

KATERI MITCHELL

PROGRAM DEVELOPMENT AND NATIVE AMERICAN CATECHESIS

▪

Kateri Mitchell, SSA (Mohawk) is a Sister of St. Ann and a member of the Turtle Clan from the St. Regis Mohawk Reserve (Akwesasne) on the St. Lawrence River. An accomplished educator, she has taught in parochial and government Indian schools in the United States and Canada and has trained native Catholic leaders for the Tekakwitha Conference and the Kisemanito Centre in Grouard, Alberta. She currently works with native communities as a member of the mobile team for ministry formation in the Archdiocese of Keewatin-Le Pas in northern Manitoba, where she leads workshops on native spirituality, liturgy, and catechesis. This essay grew out of Mitchell's work with the Tekakwitha Conference and was written for *Faith and Culture* (United States Catholic Conference, 1987), a collaborative anthology that developed out of a conference on multicultural religious education. Mitchell suggests some basic considerations for designing a native catechesis in response to Pope John Paul II's call for indigenization. Highlighting the importance of tradition and community among native people, she uses examples from her own people to show how cultural values are preserved in religious ceremonies and social gatherings. Mitchell closes by describing a basic framework for native catechesis and outlining four sample courses.

The gospel message, the presence of Jesus, is becoming more real and active in the lives of many peoples who reflect on their personal histories and spiritual journeys in a multicultural circle of faith. Therefore, how does one share a faith that is personal, relevant, vibrant and, at the same time, transforming? John Paul II gives us some direction in this matter. As he states,

> catechesis, is called to bring the power of the Gospel into the very heart of culture and cultures. For this purpose, catechesis will seek to know these cultures and their essential components; it will learn their significant expressions; it will be able to offer these cultures the knowledge of the hidden mystery and help them to bring forth from their own living tradition original expressions of Christian life, celebration, and thought.[1]

Pope John Paul II's catechetical approach presents certain challenges to us. First, we will need to use our peoples' native languages. This means not only vocabulary but cultural idioms, symbols, and thought patterns. Second, it will not be sufficient merely to adapt other catechetical materials for use in our native communities. We will need to develop new materials that will affirm and challenge our native people's traditions and culture.

Let us address the necessity for catechesis development for native people. A native catechesis is an attempt to help us Indian people root ourselves in a deeper understanding of gospel values through our lived experiences of our own tribal stories, languages, family and community orientation, values, traditions, symbols, rituals and sacred ceremonies, dances, art, and legends. In fact, the total expression of who we are as individuals and as members of a given Indian tribe, nation, or clan creates a religious experience unique to us as Indian people. Essentially, in designing relevant and inspirational catechesis, the whole person needs to be considered.

It is, therefore, indispensable to note the identifiable characteristics of a native person. First, the native way of thinking and reasoning is cyclic; that is, one goes around and around using concrete examples and stories before getting to the heart of the issue at hand. Second, three methods of communicating are particular to us: (1) in verbal expression, the concreteness of the language used depicts a visual and earthy style that is descriptive; (2) in nonverbal language, inner feelings and intuitions are transmitted with great effectiveness; (3) in silence, a deep sense of contemplation is communicated.

As we further consider points of development in catechesis, we focus on the discovery of one's personal truths centered on kinship and real life events in our communities.

> By respecting, understanding and accepting the truth about myself, my family, my tribe, the earth and the places where I live, the people I meet, live and work with, I grow in my self-understanding and acceptance of life as it is. I come to understand my gifts and my brokenness; my strengths and my weaknesses. I come to see the Creator as the source of all life. I come to appreciate the fact and many ways in which the Creater shares His life and blessings with all peoples and all creation. I come to see that my life and all life will one day return to the Creator. As I journey in life, I see how the beauty of all creation speaks to me and others of the Beauty of the Creator.[2]

Let us visualize a native community in the course of daily events. We experience the sacredness of life, of persons—especially for little children and for our elders—of teachers. Through them, we learn the sense of the sacred, respect for our Creator, respect for one another, and respect for all creation. We also learn our ways: of sharing, of hospitality, of generosity, and of being "present" to one another. It is through our interactions and inter-personal relationships that our giftedness as native peoples comes to birth and grows within ourselves, our family, our community, our nation, and our tribe. By our intratribal experiences and learning situations, we come to a greater awareness and appreciation of our creation truths.

> By understanding my traditional values and ways of walking with the Creator, I come to appreciate the gifts and sacred ways he shares with me, my family, my tribe and the world. By the stories and memories of my family and my tribe, I came to learn and to respect my tribal traditions, my own giftedness and my Indianness.[3]

To continue, let us center ourselves on *time*—that time of events, of waiting, of silence, of reflection, of contemplation, of timelessness. Think of the valuable moment or moments we can spend by observing and learning from a sacred animal, bird, or insect. They teach us ways in which we can live fuller lives as human beings. The time we stand in prayer and wait to greet a new sunrise, a new day, and to give thanks for breath and for all the gifts of life. The days, weeks, and months, we wait for our crops to grow and ripen—gifts from Mother Earth. Again, the time we take to care for and watch a child grow from infancy to puberty, then into adulthood is a won-derful gift. The hours we spend to support and to pray with a family and family members who are seriously ill; the time "to be with"; to be in silence; to pray; to meditate on the new life experience of a deceased loved one as we keep vigil are all gifts. Through the many events of our lives, we learn about our Creator, about life, about creation, contemplation, silence, and patience. In effect, it is through the life within a community that one learns to believe and to experience the depth and sacredness of life, given as a gift by our

Creator. Thus, faith is lived and gifted through our relationships. To really experience life is to be in harmony with our God and one another, with our extended family and our community, with nature and the whole of creation. In rhythm with the harmonious beat of our faith life, we celebrate life and gift through the elders—our storytellers and teachers—in our legends, songs, dances, and art; in and through our religious festivals and sacred ceremonies, whether on a mountain, near water, before a tree, in a desert, on a plain, in a sweat lodge, or in a gathering room, all speak of the sacredness of persons, symbols, and places.

Our elders tell us of the journeys of our people and how God has loved us and has been with us from the beginning and is still present in our own lives, in the lives of our people, and in our world. Our legends teach us about life and about making choices that help us lead a fuller life, a life of greater harmony.

We continue to express gratitude for life in the steady beat of the drum and the oneness of heart as we sing our chants during our solemn religious ceremonies and rituals or during intertribal social gatherings. For instance, our Round Dances symbolize the joy and love of being in union with our Creator and with one another and gratitude for the many gifts shared throughout the cycle of life. So too, our Honor Dances acknowledge the giftedness of our people and, in particular, our women who are respected as the life-givers for the tribute. Also, many of our dances are in recognition of God's creatures and are so named to show our respect for animals and birds. For example, beauty, power, and strength are shown in the Eagle Dance. Some of our dances tell a story about the life expeditions and events of our people, such as in the Canoe Dance, which is a journey; and, then, that eventful time of life—mating as expressed in the Partridge Dance.

Our many rituals, using significant gestures and symbols, bring us in closer union with our Creator, who made us and loved us from all time, and who is giver of all good things and continues to love and bless us each day. In response, we give praise and thanksgiving for a new day as we offer ourselves, our cedar in the four directions. At the same time, we recall our own brokenness and need for healing as we purify, cleanse, and bless ourselves with smoking sweetgrass and water—a continual reminder of who we are before the Creator.

As we experience the various events and stages in our lives, our naming ceremonies help us to identify ourselves as individuals and as members of a family. Furthermore, some rituals, in various tribes, initiate members into another stage of human growth and development through prayer, one's whole being. These rituals of human growth might take shape as the sun dance, a puberty rite, or a vision quest. Moreover, a person's fullness of earthly life is celebrated with deep faith and hope that the spirit is on a journey to a much fuller life, as the community gathers to share in the joy at the beginning of a new life by all-night vigils, prayer, dances, games, feasting, and give-aways. In effect, it is in all events of our cyclic life that we breathe the fullness of God's revelation to us native people. Consequently, gospel values are lived experiences in our way of life.[4]

In an insightful and sensitive article, "A Cross-Cultural Approach to Catechesis among Native Americans," Gilbert Hemauer, OFM Cap., stated that "the urgent need exists to recognize the 'good news' native American people and culture already possess in their rich traditions and ways of living."[5] It is important to bear in mind that an "arduous and deliberate process of incarnational catechesis is slow, gradual and must be freely chosen."[6]

As a result of Fr. Hemauer's concern for ongoing faith development and for setting some catechetical foundations for native peoples so that "the word be made flesh," he convened and facilitated a four-day sharing with seventeen native catechists. The November 1982 meeting on native catechesis development was held in Denver, Colorado. Sr. Mariella Frye, MHSH, USCC representative for catechetical ministry, was invited to guide the group in the consultation process.

As one of the seventeen catechists, I found it to be a time of rich, spiritual experiences of prayer. It was a time of openness to one another; a time to share hurts and feelings, sorrows and joys, tears and laughter; a time to learn one another's tribal histories, traditions, and customs. Frequently, I found myself asking the same question that Jesus asked his disciples: "Who do you say that I am?" (Matthew 16:15).

As we progressed through the process, we learned how each of us has walked with the Lord—either alone, with our family, with our native community, or with others who have helped us become who we are today. We recalled the numerous occasions when we felt Jesus' healing power and were healed from past wounds of prejudice, injustice, and mockery. In remembering the times Jesus was with us, we were able to face difficult situations. We were strengthened by many joy-filled events that were life-giving because we experienced His presence, love, and peace through each other as we were being called into a deeper love and faith. We could exclaim with Simon Peter, "You are the Messiah, the Son of the Living God" (Matthew 16:16).

As the days continued, the seventeen of us were no longer strangers but brothers and sisters—sacraments to one another. Definitely, a small community of faith was formed with love and trust. We were able to discover and rediscover, affirm and reaffirm, our own giftedness as the Creator's loved ones touched by his gentleness and presence.

We further explored and meditated on our faith, our gift of Catholicism. We came to a much more profound awareness and expression of who we are as native Catholics. We felt the powerful presence of Jesus in the sacraments of the Catholic Church. We remembered how we have experienced and been touched by Jesus' sacramental presence in our lives and how we have been changed, transformed, when we opened ourselves in God's revelation in our lives.

As the hours of retelling came to a close, we developed a tentative framework for developing a native catechesis under three main clarifications: (1) discovery of one's personal truth as learned and reinforced by our parents, grandparents, aunts, and uncles; (2) appreciation of our creation truths as we have listened to our legends and tribal stories; (3) our experience of Jesus as we listened to and meditated on his word and shared Jesus in our lives through relationships and the sacraments.

Further native catechesis development can be found in a basic, four-course outline drawn up in July 1985 by Sr. Genevieve Cuny, OSF (Oglala Sioux), Fr. Michael Galvan (Ohlone), and myself, Sr. Kateri Mitchell, SSA (Mohawk), coordinator of the summer catechesis programs, under the auspices of the Tekakwitha Conference National Center, Great Falls, Montana. These courses are offered to assist native and nonnative catechists in bringing a deeper and richer understanding of the gospel message and values to the lives of our people. In such a manner, we teach as Jesus did through our relationships with God, creation, our family, nature, Mother Earth, and the gifts of our tribal traditions, customs, and rituals.

In the following outlines, the purpose is to provide a process that will aid our people to help one another live in harmony with God, our Creator, with self, with one another, and with all creation in light of the "good news."

Catechesis I is a personal faith journey that considers three main areas: first, a discovery of one's personal truth as a native, as a Christian; second, focus on an appreciation of our creation truths, both in the tribe and in sacred Scripture; third, our experience of Jesus as Catholics called to know, love, and serve.

CATECHESIS I
PERSONAL FAITH JOURNEY

I.   Discovery of One's Personal Truth
     ACCEPT
     A. reality of sin and grace (life as it is)
     B. acceptance of individual creation truths (personal faith journey)
     C. traditional ways
     D. Christian ways
     RESPOND
     A. using gifts (individual and traditional)
     B. our loving Creator (You who have many names) shares his love, breathes his life, tells his truth

II. Appreciation of our Creation Truths
     A. His creation truth as told by my people (elders, grandparents)
     B. His truth of creation as told in his sacred Word (Old Testament)
     C. other peoples' creation truth

III. Our Experience of Jesus
    A. Catholic Church's experience of Jesus (evangelization)
    B. how I come to know Jesus (message)
    C. how I come to love Jesus (community building and worship)
    D. how I come to serve Jesus (service)

Catechesis II covers the areas and stages of human growth and faith development focusing both on the native and Christian ways and how we interact with other cultures.

CATECHESIS II
FAITH DEVELOPMENT

    I.   Human Growth and Development
    II. Native American Development Values
    III. Stages of Faith
    IV. Communication Skills in Christian Perspective
    V. Developing Sensitivities and Understanding between Cultures in Sharing Faith

Catechesis III explores the sacramental life and God's plan for salvation through the presence of the risen Lord in the sacraments and through the sacred actions of all tribes by their values, rites, ceremonies, and celebrations.

CATECHESIS III
SACRAMENTS

    I.   God Becomes Man for Us
    II. The Spirit Brings Salvation to Us
    III. The Presence of the Risen Lord
    IV. The Sacraments: Jesus Promises To Be with His Disciples
    V. God Works through the Sacred Actions of All Tribes
        A. rites and ceremonies: naming ceremonies, sweat lodge, medicine men, elders, vision quest, puberty rites, sun dance, purification
        B. values and celebrations: birth, marriage, death, hospitality, generosity, respect for life, land

Catechesis IV calls forth creative ways to share the Christian message within a cultural context and to develop native catechetical materials relevant to the different tribes.

CATECHESIS IV

APPROACHES IN NATIVE CATECHESIS

I.   Called To Be Creative in Relating Culture and Christian Message
II. Shared Christian Praxis Approach (Broome)
III. Developing Materials
    A. *Family Cluster Model* (Sr. Genevieve Cuny—article available through the Tekakwitha Conference National Center, Great Falls, Montana)
    B. *Finding A Way Home* (Fr. Pat Twohy, SJ, Seattle University, Broadway and Madison, Seattle, WA 98122; University Press, Spokane, WA 99220)
    C. *Labre Pilot Religious Ed Project* (Ashland, MT)
    D. *Builders of the New Earth*, volumes I, II, III (Fr. John Hatcher, Box 271, Plainview, SD 57748; (605) 985–5906; and Fr. Pat McCorkell, published by the Diocese of Rapid City)
    E. *Dakota Way of Life* (Palm)

To enhance the program, the Tekakwitha Center presently serves as a hub and is collecting and encouraging further development of materials by our native people that can be shared and distributed to the conference membership as needs and requests arise. Also, to date, the national center has hired a full-time director of communications, Mr. Cy Peck, Jr. (Tlingit), who is providing a collection of audiovisuals of numerous tribal events and varied workshops held in Great Falls, which are valuable resources available through the Conference to help lead our people toward greater self-awareness and wholeness.

As we continue to move forward, one of our primary program goals is to engage full time a native person to develop native catechetical materials and to provide ongoing native catechesis program coordination and program development so as to serve more effectively and to share the gospel message and values of Jesus more meaningfully with our native communities.

In conclusion, we can agree with Sr. Mariella Frye when she states that catechesis" . . . is sharing one's faith by proclaiming the entire Christian message; forming a community of believers; helping people to pray and to worship; and motivating them to serve others."[7]

NOTES

1. *John Paul II, Catechist: Text and Commentary on "Catechesi Tradendae"* (Chicago: Franciscan Herald Press, 1980), no. 53.
2. *The Story and Faith Journey of Seventeen Native Catechists* (Great Falls, MT: Tekakwitha Conference, 1983), p. 84.
3. *Ibid.*

4. National Conference of Catholic Bishops, *Statement of U.S. Catholic Bishops on American Indians* (Washington, DC: USCC Office of Publishing and Promotion Services, 1977), p. 3.
5. Gilbert F. Hemauer, "A Cross-Cultural Approach to Catechesis among Native Americans," *The Living Light* 14:1(Spring 1977): 132–137.
6. *Ibid.*, p. 137.
7. *The Story and Faith Journey of Seventeen Native Catechists*, p. 84.

14

JOHN S. HASCALL

THE SACRED CIRCLE
NATIVE AMERICAN LITURGY

John Hascall, OFM Cap. (Ojibwa) is a member of the *Midewiwin*, the traditional religious society of the Ojibwas, and a Capuchin priest; he describes himself as an "Ojibwa medicine priest." A popular speaker and workshop leader, he oversees the Most Holy Name of Jesus—Blessed Kateri Tekakwitha parish in Assinins, Michigan, and has served as president of the Tekakwitha Conference (1986–88). Hascall wrote this essay at the invitation of the Catholic magazine *Liturgy* for a special issue on cultural diversity in the Catholic church. He discusses the centrality of ceremony (including prayer, song, and dance) and the significance of tribal diversity in native religious life. Describing a water rite based on his own cultural traditions, he demonstrates how liturgical practices can be an opportunity for cross-cultural interaction and solidarity.

R eligious ceremony and worship of the one God have always been the way of the people native to these islands called the Americas. Native Americans conceive of God as "the One who had no beginning and who created all that is." We have never sought to limit this "Great Spirit" in any way, and certainly not by adding to God our human limitations or the limits of gender. In our linguistic treatment of the concept of God, there is no limiting article. As native people, we know and experience God in our relationships with all things. We experience life and God's influence in all creation. God always has worked and always will work with all creation for the good of all.

Native religious ceremonies grew out of our relationships with God, our brothers and sisters and all creation. Native dances represent our relationships with the animals, the seasons and our own emotions relating to God, creation or each other; likewise, the objects we use in our sacred ceremonies come from the earth around us. The ceremonies themselves—whether feasts of the pueblo or village, the coming-out ceremony of the young girl reaching puberty, the vision quest of a young man coming into adult life, the killing of the first deer, the coming of each season, planting or harvesting, feasts of the elders, death, marriage, sickness and healing—are centered around the circle of life. The sacred circle teaches us that we are all related to one another; our lives are interdependent and shared: human, animal, vegetable and mineral. We are one creation as the God who created us is one, though called by many names. Among our many tribes God is "Spirit," "Power," "Creator," "Mystery"; yet it is one God who created this life and is personally involved in our relationships.

Native life is lived in 450 different tribes. I am Ojibwa (Chippewa); therefore, I speak as a Chippewa when I describe the way we celebrate our seasonal feasts. In the last ten years, I have been on the road visiting and praying with many of our tribes throughout this continent. I have experienced the ceremonies and celebrations of many different native cultures. Each time I pray with the different tribes, I pray as an Ojibwa spiritual leader, and not as a Cheyenne, a Crow, a Pueblo, or other native American.

I mention this to help us realize the difficulty of trying to create a liturgical ceremony that is appropriate for every tribe. A ceremony must be sensitive to the needs and aspirations of individual tribes. The more particularity we express, the more we strengthen ourselves and those around us, thus creating a stronger community. In this article, I hope to treat the general background of our native American "liturgical" way of life.

OUR WAY OF PRAYER

We look to our elders to teach us the different ceremonies of our people. Our elders, in turn, learned the ceremonies from their elders. The prayers they spoke and the actions they performed are rituals passed down by oral tradition. Native prayer comes from the heart of the one who prays, each in his or her own way. Such prayer expresses the fullness of heart of all the grandmothers and grandfathers who have gone before us. Its content consists of all that the individual, village, season and occasion conjures in the person who is praying. Yet the person prays on behalf of all the people who have requested prayer. Communal prayer is not the custom for many of our tribes. Rather, our songs, often sung by one person or group of singers, draw on the riches of the centuries; they hand on the good and the suffering our people have endured throughout the ages.

The main instruments of song and prayer are the drum, the flute, the rattle, the voice itself. Among the northern tribes that I know best, there are many songs that express the people's petitions. Long teaching songs, of more recent origin, came from the missionaries who tried to teach us church doctrine and bible stories in the form of song. Our native songs are basically words of praise. The drummers and singers chant their prayer to the creator on behalf of the people. The drum echoes the heartbeat of all creation. As we dance with the drum, we are united with creation and each other.

Among the different tribes I have visited, I have heard beautiful songs based on the chants of the people. I have heard the songs of the Crow tribe of Montana and experienced the dance and songs of the Pueblo people of the Southwest. At a Pueblo feast, celebrated in union with a church feast, the people dance the traditional deer dance, the buffalo dance, the corn dance, the eagle dance or any other dance appropriate for the season or occasion. The drum, dance and song are central to our worship.

THE WATER RITE

All the symbols of our worship are natural gifts—like the gift of water. We begin many of our eucharistic celebrations with a water rite to remind us of our baptism and our life within the community. We seek to restore harmony in our relationships with God, each other and the world. Coming to the water for healing, we restore our relationships and renew the harmonious community into which we were baptized. For native people, water is the basis of life. We learn the value of water when we fast three or four days on the mountain, in the forest or in some other sacred place. For many tribes this means we refrain from all water and food for four days. Our purpose in fasting is to create harmony in the world and within ourselves. As we pray in the fast, we pray that all people of the earth, all nations and cultures, may be strengthened. This has been the way of our people long before we heard or knew of other nations.

The opening rites of the eucharist can take many forms; a basic one used by many of our people is a prayer in the four directions, which we call the grandfathers, a name that comes from our great respect for our elders as teachers and people of prayer. Grandfather is also a name we give respectfully to God. In this rite we look to God as creator as we experience God's great love reflected in each of the four directions of creation.

Such a water rite, used by itself or as a preliminary to the eucharist, begins with the blessing of the water. After the blessing, a bowl of water is set in each of the four directions of the place at the ceremonial grounds. As each person approaches one of the four bowls, he or she prays for the people.

First, the water to the east is pointed in the direction of the sunrise, which represents newness of life and resurrection. As we approach the water in this direction we pray for the young people, the children, the unborn. We pray that the young may be protected from all harm and evil as they grow and that they may be healed from all hurts. The water is poured into our hands. We touch our eyes, ears, nose, mouth, all our senses and body with the blessed water; then we drink it. This ceremony strengthens and heals us spiritually, emotionally and physically. It reminds us of our baptism and our relationship with God, others and ourselves. Some of us pour water on mother earth, who gives us life in the gift of water. Likewise in the sweat lodge we pour water on the hot stones and pray that our people may be strong.

Second, we approach the bowl to the south. The southern direction reminds us of woman's beauty and her life-giving role. My people use the gift or medicine of cedar for this rite. Cedar, which is also used in blessing the water, is the medicine of the woman. The woman prepares the cedar by picking it at certain times of the year. In the form of oil (pressed from the cedar berries), cedar is also used in healing ceremonies. As the south wind comes in the spring and throughout the summer, it brings new growth and life to the foods and medicines of our people. The woman gives life to our people and is thus highly respected. We pray for a deeper respect for woman in our lives, for the healing of woman and the healing of the world in respect of woman. Again to the south we strengthen ourselves, our five senses, and drink of the healing water for all people.

Third, we approach the bowl of water to the west. In the west we see the reflection of God's love for us. The thunderbirds bring water and new life to mother earth in rain and storm. This water is blessed with sage, the medicine of travel. When we drink it, we recall our journey in life and the relationships that have broken along the way. We constantly need to be strengthened and healed. In this direction we recall the eucharist and its meaning for our life as a native and catholic people. The eucharist is our food, Jesus, who empowers us for life's journey. As we pray for healing, we recall the many ways that we need healing in the world. We remember the people who are drug and alcohol addicted or dependent, whose lives are broken, or who suffer drought, famine, prejudice or discrimination; we remember all human suffering in the world, and we intercede for all the people. Again we bless ourselves and drink the water of healing.

Fourth and finally, to the north, the medicine of tobacco is used to bless the water. Tobacco, which is common to most tribes, is the medicine for prayer offerings to God. As we drink water to the north we thank God for all our medicine. We pray for the living elders and those who have passed on. We pray for their healing in mind, body and spirit. We pray that they may continue to teach and pray for us and that we may have a deeper respect for elders throughout the world. To the north we also pray for all spiritual leaders, all medicine people of all nations and cultures, that we may always walk in harmony. We pray that all may come to know God—and Jesus—as the center of all culture and life. We then pray for all Ways of prayer: the Midewiwin (Ojibwa), the Long House (Iroquois), the Sun Dance (Plains), the Kiva (Southwest) and the Native American Church (that is, the whole church). We pray in thanksgiving for mother earth and all of creation. Finally we give thanks to God for being God: Father, Son and Holy Spirit. We pray also for all we may have forgotten.

ALTERNATIVE FORMS

The form of this water ritual varies from tribe to tribe. Tribes that do not have water use corn pollen. Or this rite may take the form of a "smudge" blessing, in which sweetgrass, greasewood, sage, cedar or tobacco is burned on hot coals. The smoke is brought to the people or fanned over them with an eagle feather or ceremonial fan. In the same way that the water is used in the water ceremony, the smoke is brought to us. We, in turn, "smudge" our senses and body.

The one who performs this blessing may differ from tribe to tribe. The ritual may be led by a spiritual leader, priest or deacon, medicine person or elder or by a governor or other person of prayer. In the tribal way of life people are chosen for specific roles in the tribe, such as blessing, teaching or performing different ceremonies.

In all these ways, the liturgy of native Americans mirrors the ways of our culture. In effect, as native catholics our sacramental life must reflect our native ways so that we can grow to wholeness as a people of God to help build the body of Christ. As I go among the different tribes, I go to draw forth the Christ who has always been with our people. My prayer is that we native catholic people will continue to grow in greater harmony with our creator, with others, with the world and with ourselves through the many gifts we have been given as native people.

15

ADRIAN JACOBS

THE MEETING OF THE TWO WAYS

.

Adrian Jacobs (Cayuga) is academic dean of the National Native Bible College in Deseronto, Ontario. He was raised in the traditional longhouse religion of the Iroquois on the Six Nations Reserve in Ontario, where his father is still a faithkeeper; in 1976 he converted to Christianity through the influence of his older brother and Anglican mother, who had experienced dramatic life changes in their newfound Pentecostal faith. Jacobs attended Rhema Bible Training Center in Oklahoma and in 1980 founded the Word of Faith Center on the Six Nations Reserve, where he pastored for thirteen years. This essay grew out of Jacobs's lifelong study of native religious traditions and his experiences at a native leadership conference held at Fuller Theological Seminary in Pasadena, California. Jacobs addresses the perennial question of the relationship between faith and culture by describing four typical Christian attitudes toward native traditional beliefs and practices. His personal preference for the response he terms "sanctification" reflects his emphasis on the prophetic role that religion can play as critique of community life, and his desire to identify a unified, comprehensive solution to the problem of religious diversity.

THE MEETING OF THE TWO WAYS

A traditional Indian religionist said to a Christian minister: "Your Christianity and the Indian way are like two railroad tracks. They head in the same direction. If you look to the horizon, the tracks come together. We are both trying to get to heaven. You go by the Christian way and I go by the Indian way." The only problem with this picture is, when you get to the horizon the two tracks are just as far apart as when you started out. It is an illusion. It only appears like they come together.

CULTURE AND CHRISTIANITY

In this article I would like to address the problem of dealing with Indian culture in the context of winning people to Christ and Christian growth. I will address especially the subtle danger of uniting beliefs that come from the Bible, and beliefs that come from Indian religion. This is called syncretism.

WHAT IS CULTURE?

Culture is not easily defined. Here is my definition as it applies to this study. Culture is what is considered normal or acceptable thinking or behavior for a group of people. Culture is seen in the various aspects of their lives such as: social relationships (family, friends, kin, clan, etc.). Generally common values are held by most people within a particular culture. Most people accept and are comfortable with what is considered normal in the various areas of their lives. Ideas, events or circumstances out of the ordinary or contrary to the "usual" are met with, "that's not right," "that's strange," "that's a funny way of doing things," "Can you figure them out?"

Everyone is a part of a culture. When someone belongs to a dominant culture, or is part of a majority, he is not aware that he is part of a culture. Only when he encounters a different culture does he realizes there are other ways of looking at life. Still, when he first contacts another culture, his first reaction is, "I'm right and you are wrong (or stupid)."

CULTURAL BIGOTRY

When someone remains close-minded and refuses to accept and understand another's viewpoint and insists that his way is the only right way, then we have what we could call a cultural bigot. The greatest missionary of all time, the Apostle Paul, said, "to the Jews I became as a Jew . . . to those who are under the law, as under the law . . . to those who are without law, as without law...to the weak I became as weak . . . " (I Corinthians 9:20–22). Why? To win them to Jesus.

Culture itself is neither good or bad. Culture simply defines you as part of a people, tribe, tongue or nation. There are good or godly aspects of your culture. There are bad or evil aspects of your culture. Culture is not a sacred calf that must be preserved at all costs.

MISSIONS AND INDIAN CULTURE

When Christian missionaries cross cultures to reach another "people," values come into conflict. I believe there have been four major responses to cultural conflict. These are:

Rejection (Eliminate or discard)
Absorption (Incorporate or swallow up)
Syncretism (Uniting of opposing views)
Sanctification (Setting apart for God's intended purpose)

I believe the biblical response requires openmindedness and critical thinking that is based on the Word of God.

REJECTION OF INDIAN CULTURE

Many early missionaries responded to cultural conflict and the problem of Indians going back to their old ways by isolating their converts from the rest of the "pagan" Indians. Everything that reminded of the Indian culture was rejected. The cultural norms of the non-native-Christian missionary were forced on or adopted by the Indian convert. For example:

Native dress discarded for shirt and tie
Native hairstyle rejected for an over the ears trim
Indian name dropped for a "Christian" name
Native language discouraged for English
Native musical instruments abandoned for the piano (now guitar)
Native style of music replaced by European hymns
Native social relationships and duties substituted by nuclear family and church obligations

The result of the complete rejection of Indian culture was a "White" (please excuse the term, I don't mean to be racist at all) Indian Christian.

The traditional Indian was offended by this rejection of Indian culture because it struck at the heart of who he was. The result has been a further distancing between the traditional Indian and the Christian who wants to win him to Christ. Often, there was persecution, resulting in even less contact between the two sides. Contact that is absolutely necessary to love someone else to Christ. Let me say that there have been many dedicated, committed Christians who in their rejection of Indian culture have stood for Jesus. These stand as great examples of a desire to please Jesus at any cost.

ABSORPTION OF INDIAN CULTURE

Another response to Indian culture by the church has been what I call absorption. This is where the church swallows up the Indian culture. Here pagan, non-Christian religious rituals and beliefs are tolerated and even allowed to co-exist beside (or within) the church. This is okay as long as you are a good Christian (as defined by a particular church).

The church has its definition of what makes a good Christian. For example, it can be:

Baptism
Catechism
Sacraments
Church membership

As long as you fulfill these requirements, your "pagan" beliefs and practices are tolerated. Obviously this is not true to the Bible. "You cannot drink from the cup of the Lord and from the cup of demons; you cannot eat at the Lord's table and at the demons' table." (I Corinthians 10:21, NLB)

SYNCRETISM

Syncretism is in my estimation the most dangerous response to Indian culture.

What is syncretism? Here are two heavy dictionary definitions: Syncretism is the "attempted reconciliation or union of different or opposing principles, practices or parties as in philosophy or religion." (Random House Dictionary of the English Language, Second Edition, 1987) It is the "attempted union of principles or parties irreconcilably at variance with each other, especially the doctrines of certain religionists." (Webster's New College Dictionary, 1948)

This may be easier to understand by way of example:

The syncretist sees the similarities between Christianity and the Indian way and without qualification assumes they are the same and puts them together. The syncretist says, "the Indian burns cedar and cleanses his mind with the smoke just like the Christian does with the blood of Christ. Therefore, I will cleanse my mind with the smoke and the blood of Christ." I have news for the syncretist, only the blood of Christ can wash away sin and cleanse your conscience from the guilty feeling of doing work that is worth nothing. Nothing takes the place or stands equal to the blood of Christ.

We have many "romantic" Indians today thanks to "Dances with Wolves," and the courting of the New Age movement. It is real "in" to be Indian these days. Many of our young Indian men and women are "going back to the Indian way." Even Indian Christians in a search to be relevant and in a desire to reach the traditionalist have been caught up in the dangerous deception of syncretism. Being culturally relevant does not mean compromising the truth.

There is only one way to God and only one mediator between God and man—Christ Jesus. The gospel is: Jesus died for our sins according to the scriptures, He was buried and on the third day, He arose from the dead and was raised to the right hand of God. Jesus is coming back and we need to be ready to meet Him.

SANCTIFICATION OF INDIAN CULTURE

Sanctification means setting something or someone apart for God's intended purpose.

I believe sanctification is the proper biblical response to Indian culture. Every culture has good, godly elements and bad, evil elements. The true Christian does not need to abandon what is good or godly. The truly spiritual Christian judges all things. As the believer grows in his relationship with Jesus he puts his culture under the scrutiny of the Word of God, the Bible. Whatever can be examined and is true to the Word of God, is kept. Whatever is not true to the Word of God, is rejected.

I have retained some Indian values as they are in line with the Word of God. For example:

Respect for Elders—every "good" Indian knows and practices this.
Care of the Earth—Adam was told to "tend" or "guard" or "keep" the garden of Eden. I never littered before I became a follower of Jesus and I don't now.
Importance of Extended Family
Awareness of the Spirit World
Thanksgiving to God for all His Blessings.

There are many other things that are not a violation of the Word of God, and therefore do not need to be abandoned.

When it comes to Indian religious beliefs, this is where we must be most wise, discerning and active in our judgments. I do not pray to any intermediary, any in-between being, when I pray to God. That means I don't pray to or through an animal, bird, spirit helper, mountain, thunder, etc., but directly to God in the name of Jesus.

I do not worship "Mother Earth." I do not worship and serve the creation but the Creator. I realize my body was made of the dust of the ground and will return to dust (if Jesus doesn't come in my lifetime), but I do not pray to the earth or to any plant, animal or spirit. God is my Father and He wants me to go to Him directly.

Sanctification requires thinking and the application of the Word of God to our lives. It may be scary to let Indian Christians grow up and judge their own culture in the light of God's Word but it is what God desires. "Religion" does all your thinking for you. God wants you to grow up and judge all things in the light of His Word.

An example of sanctification of culture:

Among the Iroquois people, we have a ten day feast after the death of an individual. The teaching of the ten day feast is:

> The spirit of the person "hangs around" for ten days after death.
> A feast must be held to "feed" the spirit so it can go on its journey to where it should go.
> A ceremony with prayers and the burning of Indian tobacco (that carries prayer to the Creator) is held.

Here are the four responses to this Iroquois religious belief and tradition.

REJECTION

The Christian rejects anything to do with the ten day feast and refuses to attend or contribute. What is unfortunate is that there is then no sanctifying influence on the participants of the ten day feast, as there is no Christian to be seen. What is good is the Iroquois teaching of death is rightly rejected as not true to the Word of God.

ABSORPTION

The Christian attends the church funeral and also actively participates in the ten day feast. The believer goes along with both systems of belief. We have a spiritual "Jekyll and Hyde".

SYNCRETISM

The Christian blends the belief of Christianity and the Iroquois theology. He prays to God and "feeds" the departed spirit. He believes in heaven and hell and that the man's spirit hangs around for ten days before it goes to one of those places. He prays in the name of Jesus and burns tobacco to lift his prayer to God. The truth of God's Word is compromised, it is watered down.

SANCTIFICATION

As a minister, I have studied, counselled and helped people through the grief process. I know that death often is a great shock to the emotional system. Many people are numb and in a daze immediately after the death of a loved one.

The Christian funeral is usually done on the third day after death. Some have said they don't remember much of the funeral services and the time between the death and burial of their loved one.

Grief is a process that takes time. My study of Iroquois culture has led me to believe the Iroquois people had a better way of handling the grief process than our common Christian method that ends with the funeral service. The grieving survivor is left to his own devices after the day of the funeral. I propose that it would be a healthy aid to the grief process to meet on the tenth day after the death of the loved one. After the emotions have cooled and the grieving one has had opportunity to accept the loss would be an ideal time to have the support of friends and family. Praying, remembering the departed loved one and fellowshipping with supportive people would greatly help the grieving ones. This could be called a "Ten Day Memorial Feast" to distinguish it from the Iroquois traditional event. At the "Ten Day Memorial," the incorrect Iroquois teaching could be corrected perhaps as follows:

"Before we knew Christ, we thought the spirits of those who died stayed around. We thought we needed to feed them so that they would go away to where they should go. But now we know that when a man dies, his spirit immediately goes to its reward or judgment, that is, if he knew Christ, to heaven and if not, to hell. If we are bothered in our dreams by the appearance of the dead, it is only memories from our minds or familiar spirits that imitate the dead. It is appointed unto man once to die and after death, the judgment. We are here to pray for our living loved ones and not the dead. We are here to show our support and share together in this fellowship meal and remember the one whom we lost in death . . . etc."

I believe sanctification of Indian culture should be done in consultation with other mature believers, especially those who really understand the true meaning of culture. Newcomers to the faith must beware, as much damage could be done by unwise and rash actions. The Word of God, the centrality of Jesus Christ, His death and resurrection, and the leadership of the Holy Spirit must be foremost in the sanctification of Indian culture. Then it will have its God-intended place.

16

EMERSON SPIDER, SR.

THE NATIVE AMERICAN
CHURCH OF JESUS CHRIST

Emerson Spider, Sr. (Oglala Lakota) lives in Porcupine on the Pine Ridge Reservation and is headman of the Native American Church of Jesus Christ in South Dakota, which is also commonly referred to as the peyote religion for its sacramental use of the peyote cactus. The peyote religion combines ancient native traditions with Christian practices and beliefs, and has developed along two distinct ceremonial lines: Half Moon, which is generally considered to be older and more traditional, and Cross Fire, which is more overtly Christian in form and content. Peyotists began organizing as a Christian denomination during the early twentieth century in order to protect themselves from religious persecution at the hands of misguided missionaries, politicians, and government agents. This essay was originally scheduled as part of a symposium on "American Indian Religion in the Dakotas: Historical and Contemporary Perspectives," held in Bismarck, North Dakota; Spider was unable to attend, so he was interviewed at his home. Spider recounts the history of this intertribal religious tradition among his own people, where it exists alongside a variety of tribal ceremonies and Christian denominations. He describes the organization and leadership of their services and the power of the peyote to bring healing and insight. While many non-native Christians have supported the Native American Church in recent legal battles over religious freedom, few have perceived that they were helping fellow Christians, and Spider concludes his comments by expressing his desire that the Native American Church "be recognized by other churches."

First of all, I'm very thankful that you boys could come to the Native American Church of Jesus Christ, which was built here at Porcupine not too long ago. I am Emerson Spider, Sr., and my title is Reverend of the Native American Church. I'm the headman of the Native American Church of Jesus Christ in the state of South Dakota.

Our church began to come into South Dakota during the early 1900s. There was a man named John Rave, a Winnebago Indian. This was before I was born. I guess this man was very smart. He was in the Catholic Church. Then he ordained another man named Henry White, also a Winnebago, as a minister in the Native American Church. That man came to the Sioux in the community of Allen, on Pine Ridge Reservation. So we got our ordination by rights.

At first we weren't organized as a church. It was a Sioux man named Jim Blue Bird who organized this peyote way of worshipping as a church and put the Bible in there to be the head instrument in our church. Then he said that we should have ministers. So in 1924 we organized as a church with ministers, like any other church. Last June we had our fifty-eighth annual convention. My grandpa on my mother's side, Reverend William Black Bear, was the first headman of the church in South Dakota. Then after he was gone, my dad took over. He was sixty-six years old when he passed away. For the past seventeen years I have been head of the church.

We started out as a traditional church. We didn't have the Bible or practice Christianity. Among the Indians, we always say that it is the oldest church in the world. Gradually we learned about the second coming of Christ, and finally we accepted the Lord as our personal savior, just as in any other church. Originally, the Native American Church followed the Half Moon way. Then the Winnebagos adopted the Cross Fire way. The fireplace on their altar looks like a half-moon, but instead of tobacco smoke they use the Bible.

The Native American Church started out with the Half Moon way of the Peyote religion. They use what they call the "Generation Fireplace." On the altar they mound the earth like a half-moon, and they put a little road on that mound which represents your life from the time you were born until you come to the center, and on to when you get old and go from there to death. They put the Generation Fireplace at the altar within the tipi, and at the center of the road they place the peyote.

We know that this Generation Fireplace pushes souls to Christ. The Cross Fire way comes in after believing on the Lord Jesus Christ. In this way we put the cross at the center to represent the place where Christ gave his life for each and every one of us. So it begins with this Half Moon way and then comes into the Cross Fire way, where you believe in Christ and pass to believing on the Lord. I'm not saying that the Cross Fire way is better, but as we come along we learn about the second coming of Christ. We put the peace pipe aside and we put the Bible in its place.

When I was becoming a Christian, I heard some people say, "I'm worshipping the same God as my forefathers." I thought that was real good, but now I think our forefathers must not have had the right kind of god. I hate to say this, but it is so. In the olden days, when people from different tribes came around, they killed them. We said they were enemies because they didn't speak our language. They had the same skin as we had, but we killed them. In those days they prayed to the Great Spirit, but I don't think that's the right god. The God we found is love. He loves us all. If in the olden days they prayed to that God, why is it they killed each other as enemies?

Also, in the olden days, one tribe believed that the souls of the departed went east, riding white horses. The Happy Hunting Grounds were supposed to be over the fourth hill to the east. Other tribes said the departed souls went south, riding sorrel horses. Every tribe had different beliefs. If they prayed to the same Great Spirit in the early days, they should all have had the same belief. Christ gave His life and made a road for us to go on. That's one way: towards heaven.

Right now some traditional Indian people say this Bible doesn't belong to the Indians because the white man made it. But I never thought of it that way. I thought this Bible belongs to any wicked man, any man with a living soul in him, so that through this Bible he would be saved. This is the way I think. It wasn't for just the white men alone but for every man, every person who has a living soul within him. It's the food for that person.

I'm not saying the traditional ways are bad, but it tells in the Bible, "Choose you this day whom you will serve, whether the gods of Amorites our forefathers served; but as for me and my house, we will serve the Lord." These are not my own words; I always like to use the words of God. Some people say they are real traditional men, but Christ is also a traditional man. He's been here almost two thousand years. That's traditional; that's a long time. I was thinking that we didn't use this peyote until after 1900, but Christ was in the world two thousand years ago. I think that's more traditional than what we have been trying to do here.

In the traditional way of worshipping in the Native American Church, the leader is called a *road man*. We still have our traditional way, especially in this area. In the traditional way we pray with the tobacco and corn-shock cigarette in place of the peace pipe. I held a service like that the other night, a back-to-school meeting. I prayed for the little ones who are going back to school. So we still have our traditional way as well. I ordained some of the traditional road men as ministers of the church. I did this because if we don't it will just be tradition, and we won't be recognized as a church.

The peyote that we use is classified as a drug by the state of South Dakota. We use it in the Native American Church as a sacrament. Because we are organized as a church, the government can't take the peyote away from us. Our church is the last thing we have among the Indian people, the peyote way of worshipping. We call it *Pejuta yuta okolakiciye*, "medicine-eating church." The Native American Church is organized among the Sioux in South Dakota on three reservations: Pine Ridge, Rosebud, and Yankton. I have some ministers working on all three of these reservations. We are supposed to keep records, but I really don't know how many members there are. The other tribes still hang onto the traditional way of worshipping. They don't want to organize as a church, but the Sioux organized as a church. I think this is good, because other churches will recognize us as a church.

My grandpa and my dad told me that when they first started using peyote in the community of Allen, the Indian police would sneak up on them and stop them. They would take away the drum and the peyote. At that time my mother was real small, and she was going to the boarding school at Pine Ridge. While she was there, they found out that she had tuberculosis. In those days it was considered incurable. They placed my mother in the hospital, in a little room all by herself. No one was supposed to go near her because the disease was contagious. So they kept her there.

One day a grandma of mine was visiting the sick ones in the hospital. The door to my mother's room was open just a little bit. Her eyes were swollen nearly closed, and her body was swollen up; she was dying. As she lay there, she was looking towards the door, and she recognized the lady who went by. Mother called her name, so that lady came into the room. Although she was my mother's aunt, she didn't recognize my mother for awhile. Pretty soon she recognized her. "Is that you?" she said. "Yeah, that's me."

"Why are you lying here like this? Did you let your dad know that you're here?" My grandma on my mother's side passed away when my mother was real small, so she grew up with no mother, just my grandpa. I don't know what had happened, but the hospital hadn't notified my grandfather. So this grandma of mine said, "As soon as I get home I'm going to go to your dad and I'm going to tell him that you are here." I guess that made my mother feel real good. She said, "You do that."

Sure enough, in a few days my grandpa went after her. In those days there were just buggies, no cars. My grandpa really got mad because he had not been notified that my mother was sick. But the doctor told my grandpa not to take my mother because she had that contagious disease and was going to die anyway. Still, my grandpa took her home.

When they got home, my mother started taking that medicine, the peyote. They started giving her the medicine. My mother told me that it was towards springtime. All through that summer they would give her medicine, put her on a horse, and let her go out riding. She'd be on that horse most all day long. When she came back in the evening they would give her some more medicine. After a few months she was well. She was all right.

About that time they were caught while they were holding a Native American Church service. The man who ran the store at Allen at that time was against peyote, and he was the one who caught them. They called him *Nape Blaska*, "Flat-handed," because his hands were deformed. All of them got caught, including my mother, so they took them to Deadwood for trial. The court said that peyote was a narcotic, that it was no good. The judge asked, "Why are you using that?"

My mother's dad said: "This is good. This peyote's good. It is good medicine and I can prove it."

"What have you got to prove it with?"

"This girl here." So they had my mother stand up. "This girl had tuberculosis. The doctors gave up on her. She was placed in the sanitarium. I got her away from there. Now she's alive today."

Luckily, the doctor who had cared for my mother was in the courtroom. He asked her if she was Jessie Black Bear. "Yeah, it's me," she said.

He said, "How did you get well?"

"Through the peyote, through what we have here. I got well through that."

I guess the doctor got up and shook her hand, saying: "I thought you were gone a long time ago. I thought you were dead."

So right away the judge said, "I have nothing to do with this." "These mescal beans must be good," he said. (In those days they called peyote mescal beans.) "These mescal beans are yours; they don't belong to the white man. Give them back to them." So they gave the whole thing back, a wooden barrel full of peyote.

This is the reason that people say my mother is the one who saved the peyote. If she hadn't been there, they would have had a hard time proving that this medicine was good. After this happened, that man *Nape Blaska* went back and got into some kind of trouble. I guess he was in debt and couldn't pay, so he killed himself in the garage—committed suicide.

My dad was from Porcupine community. His family lived right across the road from here. My dad was born and raised here. He belonged to the Episcopal Church. My grandpa on my dad's side was a minister in that church. And my mother was from Allen, where the peyote church originated. They didn't tell me how they met, but anyway they got married. But my dad didn't like this medicine. He didn't believe in it. So whenever he went to Allen, and they started tying a drum for a service, he would take off. He didn't like to hear the drum or the songs. He would get on his horse and go way over the hill someplace. When they were through, he would come back. He did that for four years, I think.

My dad didn't believe in the peyote, but at the same time he was always thinking about it. He wondered, "What does it do for these people when they eat it?" Some people told him that when you ate it you got high, just like drinking. My dad never drank and never smoked. I guess he grew up like that. So he was wondering; he had it in mind all the time. But at the same time he was scared to use it because some people said it was dope.

Finally one day, when my mother and dad were alone, he said to my mother, "Jessie, I wonder if you could give me some of that medicine you eat?"

"Sure," she said. So she picked out four dried ones. She gave them to my dad and he started to eat one. This medicine is very bitter, so as he started to chew on it, he quickly took it out of his mouth. "This is awful," he said. "I don't see how you could eat it and why you would eat it. It's no good, not fit to be eaten." Then he got up. "This is not a thing to eat," he said. He started towards the stove, and although my mother tried to stop him, she couldn't. He opened that stove, threw the peyote in there, and burned it up.

Four days later, all of a sudden my dad couldn't pass any water. It stopped completely. His kidneys were swelling up, so he came back to Porcupine. His father sent for a doctor from Rapid City. That doctor came in a hurry; the Indians called him *Wasicu Wakan Witkokola*, "Crazy Doctor." He came and got his bag out and examined my father all over. I guess he told my grandpa: "If I wanted to, I could give your boy some medicine, but I want to tell you the truth. That boy's not going to live four days. You'd better get ready for it. There's no medicine that will cure him."

So my grandfather heard that. Then he wrote out a note and gave it to my father. "You take this to your father-in-law," he said. So they got in a buggy and rushed back to Allen, about twenty miles on the cut-across. When they got there, they gave that note to my grandpa on that side. He said, "Yeah, I got good medicine for that." My dad wanted to find out what kind of medicine he had. I guess he kept asking my mother, "What kind of medicine does your father have?" Finally my mother told him. "It's the same medicine that you burned here not too long ago." My dad said: "Well, that's it. If that's the medicine they are going to give, I don't want any. I'd rather die. I'm not going to eat it." "I'm not going to take it," he said.

My dad's older brother went with them on this trip. He's still alive today, over ninety years old. My dad was real young in those days. And I guess my uncle said to my father, "Brother, you're a coward." He said: "You're a coward. I'll eat it. You're scared of it. I'll eat it first," he said.

You know how young men are. When my dad heard that about being a coward and being scared, he got mad. "Well, bring all you got," he said. "I'll eat everything you got. Bring everything." So right away they told my grandfather. "Okay," he said. They got everything ready in no time. They boiled some of the powdered medicine in water to make tea, and they started giving my dad some of the dried medicine to eat. My dad said he didn't know how much he ate. "A lot of it," he said, "and I drank a lot of tea." His stomach and his kidneys were so swollen he could hardly walk. "I could hardly move," he said.

They were beating a drum, but it seemed to my dad that they were very slow to begin. My grandpa went after some boys, and pretty soon they came back and started their service. That morning my dad had to be excused, so he went out. There was no longer anything wrong with him. Back there about three gallons of water came out of him, I guess.

This is the way my dad told it. He said, "That's good medicine—real good medicine. It could cure anything. But the way they're praying with it, that's another thing." He grew up in the Episcopal Church, so he didn't believe in the Native American Church. "How can they pray with that peyote? How can they say that it is holy and leading a man to Christ? How could it be?" My dad kept going to church. Then one day he took some medicine, and I guess it showed him. Although he never brought out what happened, he learned that those who were weak in faith could benefit from using the peyote, that it was put here for the Indian people to lead them to Christ.

Now some of us are Christians—you might say born-again Christians. That's what we are. As we come along, we try to do whatever other church-es are doing. In the past we had the Half Moon way of worshipping, and we used the peace pipe in our services, because the peace pipe is the tradi-tional way of worshipping among our Sioux Indian people. As we came along, we put the peace pipe away, and in place of it we now use the Bible, so that we may be saved in the end. I know and believe that the Great Spirit in heaven did this for the Indian people, so that through this medicine we would find Christ.

In my own life I have experienced this, and I've told a lot of people about it. Indians from all tribes went out to hunt for roots to use as medi-cines, so God put this peyote here for the Indians to find. They call it peyote, but we say *pejuta*, which means "medicine" in our language. All the differ-ent tribes call it "medicine" in their own languages. Because God loves all of us he put this medicine in the world so that the Indians would find it and through it they would come to Christ.

Today I am well-known among other tribes as a good person because I have the fear of the Lord and I love God and I love Jesus Christ. If you live this way you'll get somewhere. I went to school as far as the fifth grade at Holy Rosary Mission at Pine Ridge, South Dakota. Some of the teachers there talked against our church and said that I was a dope eater. The boys I played with got scared of me. They said, "Don't go close to Spider cause he's going to poison you. He's a dope eater. He's no good." Sometimes I cried in the classroom, or on the playground, because I wanted to have friends but the boys didn't like me. They always said things like that to me as I grew up.

About two years ago they called me to that same place where I went to school. The people there used to hate me for using this peyote, but now they wanted to find out more about it. I didn't refuse them, because I have the love of God. I went back and told them about what the peyote had done for me.

To start with, we had our services in a tipi, with a fire burning inside. Our instruments were the drum, rattle, and feather fan. And we used God's plant, the Divine Herb. Through that, some of us—not all of us, but some of us—have become Christians. We're walking hand in hand doing the Christian walk. It's pretty hard to put in words; I think it's a mystery of God and no one can bring it out in words. But I'm going to try my best to explain some of what happened to me.

One time, before I became a Christian, I was sick. At that time I used the Divine Herb and I was healed by Christ. I got hurt when I was fifteen years old. The sickness I had was osteomyelitis. The doctors told me that it's incurable. There's no medicine on earth that will cure it, they said. And sure enough, the peyote eased my pain, but it didn't kill the disease. They said it's in my bones. I got hurt when I was young, and it started from there. When I was sick, I got double pneumonia, too. I was on my deathbed. I overheard the doctor talking to my parents, and he said if I didn't make it through that night, I would die. The doctor was telling my dad and my mom to be ready.

That day a preacher came into my room, passing out tracts. He gave me one, but I couldn't read it. I had poor eyesight, so I couldn't read it. So I just put it on the table. I was lying down. I couldn't get up from bed. I couldn't sit up, and I could hardly talk. That morning—I think it was a Sunday—it was coming daylight, and I remembered that the old people used to tell us that that's the time to talk to God. If you tell Him something, He'll hear you, they said. So that morning I was praying on my deathbed that if it's at all possible, I wanted to live longer.

God must have pitied me, because that morning He called me by my name. It was real loud. It was the first time I heard something like that, and it really hit me hard. The voice said, "Emerson!" real loud in the room. I couldn't get up from the bed but I answered that call. I said: "What? I am over here. I'm lying here." I thought it was one of the other boys in the room with me. There were about four other patients who were about to die, too, so they were placed in the room. But when I looked around they were all in bed asleep. I just started to go back to sleep again when I heard it a second time. It got me out of bed, sitting up. I noticed I was sitting up as I said, "Hau! I'm over here. What do you want?" But there was no answer, so I lay back down again.

The third time the voice got me to my feet, standing up. I knew that I was on my feet standing up. I walked towards the aisle and looked around, and here it was, the high calling of God; and it seemed like cold water on my face that morning, like it tells in the Scriptures about spiritual baptism. And that morning Christ healed me from my sickness. So I rejoice in the Lord every day of my life. Every time in the morning, ever since then when I get up I praise the Lord. I give Him thanks every day of my life. That's the life I'm leading now.

When I came back to the bed, I noticed the tract that had been given to me. I picked it up and read it, and it said, "Come as you are." Christ was speaking. "Come as you are." I knew it meant me, because I was a real sinner. I was no good, but it said *as I am*, He wants me to come to Him. And it says in there, "If any man comes unto me, I shall in no ways cast him out." So I know Christ called me by my name to be a leader of our church. I was supposed to stop sinning and try to be a good person because I was going to be the leader of the church. I was married when I was twenty-one, and when I was twenty-three years old I stopped drinking and smoking.

While I was coming along, there were some Christians who said to me: "You should come to our church where you won't be shedding tears for your people. Although you try to tell them right from wrong, they don't listen to you. Our church will listen to you," they said. But God wanted me to go where the church wasn't doing right, to tell them about the second coming of Christ. So actually God sent me to this Native American Church. He used me as a tool of the church to be the head man to try and guide them in the right way.

In our church we have leader helpers who can hold a service if there is no leader present. I remained a leader helper for a long time. Then I became a candidate leader. And then I became the chief leader. I gave information on how to hold a service. Gradually I became the headman of the community; you might say a minister of the community, the headman of the local branch. Then pretty soon, when the assistant man who sat next to my dad passed away, they appointed me his assistant. So I came to it step by step, and then when my dad passed away, I became the high priest.

Before my dad passed away, he said: "This is my best. I want you to make it right for me." So that's what I'm doing now. I'm trying to make the other non-peyote people see that I can lead a Christian life in the Native American Church. I stand up for my church and say that it is a good church.

By rights we can hold our church services most any time. During the summertime we can have our services any time of the week, but during the wintertime we have to have services on Saturday because the kids have to go to school Monday. And lately some of the church members have been working, too, so we have to consider them. Also, the cost of the medicine we use is getting real high. Usually we go and harvest it ourselves, but the trip is very expensive. I know just lately there are people selling land to get the money to go and harvest peyote and bring it back.

It takes four persons to run a service: the leader, the drummer, the cedar man and the fire man. They don't pick out just anybody for these positions.

The man who takes care of the drum is supposed to be a certain kind of man who knows how to hit the drum. He can't live a wicked life and handle the drum. It's sacred to the Indians. Indians really like the drum. It is made into a great big drum which they use at powwows and things like that. We use that same drum, but we make it into a real small drum, and we use it to praise and sing unto the Lord. For that reason the drummer has to be a certain kind of person to hit that drum. He has to know how to sing, how to hit the drum, and how to live a good life. He must know how to make instruments in the church.

The man who takes care of the cedar throughout the night has to be a man who knows how to pray to the Great Creator, to the Great Spirit. He has to take care of the prayers. Every time a person prays, he burns cedar. We use the cedar smoke as incense, just like the Catholic Church. We were told that a long time ago the old people made smoke signals in order to send messages to others far away. We were told that we're doing that. That's the reason they used the peace pipe to pray to the Great Spirit, making smoke signals to pray with. During our church services in the tipi we burn that cedar whenever somebody prays, so that the smoke goes up. Our understanding is that we are making smoke signals to the Great Spirit so that He will hear our prayers. That's what we have been told.

The fire man is supposed to know how to build the fire; they don't just throw the wood into the fireplace. This man has to know how to chop and gather wood, how to build a tipi, and things like that. We have a fire going inside the tipi all the time, so this man takes care of it, he watches it. He's the only man who moves in the church, like an altar boy in the Catholic Church. He goes out, brings wood in, and keeps that fire burning. In our church building we have lights, but when we hold traditional services in the tipi, we have to keep the fire going all night.

In the traditional way our services started at sundown and continued until sunrise. That's the way it used to be. But nowadays the people come late. When the leader, drummer, cedar man, and fire man all arrive, then we start our service.

There are different instruments that we use in our services in order to praise the Lord. To start with we use this staff, which we call *sagye*. That means "cane" in our language. Each man, when he sings in the service, holds onto this cane.

We use this small drum, tied in a certain way, with water inside. Only a few men know how to tie and beat the drum. We call it a holy drum.

We use this drumstick, which can be made from all kinds of wood. One kind is called snake wood. It makes a really good-looking stick.

We use this gourd rattle, which each man holds when it is his turn to sing.

We use this sage. From the beginning of our church, the Half Moon way, we have used this sage. It was used as a traditional way of praying. They were told that they should use it to refresh themselves, to cleanse themselves, before going into a ceremonial like the Sun Dance or sweat lodge or fasting. If you wipe yourself with it there is a good fresh smell and it cleans you. That's the reason they used it all over the body in the sweat lodge. For that reason the traditional way of worship in our church uses sage. They hit themselves all over with that sage to clean themselves. Then they partake of the Divine Herb.

We use this bone whistle, made from the wing bone of an eagle. The leader blows it in a ceremonial way during the service.

We use this fan, made from different kinds of bird feathers, to perform holy orders. To start with, they used to use a feather fan made from two swift hawk tails, twelve feathers on each bird, a total of twenty-four. These feathers are arranged to form a circle. On the outside are four eagle feathers, and inside, at the center, is an eagle plume. They say this swift hawk is the swiftest bird in the world, and they say the eagle is the fiercest bird. The plume inside the fan represents the living soul that's in a person. We were told that the tail feathers are there for the swift hawks to try to catch the living soul, the spirit of a man, the soul of each person. They can surround him and catch that living soul. The eagle plume is there so that if any bad spirit comes, the eagle will fight that spirit away. This is the way we were taught by our elders. We should use this type of feather fan to come out of the traditional way into a Christian way of worship.

Today they make fans from red and blue macaw feathers, and what they call scissortails—real pretty feathers. They bring all these different feathers into the church. They're good, they're God's creation, but it didn't come to us like that from the start.

Finally, we use the Divine Herb. When a person takes the peyote in a service, if he has teeth, he usually eats it dry. When I was young, when I had teeth, I could eat it dry. Sometimes they grind it up. Then a person can put the powder in his hand and eat it like that. Or he can mix it with water and make it into a kind of gravy and eat it like that. We also make tea out of the powdered peyote, using warm water. The peyote is very bitter. If you can eat four of them it is good, and if you can eat more, it will do you a lot of good.

When peyote first started to come into our area, we used our native tongue all the time to preach the word of God. I have a Bible that's written in our language, and I can read it well. Gradually our young people have gone to school and gotten a good understanding of English. The man who had this church building built is half Sioux and half Shoshone, but he was raised in a city, so he didn't learn either the Sioux language or the Shoshone language. He speaks just this whiteman language. So when we have our services and there's no person who doesn't speak our language, we usually talk in our own native tongue. But when somebody who doesn't understand our language comes into our church, we try to perform everything in English so it will be understandable. But some things we can't do in English, because we were brought up in a certain way and it has to be that way. It doesn't have to be understood by other men, just so the Great Spirit will understand us, listen to us, hear us. We believe that way.

During the service we sing songs in groups of four. Some are in Lakota and others are in English. These are the words to one set of songs. I composed the first song using words from my favorite gospel hymn; the words of the third song are in English, and the other three are in Lakota:

(1) I have decided to follow Jesus.
No turning back.

(2) Jesus I love your words
Because your words are eternal life.
Give me life.
I love your words.

(3) Praise our Lord Savior Jesus.
Did you know that our Lord Savior Jesus died upon the cross for our sins?
Praise our Lord Savior Jesus.

(4) God, look upon us Indians,
We want to be saved.

After the service we eat a breakfast of four symbolic foods. They are sacred to the Indians and are eaten not for the body but for spiritual strength.

The first is water. They say everything lives by water, so in the morning we have a woman bring in water and pray over it. This is because in the beginning it was a woman who first found the peyote. Later, when the Indians learned to read the Bible, they found out about the well of Jacob, and about Christ saying "I am the living water." They found where Christ says: "The water you will give me, I'll be thirsty again, but the water I'll give you, you will never be thirsty. You will become a spring within yourself." This is what it tells in the Scripture, so they pray over the water for spiritual strength.

The second is corn. Usually at this time of year they have fresh corn on the cob, but in the wintertime they used dried corn, which they cook so it comes out just like it was fresh. We have been told that before the white men ever came across, the Indians knew how to plant corn. They already had that here and they lived by it. They use this to pray that their gardens will be good; they pray over the corn that in the summertime everything will grow real good.

The third is meat. A long time ago they used only dried meat, but today they use any kind of meat, usually beef. They boil it and serve it with soup, although some pass around just the meat itself. In the olden days the Indians used to have a lot of livestock, cattle, and wild animals like deer and buffalo. So they prayed over the meat that the hunting season would be good, that their children would have good food.

The fourth is fruit. The old people prayed over the fruit so that the wild fruits along the creeks would grow for the Indians to use. They pounded the fruit up and dried it so it would keep.

All the church services we have are not alike. We have services for birthdays, healing, marriage, baptism, prayers, funerals—anything, we have it all. Every service is different. That's the mystery of God.

One time we had a healing service here which pretty much surprised us. We had a man who was going to have surgery for gallstones, and we had a healing service here and gave him medicine. He was seated right near the altar. A girl suffering with arthritis was seated across the room, against the east wall. We performed their healing. Lately we're trying to get the healing of Jesus Christ. We don't give sick people a whole bunch of medicine like in the olden times, but we just give them so much. One Scripture I used was, "Any man sit among you, let him call the elders of the church that they anoint him with oil, pray over him that he may get well, and if he commits any sin, it shall be forgiven." These are the Lord's words, so I used them. That man was healed right there that night. And the girl, even though she wasn't out in the center of the church, was also healed. So things like this happen. It's altogether different than the works of the peyote.

I might put it this way. When people come to a service and partake of the Divine Herb, it works on them in different ways. That's the mystery of God. Sometimes, even if a person is no good, the peyote will work for him. Through the peyote he will throw away the evil and give himself to Christ. In this way some of our church members have put away alcohol, become Christians, and gotten good jobs again. And they help other people in the church, too.

One time my dad went to a prayer ceremony. He must have eaten a lot of medicine, and the service was going on and on. And all at once he saw the door open, so he looked over there and here was a man coming in. It seemed like nobody else noticed that man coming in. But my dad kept watching him, and that man came up to him and said: "I've been looking for you all over. I couldn't find you. I heard that you were in a meeting someplace. I went to one meeting but you weren't there, so I came over here." He sat beside my dad and said, "Tonight I'm going to pray with you, sing with you." So my dad was happy. My dad wasn't a drummer, but he was a good singer, had a good voice. And my dad was a minister and a good man. The visitor had a box with him, so he took his instruments out. Everything he had was perfect. When the singing came to them, the visitor sang first. He sang good songs, real pretty songs. Then he hit the drum for my dad, but he made that drum sound different, a good sound. Then he talked and prayed, prayed real good, prayed so interestingly that the people started crying. He was really good at everything.

My dad was watching him, but he never did see the man talking. Then he saw that the man was going around to every person in there, looking at their prayer instruments, opening their boxes up and taking a good look at their instruments. Then, finally, he came to where the altar was, and he looked at everything there. They had this Divine Herb there, which they were partaking of. My dad saw him open it, and suddenly it seemed like somebody had hit the man in the face and knocked him toward the door. When he landed by the door, my dad could see his tail and horns. As he was going out, he looked back at my dad and said: "I'm going to come back and visit you again. Someday I'm going to come back again."

From this we know that the Evil One can come into any place, even a church. The Evil One can read the Bible, he can talk, he can pray, but he doesn't believe in Christ. He says he believes in Christ, that he knows Christ, but doesn't believe it. He's that powerful, fooling people all over the world. So a man should be aware that the Evil One can come anywhere.

Through my work in the church I came to know many things. One thing I wanted to find out for sure is where the souls of our departed ones are. I went around to different ministers, different churches. "I want you to tell me the truth of it," I said. "Where is paradise?" But no one could answer me. So I came back to my church and finally learned that the departed souls are here. They're not going any place. When we pray in the prayer service, and we are thinking about our departed loved ones, they come near us. They come right close to us. The only thing I found out about it in the Scriptures is that the departed souls are just like they are behind glass. They're on the other side, we're on this side. They see us, but we can't see them; they hear us, but we can't hear them. That's how it is. I found this out in our church and by reading the Scriptures, that the departed ones are always here with us. I thought this was real nice.

We are Indian people, and we still have some of our traditional ways. One thing we have, which the Indians grew up with, is what we call the spiritual food for our departed ones. Long ago, when people were eating something good, they would think about their loved ones who had gone beyond. Then they would take a little bit of the food they were eating and throw it outside, saying, "*Wanagi le iyakiya*," which means, "Spirit, find this." When my grandpa and my grandma were alive, I saw them do this, and we still have this. We couldn't part with the things that the traditionals had, so we still have them.

They prayed for these departed ones, too, and they talked to them. They grew up with that. The Bible says that when a person dies he knows nothing, he can't hear, he can't see. But the Indians say that for four days that body is holy. It can see you, it can hear you, they say. One time I went to a gospel mission. The preacher was a white man. His wife had just died, and they were having a wake service. I said: "This lady is not dead, she's sleeping, I think, resting. So she sees you." And that man started crying. He said to me, "Those are comforting words that you brought here, words we never heard before."

"That's the way I was taught," I said, "and that's the way it is." So I prayed over her, and I talked to that dead body, because that's how I was brought up.

There are some traditional things that we still have in the Cross Fire way, things we still hang onto because we grew up with them and we're Indians. But actually I don't know about the next generations, the coming generation. I notice that every generation changes. Things are changing.

I was told that God created all men equal, so this was the reason He put the peyote here for the Indians. Some of us didn't find out about it for a long time. But it is a good thing that my grandfather and my father found out about it, because it helped us to find Christ. Lately I have been going around to other churches and to schools telling about what our church is doing for us Indian people. For this reason I am happy to put my talk in a book so that people will read it and learn about our church. The days are getting short. The second coming of the Lord is at hand and we're getting ready for it. People will not be judged according to their beliefs, or according to which church they belong to. God will not say, "What kind of church do you belong to? What ways do you have?" It's not going to be that way. The bad things we've done and the good things we've done shall be weighed; and if we do good we'll be in the arms of Christ. It doesn't matter what church we belong to—the church will not save us. These are things I want to bring out to people, especially to the younger generation.

I would like you to understand that the fear of the Lord is the beginning of all knowledge. It says in the Scriptures that it doesn't matter if you gain the whole world's knowledge if you don't have the fear of the Lord. You have to be good in every way and put Christ ahead of you all the time so you won't go wrong. If you put your beliefs or anything else ahead of Christ, you'll be wrong. This world will come to an end. Everything must be stopped. So you need to have the true love of God to be saved.

Some people tell me that the knowledge of this world is the key to tomorrow. That's what they say. This earthly knowledge is good; it's necessary to get by in this world. I wish that the boys and girls will stay in school and learn—but put Christ ahead of your schooling. Read your Bible and you'll be safe in the arms of Christ. There is no other way to salvation.

If you come to the Lord, no matter what sickness you have, you can be healed. I was healed and now I'm a born-again Christian, and I'm working for my church. It used to be that when we had the traditional way of worshipping, we believed in earthly life. Now we believe in the second coming of Christ, although we still have our traditional ways. We still believe in them. I believe in the Sun Dance and fasting and all the traditional ways. I believe that they are sacred and I believe that they are good. But they are earthly, so by them alone no man will be saved.

The second coming of Christ is the only way to salvation. So I want you to know me and I want you to understand my church. There are some Christians who don't know our church, who may even think we are uncivilized. I want the Native American Church to be recognized by other churches. And I want people everywhere to pray for us, too.

...4.......

TRANSFORMATION
AND SURVIVAL

. . . .

17

JUANITA LITTLE

THE STORY AND FAITH JOURNEY OF A NATIVE CATECHIST

Juanita Little, OSF (Mescalero Apache) is a Franciscan Sister currently working in Mescalero, New Mexico, as a counselor with the Center of Protective Environment, a state-funded agency that intervenes in situations involving domestic violence. She previously served on the parish staff at St. Joseph's Mission in Mescalero and has also worked as a teacher. She first presented this essay at "A Consultation in Native Catechesis" sponsored by the Tekakwitha Conference; it grew out of her work at St. Joseph's at a time when they were beginning to develop a parish mission statement and a liturgy that would cultivate leadership and empower the local community. Little describes her cultural and religious background and recounts some examples of mutually beneficial interaction between contemporary Christians and traditionalists at Mescalero. Her "story of Jesus" as gift, guide, friend, provider, and protector is also the story of her reluctant journey back home to work with her people, and of her growing conception of an inclusive, global human community.

I'm Sr. Juanita of the Mescalero Apache tribe. I am enrolled in that tribe. My grandfather was captured by a band of Apaches near the Chihuahua area in Mexico when he was six years old. They brought up my father according to Apache ways. My mother is San Juan Pueblo. I really consider myself a real New Mexican. My grandmother was a Spaniard and I'm really proud of that fact because we have a little bit of all the cultures of New Mexico in our family. The Spanish, Mexican, Pueblo, and Apache. Now our younger members in the family are marrying non-Indians and when we get together, we are quite a nation. It is lovely. It is beautiful! We do have, in some instances, trouble within the marriages because those who have married the non-Indians eventually notice the cultural differences. We've had to cope with that as well.

My dream for myself is to build the Kingdom of God among the Apaches. When I first entered our community, the Franciscans of Our Lady of Perpetual Help in St. Louis, that was in the back of my mind. It was lost through the years while I was being educated in the various colleges in the midwest. (I'm the only Indian Sister in our community). Eventually our Sisters took on a school which was only fourteen miles from the Mescalero Reservation. I was back in contact with our people. I was very, very saddened to see that very little was being done for them, spiritually, through the Church. They're also losing their traditions. It hurt me very much to go to the feasts, dances and see it so abused that it was becoming just a performance. I didn't know what was happening. My world began to fall apart, too, because my people were falling apart. Our Sisters withdrew from the school. For about three summers no one really taught catechism. There were no first communion classes, no confirmation, nothing. The priests didn't seem to have any interest in really teaching the people or in really being concerned about preparing the children for their first communion. Every year when I came home for vacation the people would come crying to me about this. So, I began to speak about this need and the people began to tell me, "You're the one who is to respond to this need. You know best what the needs are." I couldn't seem to get this across to my community. I was becoming very bitter. I was very much burdened by this call that I couldn't respond to. I asked for a formal interview with the council in our community and they began to hear me. The diocesan priest helped me by presenting my need to the Bishop and writing to the council. The council decided that they would allow me to work at a school thirty-five miles from the reservation part time and work part time on the reservation. That meant travelling about 100 miles every day in the afternoon.

We have a very beautiful Church, a very famous Church, in fact. It's called the Cathedral of the Mountains. Fr. Albert Brown built this Church with local native materials. Huge stone was cut out of the sides of mountains and the people themselves were very much involved in building this great Cathedral. I think it speaks of us. It's very rugged. It's unfinished and people come and say, "You really should finish the Church." I say, "No, that speaks of us—we're not finished yet. We're just starting, and we're rugged and we're strong." When I first came I was cleaning and repairing. Then I felt, "Well, if I just keep doing this, this is all I'll do and there'll be no people coming to church." The Church is out there with the people.

I began visiting. In order to build a kingdom, I realized I would have to get to know what kind of foundation I was building upon. I found we had a very strong foundation with very prayerful people. People that were very humble, very dedicated, very self-sacrificing. We only have one real prayer form, the "Crown Dance." It has to be done for two or four nights. Part of that is feeding the entire tribe. It takes a lot of work, a lot of self-sacrifice, and a lot of dedication to go through this prayer form. I see the people doing it joyfully, perfectly. I think to myself, "Why can't we bring this forth from people in their prayer form, in Church, in our liturgy?" It didn't have that much meaning for them yet, but I think it will.

I'd like to share a few experiences that I have had. About three years ago, we had a call from the "Real to Reel" producers in Washington, D.C., who, I believe, are funded by the Catholic Bishops Communication Dept. They asked if they could come and film a videotape of the Catholic Indians and the way they live out their faith in the community. That really blew my mind. I said, "How am I going to do this?" I went to the president of the tribe and I asked for permission for the people to come to the reservation and do this filming. I didn't know how much to allow them to see, so he directed me to another council member who was in charge of cultural programs. We sat down and we talked about the things that we could allow these people to see, to share with us. She said, "Why don't you ask one of the clan members to do our Crown Dance?" I hadn't ever dared to think about it because they wouldn't do it as a performance. When I asked the clan leader, he said that he had just been waiting for a chance to be blessed by Father and to be blessed by the Church. He said he'd be glad to do the Crown Dance but it had to be done the right way—for two nights. The clan leader came over and instructed both Father and I on how to prepare a feast. We had just three days in which to do this, but the word got around and the people just cooperated beautifully. The religious leader called me aside and told me what to get ready. I forgot all about the filming because we got so much involved in this parish renewal. This is a big thing in our diocese. Everybody was asking me, "When are you having your parish renewal?" and I answered, "I don't know." I just let things happen and it did happen. That was our parish renewal done in our own way. It was a tremendous learning experience for me. This clan put so much trust, so much faith in me. We revealed to these producers so many of our native traditions, especially the prayer form never before done in public or put on film. I was very much frightened about it, but I was assured that the clan leader knew what he was doing.

I hope that this prayer form will be very much a part of our Catholic prayer, a part of the liturgy. I see that it is coming, very subtly, very quietly, and I'm not pushing it.

This year we had three major teaching experiences with this particular clan which is trying to renew its roots, its traditions. These people went back to their sacred mountain, which is in the Guadalupe Range right on the Texas-New Mexico border, for two days in March. They had visions. They heard things. They felt the presence of the ancient people with them. They asked me to go with them, but Father was ill and I felt I could not leave the mission at that time. They went back again in August, and this time they stayed four days, which is really the full time. Instead of just having a prayer meeting, they had the puberty rite. Again they asked me to come; I wasn't able to go all four days, but I went there the last night of the prayer. We had to travel for five hours way up in the mountains. It was quite a journey. When we arrived there, the people were so happy to see me. I couldn't believe the peace, the joy, I saw on their faces. I hadn't seen that before and I couldn't imagine why they would be so happy to see me. Then I realized how much it meant to them that I would be with them. This meant that the Church approved this prayer form. Later on, one of the women took me aside and told me that some of the women—the religious leaders—of this clan (who are also fallen away Catholics) had dreamed about the Blessed Mother. She said they were taking that as a sign that they should come back to Church. They told me of many other visions they had experienced. When we arrived there, the children came running to me full of all these wonderful things that had happened. They were not afraid. They said that this was their ancestors letting them know how happy they were that they were renewing themselves. The children all went back to one of the tents. They came back later and said, "Oh Sister, you should have come with us; the clan leader was teaching us." I was sorry that I hadn't been with them. When the dances began at sunset the songs were so beautiful, so prayerful. I had never seen the Crown Dance performed in such a prayerful manner. I can't explain. It was very moving and a very spiritual experience for me. One of the ladies invited me to join them in the dance. Another lady, a non-Catholic, came to me and said, "We've been dreaming about Father and we've been praying for him, is he all right?" I said that he hadn't been feeling too well and she said, "We want him to bless us again."

The head dancer always carries a cross in the dance. The Feast Giver must give the dancers and singers a gift. I asked the clan leader what might be appropriate. He said a rosary for each one. I went looking for rosaries but I saw these little wooden crosses and thought they would be more appropriate. I brought one to the clan leader and he approved. The head lady showed me how to fix these little crosses and now the dancers wear them all the time in their ceremony. I'm very proud of that. I always feel that they're praying for me and I have been assured that they are. So, to me, that was another tremendous learning experience. It made me aware of how much confidence and trust they were placing in me.

The other experience was the Confirmation Ceremony. We hadn't had a confirmation in our parish since 1968. We were supposed to join the other parishes for confirmation in June, but we asked if we could have it in our own mission, in our own way, and make it a big feast. This was the first time that adults would be really prepared for confirmation. It took us eight months and people came with great dedication. We started out with thirty-two in the class and we had sixteen confirmed. Ten teenagers and six adults. Three of these were converts. I tried to include these people in planning the liturgy and one of the things suggested was that the women make their own ceremonial shawls and the men should wear ribbon shirts. We made it a simple ceremony, but it was very beautiful. We had the big feast and I think now I'm learning how to put on a feast and who to call. The Bishop who came had been a Bishop among us for thirty-five years and had been retired for five years. During that five years we've had two Bishops and not one of them ever came to our mission. We were not invited to be a part of the installation ceremonies. The people were so happy to see that Bishop Metzger would come because he was an elder and this was someone they really knew. The people had never felt they had anything to give the Bishop. I said, "Well, part of our tradition is to give, what do you suggest?" One of the ladies beaded a medallion of the Holy Spirit and it was presented to the Bishop. He was very moved by this because this was the first time he had been given anything from our tribe.

We have a new Bishop now, starting a new Diocese of Las Cruces; it's very exciting. We were invited to participate in the installation. We have three tribes in this Diocese, but only the Apache tribe is officially recognized; the other two had integrated so much within the Mexican community that it's only once a year they come together as a tribe. The Bishop requested that these tribes be the honor guard for the procession of the hierarchy. Fr. Diego was there with us. I went to one of the women involved in the powwow group and she told me who to contact. We got a group of dancers in their Plains Indian costumes to be part of this honor guard. I was so proud of them. They stood so tall and straight. They considered this a privilege and they were just beaming. They added the color to the whole ceremony. We were asked to present a gift to the Bishop that would be something from ourselves. I had something like five days to prepare and I went to several of the women for their suggestions. I go to the women because we are a matriarchal society. They are the real leaders of our tribe. They told me to go to the artist of our tribe, Ignatius Palmer, whose work is very much in demand by collectors of Southwestern Indian art. They told me to ask him to paint a picture of a Crown Dancer and to be sure that all this light would be behind it so that it would give the idea that we are really praying to a deity. Many people call the Crown Dancers "Devil Dancers" and "Devil Worshippers." It's not that at all. We didn't want to give this impression. I went to the artist and explained what we wanted. In five days, he created a masterpiece. The moment I saw it, it gave me a joyful feeling, a feeling of resurrection. Miss Mescalero, in her buckskin costume, presented this gift to Bishop Ramirez. They asked for two of our children to be among those who would go to the Bishop for the "Kiss of Peace." We dressed a little boy and a little girl and the president of our tribe sent one of the Council members to officially welcome the Bishop and congratulate him upon his installation. You can see that we were very well represented. The people were just so proud of this. Now they say, "Sister, when is the Bishop coming? You know we have to make a big feast when he comes."

These are just the highlights. The greatest challenge for me is when people come to me and they don't ask me to pray for them; they ask me to pray with them. That really challenges my faith because I have to ask them to have faith and that calls forth the faith in myself. We have a prayer group, one of the first things we tried to establish, for our main support. Now people are saying, "We're having trouble in our family, will you come pray with us?" Our main prayer is the rosary because I've discovered the people have a great devotion to our Blessed Mother. They pray the rosary and I use this as a way of teaching. In using the scripture, I pray at the same time. We are being invited into different homes where they are having experiences—family problems—to pray with them. Sometimes when I am in the community center I am asked to pray with someone. They never ask me to pray for them but to pray with them. This is very challenging to me because it challenges me to really be authentic also. . . .

MY STORY OF JESUS

Jesus is many things to me at different phases of my life and my journey. The realization of Jesus being "Gift" was very strong last Christmas. Our people, and myself, have a deep sense of the "Fatherhood" of God. I think my father has really influenced that. I think of Jesus as a gift from the Father to be our Brother. This Brother has a message for us. He is a Teacher sent to tell us about the Father. Especially how the Father loves us so very much and is waiting for us at the end of this journey here on earth.

Our people are a wandering people. Their history is one of wandering all over the southwest and into Mexico. So the Chief, the Leader, the Guide, is a very important person among the people. This Guide has to clear the way. I see Jesus as One who has, first of all, won us a freedom through His suffering and death. He has cleared the way for us but He still walks with us on this journey. He walks with us as guide, as provider, as protector, and healer. Being one of us and sharing the joy and the sufferings of this journey. As I look at my own personal journey with Jesus, I am impressed. I can see that He has sent certain people, has put me in certain places at certain times to keep me on the way.

In our mission there were no Sisters. Yet, as a very young child, I always talked about Sisters or that kind of life. My parents tried the best they could to answer my questions about the type of life a Sister would live. They didn't know much about it themselves. When I first met Sisters, I was in the sixth grade. I wanted to be a Sister, not particularly in their order, but I knew I wanted that kind of life. When I was in the seventh grade, my father was transferred to Ft. Defiance, Arizona. The "White Sisters" were there. They taught catechism to the little ones. They didn't teach us. They were very distant from us. They walked like angels. I was afraid of them, but I still wanted to be one of them. So, I'd ask the Fathers about the Sisters. The Fathers tried to tell me about this kind of religious life. When I finished eighth grade, there was no high school in Ft. Defiance, so I would have to go to boarding school. My parents had been through boarding school all their lives. They didn't want that for their children. My father went home to see if he could find a job or get a transfer so I could go to high school. He stopped in Gallup and met Fr. Gil. Father asked him if I was still interested in becoming a Sister. He asked if I would be allowed to go to St. Louis to the Academy. Dad came home with the news that Father would be with us the next evening to talk about it. I didn't know where St. Louis was. I'd never been outside of New Mexico. When Father came, it was agreed that I could go to St. Louis. I was only thirteen years old.

During the summer, Father would take me to the Brown Franciscans. Those were our Sisters and they were working at the Community House, the Monastery, at St. Michael's. They're not there anymore. They were there just for the moment—long enough for me to be acquainted with them. I spent a few days with them off and on through the summer and I liked them very much. Father told me, "They're very human; I'd like for you to go with them." So I went to St. Louis for one year.

When I came home for summer vacation, my parents told me that they thought I was too young to make such a major decision. They wanted me to wait a little bit longer. I told them that I would wait on the condition that I could go to a Catholic boarding school. I didn't want to go to public school because I was afraid I would lose my vocation. My parents let me go to St. Michael's for one year. I stayed home my third year. My parents weren't able to afford to send me to boarding school or St. Louis.

At that time our community was accepting girls into the postulate at the age of fifteen. I entered the postulate when I was fifteen and began my training. When I first went, my father said, "Don't even think of coming home the first year." After I got through the first six weeks, my first year was all right. During my last year, my novitiate, I became very, very lonely. That's when I found Jesus as my friend. Throughout my different assignments, I have experienced a great deal of loneliness. That loneliness always seems to be in the cities and parishes that were affluent. I have found Jesus more in the poor places among poor people. I'm more comfortable with the poor people. That's where I belong. I've experienced Jesus as Friend, Healer. I always knew, in the back of my mind, that this calling I had was to be shared with my own people.

The community that Jesus sent me to is a story of guidance, of His putting the right people in the right place. When I came home in the summer, the Sisters from St. John, another Franciscan group, were teaching catechism in our parish. Father kept asking me, "Why don't you go with these Sisters?" I'd be closer to home at St. John's in Arizona. I said, "No, I feel that my place is with these other Sisters." They weren't anywhere close to my parish. I felt that somehow Jesus was going to find a way for me. When I was at St. Michael's, Mother Charles was trying to get me to join their community. But the Franciscan Community was the community I wanted to join. The year I took my perpetual vows was the year that our community was invited to establish a school fifteen miles from my home. The year after my perpetual vows, I was assigned to this school. I was teaching Catechism there on weekends, getting closer to my home. I said, "All right. Now I know where my journey is leading."

A year later our Sisters withdrew from this particular school. No one was teaching the children. Then I began to be burdened by my people. I felt them on my back no matter where I went. I tried to put distance between us. I asked for a transfer to St. Louis, to Illinois, to anywhere. I was even more burdened. I couldn't suppress this call, this need to come back. My community wouldn't listen to me. They kept telling me that I belonged with them and had to go where they asked me to go. I felt like I was being used and became very bitter, angry. There were many hurts. Until one of the Sisters told me to write a letter stating this need to present my personal apostolate to the council. At last some of the Sisters in our community helped me. They prayed for me and they showed me, Jesus gave me the strength and the courage to face the council members and tell them what I needed to do and what I needed from them. The council listened a little bit. They told me to get letters from the Fathers at the mission and from the Bishop to really verify the need. That made me angry. I said, "I'm the one who should know that need. Don't they trust me?" I was hurt but I did it. I got all the necessary letters. Finally, Mother called me and said, "We will send you to the school thirty-five miles from your home and you can teach half day and be at the reservation the other half day." I said, "All right. It's a beginning." I did that for two years.

All during that time there was very much healing taking place in my life. I couldn't come to my people with all these hurts. I was burdened and broken. I wouldn't have had the strength. I was healed gradually. I became whole again. Then Reverend Mother came to me and said, "Sister, we have to do something about this Mescalero business." My heart went to my feet. I thought she was going to tell me that this was the end. But she said, "Can you find a home to live in? Preferably near your parents." My parents lived four miles from the mission. My cousin had just asked me if I needed his home, which had been my grandmother's home where I had been born. He asked me if I needed it for the summer for when the Sisters would come. I told Mother, "Oh, yes, yes I can." I went to my cousin and asked if I could have the house for a while. He said, "You can have it for as long as you need it." I brought Reverend Mother and she looked the house over. She said, "It's a nice little home, how much are you going to charge for rent?" My cousin said, "Nothing. This is our home. This is where Sister was born."

That is the story of Jesus as my Guide. He continues to guide me all the time. I start out my day sometimes not knowing where I'm going. Suddenly, I find myself in homes with people that I hadn't really intended to see. They say, "Oh, Sister, I'm so glad you're here." Sometimes I'm walking by and they'll wave me in and say, "Sister, I was hoping you'd come by here today." This is Jesus guiding me and providing for me and being my Protector. I travel and do things that I would never have done before. As long as I know that I'm doing it for Jesus, I do it. . . .

This is how Jesus walks with me. As my Guide, my Provider, my Protector. I find that when He provides me with anything, He's also providing for other people. I think that our people can see Jesus in this way. They're very conscious of the guiding element of Jesus in their history and in their present life.

THE CATHOLIC WAY OF LIFE

For a long time I thought I was a Catholic Indian, but I'm beginning to see myself more as an Indian Catholic. I was baptized in the Catholic Church. I made my first confession and first communion and was confirmed.

My family really didn't go to Church that often. My father was too busy making a living for all of us. Church going wasn't that important. Our prayer life was. My mother taught us to pray. A Spanish priest used to come and teach us catechism. I was ten years old before I made my first communion because of the language problem. I'm glad I waited though, until I was ten. I will never forget when I made my first confession, Father asked me, "Who taught you how to go to confession so well?" I said, "My mother." It wasn't any of the catechisms, it was my mother.

It never bothered me to be Catholic and Indian. I guess I never gave it much thought until I was thirteen years old. I asked my father if I could go through the puberty rite. My father said, "You're a Catholic. If you go through the puberty rite, that's not just a social activity. You have to believe what they tell you in the Indian way. You have to take it seriously." So I thought that I'd better think about this. Going on to school in St. Louis and becoming a Sister just took this opportunity away from me.

In my years in Catholic school, the sacramental life of the Catholic Church became very important to me. The Eucharist, the confession. This is what I want to share with my people at home. The Father image is very strong. We understand that. We need much healing. We need nourishment. We will find it in the Church. In the encounter with Jesus, the Healer, the Nourisher, the Protector, the Conqueror of Evil. The Church demands to give all. If you really love God and Jesus you have to respond in service. When I make that response, when any of us Indians make that response, we make it with all our Indianness. This is the only way we know how to express ourselves. In our Indianness, our language, our prayer form, and our art.

That is why now, through this process, I'm beginning to see that I am an Indian Catholic. I want to tell my people. "You can be Indian and you can be Catholic. They are both the same." Except, that in the Catholic Church, we are members, not just of the tribe, but of the world-wide family. We meet the same Jesus. We are healed in the same way. We are nourished in the same way as everybody else. If we can see ourselves in that way, we can see that we are made equal. We are all brothers and sisters with all other nations. That is what it means for me to be an Indian Catholic.

18

KAROL PARKER

RETURNING

Karol Parker (Mandan-Hidatsa) is a clinical social worker with the Community University Health Care Center at the University of Minnesota. Convinced that mental health problems among native people are the product of a broad pattern of economic inequity and government policy, she is involved in a variety of social justice issues and was a co-founder of the American Indian Community Mental Health Association in Minneapolis. Parker is also an active member of the Council for American Indian Ministry in the United Church of Christ (UCC). She originally presented this essay at the Second Biennial Assembly for UCC Women and subsequently published it in the UCC magazine *Common Lot*. Unlike Little, Parker's early experiences in Catholic schools drove her away from the church, and she found a new sense of purpose and identity in the political movements of the sixties and seventies. Family considerations eventually led her back to an organized religious community, where she found a comfortable combination of support and activism.

I am a member of the Three Affiliated Tribes of western North Dakota. The Mandan, Hidatsa, Arikara were regarded as "peaceful" and, since they had lived in close proximity for many years, they made treaties with the U.S. government for lands along the Missouri River which the Mandan and Hidatsa had occupied for hundreds of years. Our people, like many tribes, had farmed the rich river bottomlands and made a pretty good living at it. This process must have felt irrelevant and unnecessary since our people already knew who "owned" the land. Once the U.S. government had "established" a reserved spot where our people were to remain, the needs of the white "settlers" seemed to be satisfied because, by and large, our tribes were left alone without any serious disruptions until the late 1940s and early 50s. During this period, the Army Corps of Engineers began a project which culminated in the building of a series of earthen dams all down the Missouri River. A quick scan of the river shows that these dams were strategically placed below Indian reservations. Our people were the most seriously impacted.

When our people were forced to move from the river bottomlands up to the top prairie lands, I was about three years old. Even at such a young age, I was aware of the great pain and sadness this caused. Some of the older people had to be physically removed from the area which was to be flooded. Families who had lived as close friends and neighbors in the old community of Elbowoods were moved to new communities which were geographically and psychologically miles apart. Vital community institutions in Elbowoods were slow to be rebuilt, or in some cases never replaced, in the new communities. I grew up in the midst of this disruption and, for my generation, it became the norm. We had no realistic idea of the supreme sacrifice our families had been forced to make. The enormity of the disruption is still being felt today; our people still mourn the loss of lands which had been home to our ancestors for hundreds of years.

But this loss of land was merely one way we were impacted. Religious missionaries of various denominations had staked out their claims to our reservation and went about the business of converting souls. Thus, for the most part, we are either Catholic or Congregational. More recently, the Mormons and Fundamentalists have moved in.

My maternal grandmother was converted into Catholicism. As a matter of fact, she very nearly entered the sisterhood as a young girl. Apparently, this step into the inner sanctum of Catholicism was not completely acceptable to her parents, as they intervened and took her out of the nunnery. My mother's experience was a mixture of respect for the religious training with a strong distaste for the treatment received at the hands of the nuns. Most employed corporal punishment and forbade the speaking of Hidatsa. Despite this, my mother still raised her family Catholic.

Growing up Catholic on the reservation was quite an experience for my older sister and me. Each summer, we spent perhaps two weeks (which seemed like eons) at catechism. We attended mass at least twice a day, learned the Ten Commandments, the Seven Sacraments and stared fearfully at the larger poster size pictures of hell and purgatory. We learned about many things which seemed to be steeped in ritual, mystery, and fear. There was no acknowledgement of our culture in any form in the Catholic mass. But in those days, that was the least of my concerns; most "white" institutions were totally oblivious to any culture other than the Euro-American. Thus, my early religious experiences were not happy.

I gradually moved away from the church over the years, until, in high school and college, I did not attend church at all. My attention was directed to more relevant causes, such as joining the Poor People's Campaign after Dr. Martin Luther King's death, the anti-war movement in college, and then experiencing a heightening of consciousness regarding Native Americans. This became my one and only interest. From this perspective, Christianity became a vehicle of oppression and an extension of colonialism.

I met my husband in college and learned long afterward that he was also an "ex-Catholic." We implicitly agreed to stay away from the church. It, undeniably, offered us nothing. Later, as our daughters were born, we did make a feeble attempt to return. That is, we had our two oldest daughters baptized. But I still felt no connection. One day, my oldest daughter was hospitalized and lay in bed staring around the room. She asked, "Mom, who's that little man hanging on the wall and what is he on and what is that stuff on his head?" I looked at the crucifix and realized that my husband and I needed to talk about our decision.

We acknowledged that this society's culture encompassed too much of Christianity to avoid it totally. We decided to proceed cautiously by providing exposure to a Christian church for our daughters. We began by attending various churches in the small reservation town. As we "sampled" the various denominations, we realized we felt most comfortable with the United Church of Christ's philosophy and its commitment to social justice issues. For me, an immediate connection was made when the pastors (our church has a husband and wife co-pastor team) were lifting up some of my people's beliefs and culture. (In fact, one of them had taken a Hidatsa language class). Equally important was how our family was welcomed into the small congregation and our children were encouraged to develop their talents and strengths. For instance, one daughter had begun reading at a rather young age and she was approached by the pastors to read a passage one Sunday. This was her first experience in "public speaking." We nervously watched and listened as she stood, a tiny four or five year old, at the front of the church, loudly reading her passage. Such encouragement in the church just was not present in my childhood experience. It was wonderful!

My spiritual journey has been a combination of both negative and positive experiences. I chose not to remain in the church I had grown up in, then wandered away from Christian beliefs—I thought, permanently. But our family returned, by choice, once we discovered that religion can be nourishing, encouraging, and uplifting. This is how we came to join the United Church of Christ.

19

CLEM BEAR CHIEF

PLUCKED FROM THE ASHES

Clement Bear Chief (Siksika) is director of welfare for the Siksika Nation in Gleichen, Alberta. He is active in the Strathmore ward of the Mormon Church and serves as a group leader for the high priesthood, an organization of older men in the local community. Bear Chief's account of his religious experiences was written for the Mormon journal *Dialogue* as a personal testimony for the benefit of other Mormons, not as a tool for conversion or object of theological debate. He was raised in the Anglican church and learned traditional ceremonies from his grandparents, and later prepared to become a priest by studying religion in college. In this essay, Bear Chief describes his childhood fear of Mormon missionaries, his struggle with alcoholism, and his subsequent involvement in the Mormon Church. Dreams and visions have played a prominent role in Bear Chief's spiritual life, and have led him to find a sense of meaning, purpose, and identity in the Church of Jesus Christ of Latter Day Saints.

While growing up on the Blackfoot Reservation near Gleichen, Alberta, Canada, I lived with my grandparents. On Sundays around noon, two well-dressed white men would drive up to our home. For some unknown reason, I always ran for the nearby forest and hid until they drove away. I learned from friends, neighbors, and our church ministers that these well-dressed men were Mormon missionaries, and not welcome. From then on, and although they had done nothing to me, I had a great hatred for these outsiders and their church.

After getting married and entering the white man's world to earn a living, my wife, Theresa, and I had occasional visits from the Mormons. They had good visits with my family when I wasn't home, but when I was, I either frustrated them out of our house or simply told them to leave. It seemed that this happened about once a year. One time some of our good friends met with the missionaries. I was furious. I told my friends everything I could think of to turn them against the Mormons, and it worked—they told the missionaries not to come back.

Like many of my friends, I became addicted to alcohol; the quality of my life began to drastically decline. By 1975, my marriage was barely holding together; our quarrels were frequent, and Theresa often felt the brunt of my unhappiness. In the late spring of that year, we had a bitter spat during which I chased her and the children out of our house. They went to live with Theresa's parents on the Blood Reservation. I was alone with the house and little else.

Since my family was no longer with me, and since I still had money, I decided to go downtown and drink myself to death. For many days I was never sober and often awoke to find myself in some back alley. I finally sobered up and went home. It was then that I realized just how empty and alone I truly was. I felt so helpless. Who could I turn to? In my despair, I again headed downtown to drink. During this binge something very odd happened to me, something which, to this day, still causes me to wonder.

Although I had no money, I managed to find friends who bought me enough drinks to start me on my self-destructive path once again. When the alcohol didn't kill me, I went back to the bar and deliberately provoked a fight with some strangers. One of them threatened to cut me up with the knife he held under his table. I thought I had wanted to die, but, when faced with the reality, I backed down and apologized to the strangers. Things seemed okay again, but I sensed they were still angry. I excused myself to go the bathroom but instead, I went out the rear entrance. To my horror, I now stood face-to-face with the very men with whom I was at odds inside the bar. The one with the knife came towards me and swore that he would teach me not to pick a fight with them. Just then, two men emerged from the shadows. I could not see their faces, but they seemed to be wearing either overcoats or some kind of long robes. When my assailants saw these men, they ran away as if they were frightened. Immediately I approached the two men to thank them for their help, but as I moved closer they too disappeared into the shadows. I tried to follow them but walked straight into a solid wall—there was no door. Now scared and quite sober, I was able to catch the bus home. Throughout the night, I wondered if what I had experienced was real or just a hallucination. And although I was terribly hung over, the next morning I went to town to survey the spot where the previous night's incident had occurred. It was just as I suspected. There were no doors within a block of the door leading into the bar. This caused me to more deeply question the reality of the two men, and what the experience meant. Again, I had no answers.

After a time, I began to suffer the withdrawal symptoms of an alcoholic. I suffered alone with no one to comfort me. I called our local parish priest, but he told me that I must work out my marriage and drinking problems by myself. I called the pastors of other churches that in the past had shown an interest in my family. They offered no solutions, only excuses. They claimed to be either too busy or simply untrained in marriage and alcohol counseling. In desperation, I took out my Catholic missal of prayers and rosary and knelt before a crucifix and a picture of Mary, the mother of God. I recited a number of "Hail Marys," "Our Fathers," "Acts of Contrition," and whatever else I came to in the missal. Over and over again, hour after hour, I prayed from the prayer book, still utterly alone in my empty house. In spite of my pleadings, I felt no sense of relief. I decided that God must be very angry with me and was simply not listening. He must have given me up to Hell to suffer out my last days. I thought of suicide again. My family was gone, I had no friends, and even the priests and pastors, men who were supposed to be my spiritual guides, had offered me no word of comfort.

Although I managed to get some sleep, my rest was interrupted by terrible nightmares which kept waking me up. During the times I was awake, I knelt before the crucifix, crying and pleading for comfort. As I lay exhausted on the couch, my thoughts went back to my boyhood and to my grandmother. I remembered the times when I would listen to her talking to an unseen being whom she always addressed as "Nin'non." My people use this term, meaning "dad" or "daddy," whenever they approach a loving father for some favor or request. As a last resort, I resolved to call on this being from the unseen world. I sat up and addressed "Nin'non" in much the same way as grandmother would: Daddy, Daddy, look down on me with compassion. Look upon me with pity. I am so lonely, I am so sad, I am so sick. If you are real and do exist, please hear me. I have been very bad. I have driven my family out. I have no more family to comfort me. Daddy, Daddy, I want to change. I want my family back with me. If you are real, if you are here, please hear me. If you bring my family to me, I will try my best to be a good father and a good person. Please do this for me if you are real and can hear me. Please send us one of your churches so we can join it without question this time. For the first time that night, I felt comforted and somehow peaceful.

I made a similar plea the next day. However, when the third day came and my family had not returned, I began to doubt. On that same day, the phone rang and I was very relieved to hear my wife's voice. Though I had called before to plead for her return, this time she said that she could no longer live on the reservation because of the overcrowded house, lack of privacy, and the pervasive alcohol. She would rather put up with me than remain where she was. As a condition for her return, she made me promise that I would not repeat the circumstances which led to the split. I agreed.

That same evening, my family came home. As we sat up talking, Theresa and I agreed that we needed God in our marriage and in our personal lives. We wanted to join a church which would truly help us better ourselves. We also agreed that since the Four-Square Gospel Church, the Jehovah's Witnesses, the United Church, the Bahai's, and the Pentecostal churches had all shown great interest in us, we should probably join with one of them, one had to be right for us. We resolved to join, without hesitation, the first church that sent representatives to our door.

Days passed and no one came. I was about to call (without Theresa's knowledge) the Jehovah's Witnesses since they had been quite nice to me on their previous visits. For some reason, though, I never made the call, and that omission would greatly affect our lives. However, that same evening we heard a knock on the door. I was excited because I thought perhaps the Jehovah's Witnesses had decided to visit us. I asked my wife to answer the door. She returned and hesitantly told me that a man and his wife were asking to come in to talk to us. She said that they were Mormon missionaries.

My heart sank to the bottom of my soul, and anger welled up inside me. I thought to myself, "Oh, *Nin'non* how could you have sent the very people I hate so much?" I rationalized that I could still chase them away since they were not considered Christians and did not count. I then remembered what I had said in my prayer and told my wife to invite them in. I would listen to what they had to say, but I decided to give them as hard a time as I possibly could.

As the weeks went by and they continued to visit, I unloaded all my prejudices on them, but it didn't seem to bother them. They kept on with their lessons and patiently answered all my questions. I asked them all the questions that had stumped representatives of the other churches. These Mormons seemed to have the answers for what the other churches called "holy mysteries," questions pertaining to the unseen world, this world, and the world above. They took us to their Sunday services and to other meetings which were uplifting and inspiring. The other members were so friendly and helpful. Suddenly I began to love the very people I had hated so much. I was sometimes almost afraid to attend because I would be hugged, even by the men. They were ordinary people like us and faced the same difficulties, temptations, and problems that we did. I was also filled with remorse. I wanted to meet all the missionaries who had ever knocked at our door and apologize for the rudeness I had shown them. My chance was lost, though; they had already come and gone. The only thing I could do was express my thankfulness to these new missionaries, Elder and Sister Andrus, for coming to us.

In August 1975, the Andruses asked us to be baptized, and by then I was convinced that this was the church for us. However, the night before our baptism, something happened that almost shook me to a point of backing out. Theresa and I had stayed up late wondering about our decision when we heard noises we had never heard before. There were footsteps, creaks and groans, and we felt a presence in the room which we had also never felt before, an unwelcome one. We saw with our own eyes a box move by itself along the hallway and into the kitchen. We saw a knife leave the fireplace mantle and embed its blade in the wooden floor. It seemed that something evil wanted to stop us from joining the Mormons. We were shaken but went ahead with our baptisms on 16 August 1975.

Around September we went to a stake conference. At the time I had no idea what that was, and so I agreed to tell the conference about my conversion. When we arrived, I became frightened. I had never seen so many people. I thought this was something more than I could handle and wanted to back out. However, the missionaries assured me that it would turn out for the good. By the time my turn came, I had this warm pleasant feeling like I was half in the air. While I was talking, I saw myself, whether imagined or not, standing across a river from Satan himself. He stood before what appeared to be an army that was ready to attack. He pointed the tip of his sword at me and shouted a warning that he would try to kill me. For some reason I felt uncomfortable, rather than afraid of his warning. I did not respond, and the scene disappeared. I do not remember much of what I said to the congregation, but as I left the podium I noticed a lot of people with tears in their eyes. I felt extremely ashamed and went back to the safety of the missionaries. I whispered to Brother Andrus that I wanted to leave because I must have said something bad to make these people cry. He tightened his grip around me and whispered back in a reassuring way that I had not said anything out of place. Although this gave me some comfort, what happened in the following months made it seem as if Satan's warning had come to pass.

On 4 October of the same year at 2:30 A.M., we received a telephone call that my wife's father was critically ill and was near death. We gathered ourselves together, knelt, and prayed that he would stay alive at least until we got there. We rushed to his bedside, but he had already passed away. I was very disappointed. I asked the missionaries why he had died after we joined the Church. Why didn't he die before we joined it? Why now? Then a warning from the past came back to haunt me, a warning that our priest had given us years ago. God would punish us, he said, if we ever left the Catholic church. Had God cursed us for joining the Mormon church? The missionaries explained to us that this was a trial of our faith, and I was pacified. Two weeks later, we received another phone call in the morning telling us that my wife's auntie's daughter had been shot to death. I thought about the warning again. I told my wife that for sure God had cursed us and the curse was now spreading to her relatives and maybe will spread to mine until we renounce our membership in this church. Again the missionaries managed to help me understand.

However, things did not improve. On 7 November 1975, we received another urgent call from my wife's family that her mother was very ill and close to death. Once again we prayed for her recovery or for her to stay alive till we got there. By the time we arrived at the hospital, she had died. This really shook me. I told the missionaries that I now knew that this church was not right and that we must go back to the Catholic church because God was punishing us for leaving. I told them I wasn't going to church anymore and wanted out. With great patience, the missionaries talked to me, explaining and comforting us. Their understanding and love calmed and strengthened us. These missionaries, Doug and Vea Andrus of Idaho Falls, Idaho, stood with and by us throughout all these difficulties and doubting periods, reassuring us that all this should pass and that the Lord would bless us yet.

As the times of trial passed and the year progressed, I came to see that this was true. Before joining the Church, I had accumulated a sizable debt, due primarily to my alcohol problem. The Christmas season was approaching, and I found that I was quite a bit behind on some of my payments, especially my rent. My landlord and the other creditors were constantly hounding me for payment, causing me great pain and worry. In desperation, I confided in the missionaries, hoping that they could help me. Elder Andrus suggested that I should go and ask our bishop for advice.

I went for an interview with the bishop, a man who had been very friendly to us since our baptism. I sat across from him and related my problems. He listened without showing much emotion. He looked at me with compassionate eyes and then asked, "Brother Bear Chief, have you paid your tithing since you were baptized?" I thought to myself, "Oh, oh. They got my soul. Now they want my money, too." I asked him if he heard me correctly the first time. I could not possibly pay tithing. All my money went to debts and rent and food. He seemed to ignore my problem and again asked me if I was paying my tithing. I thought again to myself, "I came to you for some help and all you can ask is if I pay tithing." I became angry and was about to walk out when he stopped and explained tithing to me. He asked me to set aside ten percent of my paycheck each payday to hand in as tithing and see what happened. I reluctantly agreed to try to do as he suggested.

It was getting close to Christmas, and my landlord and creditors increased their pressure on me. However, I was determined to find out what would happen if I paid my tithing. I admit that I did so more out of curiosity than from any great faith. A week before Christmas, nothing had happened. I was about to complain again when one evening the doorbell rang and the children ran to answer. There was no one at the door, but someone had left two bags of groceries. The next evening the same thing occurred. This time, however, I found an envelope in the mailbox containing a check that was large enough to cover all my bills and the rent.

The next day more groceries arrived at our doorstep. At work, I was approached by a co-worker who was a United Church lady. She asked if we could use some groceries for Christmas because they had some left over from their annual giveaways. That evening the United Church members arrived in a pickup whose bed was loaded with groceries of all kinds. We ended up with so many groceries that we did not have the room to store them. We had to leave some in the hallways and in the living room. I was able to provide presents for my children in addition to those that were mysteriously left at our door. For days, my eyes watered my desk at work. My co-workers wondered if they could help me with whatever was bothering me. All I could say to them was, "No thank you." The Lord and his people were truly good to us, and I have grown to love them and have come to know the kind of people they are. All the bad things I heard about Mormons were dashed to pieces.

At this point it seemed that God had blessed us with more than we deserved. However, he was not yet finished with us. About this time, I began to have experiences which prepared me for even greater blessings. Not long after the holidays. I had a strange dream. I was in an open field lit only, it seemed, by moonlight. A man in white clothing stood beside me and asked me to go with him. I followed until we came to a hole in the ground large enough to walk in. I saw that there were stairs leading down into the ground. We went down the steps to the bottom where we entered a long, dark hallway. I immediately noticed a lot of commotion which seemed to be coming from the walls themselves. Above the sound of all the other voices, I heard people calling my name, I tried to answer, but they could not hear me. I recognized some of the voices as those of friends and relatives who had passed on long ago. For a moment, it seemed that the walls were transparent and that I could almost make out who these people were. Finally we came to a small, dimly lit room where I had to squint in order to see. I recognized friends who had recently died. Though I waved to them, they made no move to indicate they knew me.

We then came to a huge, open room which resembled a church cultural hall. Many people were sitting around the room holding their personal belongings. Occasionally a voice called out a name over what sounded like a loudspeaker. When this happened, one of the people would get up and ascend some stairs leading to an upper room. As they opened the door, a very bright light poured out, a light so bright that it almost blinded me. I turned and asked my guide what was happening. He explained that all these people were waiting for people on the other side of the room to be baptized on their behalf so that they could enter that brightly lit room. As I had not been to the temple nor been instructed about it, this seemed quite strange.

I was curious and asked if I could go up to that room and just look in. He told me that I could not go in since I was not dead. He then motioned that it was time for me to go back.

As I passed back through the rooms and the hallway, I again heard the people calling my name and again I tried to answer them, all to no avail. They knocked on the wall as they called my name. I'm not sure why, but I avoided them. For no apparent reason, I became very sad and started to cry. My companion and I climbed the stairs to the open field where once again I found myself alone. I felt afraid and very sad, and I wept for those people down there. It was then that I awoke from this dream to find that both my pillow and my eyes were wet with tears. As I mentioned I had no idea what the dream meant because I knew nothing about temple work. Much later, my wife and I did some temple work for our parents, grandparents, and others. We were seated on some benches around the temple baptismal font when I suddenly had the strange feeling that I had been there before. My mind wandered back to the dream, and as I looked around me, it appeared that this must be the same place. This time there were no people waiting, but I noticed the stairs leading up to a door which led to the main part of the temple. I could not help but feel that I was doing the work that those on the other side desired of me. I dare not say that this was the same room, but I knew that those who had been calling my name could now hear me answer through the work I was doing for them. God had allowed me to see what must be done, and granted me the opportunity to do so.

On 25 August 1976, my children, wife and I were sealed in the Salt Lake Temple. Brother and Sister Andrus, who by this time were like grandparents to us, accompanied us. I remember that before I had ever heard of temples, I had been a picture of the one in Salt Lake City. Even then I revered it above all other churches. So when the time came for my family to be sealed, it seemed the natural place.

After our sealings, we were treated to a wonderful surprise. Brother Andrus invited us to tour Temple Square, then told us that we were going to meet a very special person. We went to the Church Office Building, and Brother Andrus told us we were going to meet the Prophet of the Church. In the elevator I centered my thoughts on this man called "Prophet." I thought to myself, "I'll bet we will be seated in a huge room with gold-covered things all around. Huge doors will suddenly open and in will come this man clad in fine golden clothing. He will be seated on a throne borne by six servants. Perhaps we will then have to bow to him and possibly kiss his huge, diamond-studded ring of authority. He will greet us and then be carried back into his comfortable quarters."

We left the elevator and met Brother Boyd Packer, who greeted us with great respect and ushered us into a small office decorated simply with souvenirs from other lands. As I entered the office, I passed a humble looking old man dressed in an ordinary suit. I paid little attention to him, thinking that he might be one of the servants, perhaps the doorman. Brother Packer brought the old man forward and introduced him as the prophet of the Church, Spencer W. Kimball. My immediate thought was. This humble, ordinary looking man is the prophet? You've got to be kidding. Where is his scepter? His cloak of authority?

He hugged each of us and shook our hands. He had us sit down, asked me to push my chair a little closer to him, and looked me directly in the eyes. Then he said something to us that I had never heard from any leader of any church or organization. He said, "Brother Bear Chief, I want you to know that I love the Indian people." This one sentence gave me more spiritual peace than any other words of comfort that I had ever been offered. Even though a man had spoken them, the words seemed to come from a higher source. In those few moments, I recalled the many times that my family had been driven from place to place, searching for good neighbors with whom we could live and work. How I had hated those who shunned us. How I had wished bad things upon them. President Kimball's words touched me so deeply that I melted inside. I felt as if I had found a long-lost father who had greeted me with open arms and would remain with me forever. I knew then that he had to be a prophet of God.

God, through his missionaries, plucked us from the ashes of a miserable existence and led us to one of joy, peace, and happiness. Although we still suffer many afflictions as a result of the environment in which we live, we praise our God for finding us and bringing us to the new life we now enjoy. Had we not passed through these many experiences, good and bad, our testimonies would have crumpled and we would have fallen away long ago. God has taken away all the hatred I had towards this church. I have come to believe that those who hate the Church do so because they still do not understand its teachings. We do not profess to fully understand it either. But we do know this: the Lord has shown us through his church and its people the real meaning of Christian love. He has caused us to feel that we are in the arms of loving parents.

The Church has not made us rich financially. Nor has it caused us to have stiff necks toward others. It has, however, given us a fuller understanding of life, a more comprehensive view of why God bothered to create us and put us on this earth and what his total plan is for all of his children. It gives us a sense of where we really came from, what is the point of our existence here, and what happens after we leave this earth. We have learned to view life in terms of an eternal existence. Most important, the gospel gives us identity. It answers for us the slippery questions that still perplex so many of my people: What am I? An Indian? An Aborigine? An indigenous person? A grassroots person? First nation? The Church, through its prophets and scriptures, answers these questions. Because of them, and as a result of my many personal experiences, I cannot and do not doubt.

TWEEDY SOMBRERO

TWO PATHS

■

Tweedy Sombrero (Navajo) is pastor of the Garfield Indian United Methodist Church in Phoenix, Arizona. A graduate of Haskell Indian Nations University and Ottawa University, she earned her Master of Divinity degree at Iliff School of Theology, where she studied with George Tinker. She has held a number of pastoral and counseling positions and serves on numerous committees of the United Methodist Church at the local, regional, and national levels. Sombrero presented this essay at a consultation on "Racial Ethnic Women in Ministry" sponsored by the National Council of Churches. Organizers of the consultation wanted to hear about the ordination struggles facing racial/ethnic minorities, so Sombrero decided to talk about her decision to become a minister, since many of her own people were questioning this choice. She describes the important guidance she received from her grandfather, a Navajo medicine man, in discerning her own spiritual path.

"There are two paths that you can follow. You need to choose one!"
When I was a little girl, I would always hear my Nahlee Man say these
words. Who is Nahlee Man you ask? Nahlee Man is my grandfather, my
father's father; Nahlee is the respectful name for such a person. Nahlee Man
is my teacher, my minister, my counselor, my doctor and my friend. To others he is just the medicine man who lives at the top of the hill.

At the age of five, I can remember my Nahlee and my father getting us up
at five in the morning to run. This ritual had no real meaning but without fail
we did it faithfully. Finally at the age where we could understand what we
were doing, my Dad took us aside and said, "the Creator comes everyday and
we must show that we are not lazy." So in the morning when we run, we run
to the Creator with thankful hearts that all is well and even when all isn't well,
we thank the Creator for giving us another day and a new beginning. For we
run to the East which means a new beginning, a new day. And one great day
the Great One will come from the East on the path of the rainbow to gather all
the children! Be ready and prepared! My Dad is going to be seventy years old
on Friday the 14th of this month [September 1984], and he still runs East to
the top of the hill to Pray, Praise and give Thanksgiving.

All through my childhood, my Nahlee and my parents taught me about
our culture and heritage. In 1972, I entered college and I remember my Nahlee
teasing me, "Oh, so you're going to go to a white man's school. Are you going
to learn how to be a white?" In college, I learned that there were other denominations besides the Mormons, the Presbyterians and the Christian Reformed.
I happened to come upon a United Methodist Minister and he shared with
me the beliefs of the United Methodist Church, for I had never heard of
the Methodists before. It was interesting and I was curious, so I started to
attend his church. I liked what I saw and I liked what I heard so I became a
United Methodist.

Little did I know what I was getting myself into, but God knew! Upon
returning to the reservation after graduation, my Nahlee sat quietly and listened to my adventures of college. When I was finished, he stood up and
said, "It is time to teach you about the Creator, for now is the time to choose
your path." The First lesson is to wonder about the Sacred path of the
Creator. Nahlee took me to the canyon and for hours we sat and talked
about the rocks, the trees, the insects, the sky, the clouds and everything else
around us. For everything I see is a part of me. Always wonder everyday
about the Creator. Second Lesson, Pray every minute, every second and
everyday of your life. Be thankful for everything that happens. For everyday
the Creator is with you. Third lesson, give of yourself for it is a way to show
the Creator that you are using the gifts and talents that is bestowed upon
you. For everyday the Creator gives us something.

On the fourth day, Nahlee and I sat at the top of Navajo Mountain and
looked out into the valley. "The paths lay before you and there will always

be two paths for you." As I sat silently beside Nahlee, my thoughts quickly ran through my life so far. I could see that my life was rough, but then whose isn't? I could see the tribulations I've been through since I started my quest for wholeness. First I saw a marriage that started out good but ended in divorce. During one part of the marriage, I watched as strangers walked away with my baby; for a doctor had accused us of child abuse. For five whole months we battled in court to get our baby back. Little did we know about the court putting our baby up for adoption. How could this happen? My husband had dropped Rolena giving her a spiral fracture on her right leg. Many people of the United Methodist Church and of the American Indian Movement came to fight for us and in February of 1977, we had our daughter back home. I also saw myself standing close by as I watched my twin sister suffer a severe asthma attack that almost killed her. As these things crossed my mind, Nahlee put his hands on my arm and said, "It is time." I took a deep breath and said, "Nahlee, I would like to be a minister." He laughed and clapped his hands, then he said, "There are two paths from which to choose; one of them is a nice smooth and clear path. The other one is a rough, rocky path and there is an obstacle all along the way. The path you have chosen is the second one, but my dear child you will make it, if you keep those three lessons in your mind and in your heart."

In the month of September 1980, my Nahlee passed away at the age of 110. . . .

> There's a certain love I have for a very special Indian person—my Nahlee Man. I talked with him, laughed with him, wept with him, but there was one beautiful thing I admired and will never forget which only he possessed, and that was his mind. I loved him for what he was. He taught me the great undying pride of our heritage. We'd spend hours in the warm days talking of everything under the sun, while I listened carefully to what he had to say. He had a full rich voice which I still dream of . . . then we'd laugh together of little things that we'd found humorous. If I had my way, I would have spent the rest of my hours with him and learning of things. But, I had to leave one Spring afternoon as the flowers were blooming. I was young then but learning from him made me feel older and wiser, sometimes I dream about him, and when times are bad, he seems to smile and say, "Yes. . . . I know it's bad, little one, but dry your eyes and try again."

In the past three or four years, my path has been rough, I've dealt with racism, in some of the worse shapes and forms. I've dealt with sexism. I feel sad because the racism came from seminary students. The sexism has not been as great as the racism but it is there. I've dealt with people of my tribe as they do not understand why I entered seminary at all, and I've dealt with evangelists coming onto the reservation telling the Navajos that they are devil worshippers and then some of those Navajos turn to me and accuse me of the same act. I remember after such an incident, I went crying to Nahlee and as I sat there crying, he sang the Blessing song for me. Then he said, "there will always be two paths for you, for you see, you can change your path but what will you have accomplished?"

So why do I put up with such tribulation and why do I continue this path? For the simple reason that I do believe in a living God! For you see, people do not fail, they give up trying. God will not look me over for medals, degrees or diplomas, but for scars. Trouble and perplexity drive me to prayer, and prayer drives away perplexity and trouble, for in the midst of the my struggles is my spirituality. Christianity has not been tried and found wanting, it has been found difficult and not tried. Besides, trouble are often the tools by which God fashions us for better things. In great attempts it is glorious even to fail. That which is painful to the body may be profitable to the soul.

So why do I not take the first path? Because my path had been chosen for me long before I chose it. And because Jesus said, "Pick up your cross and follow me." I know now, why my Nahlee laughed and clapped his hands. When I look back on my path, I thank God for every bit of tribulation. And if I could, I would live my life over and not change a thing.

Without God, I am nothing and I would be no where, but with God, I have everything and I am everything which makes me a whole person. . . .

Laverne Jacobs

The Native Church
A Search for an Authentic Spirituality

■

Laverne Jacobs (Ojibway) is the national coordinator for native ministries for the
Anglican Church of Canada. An ordained priest originally from Walpole Island First
Nation in Ontario, he has served in several Ontario parishes and is involved in
many other denominational and ecumenical activities at the national and
international levels. His work is guided by a desire to promote healing and self-
determination in native communities and to address the basic crisis of identity
facing many native people. Jacobs wrote this essay in response to an invitation
from *Ecumenism* magazine to contribute an article on native traditions; he felt
qualified only to write about his own experiences, an attitude that many native
people share. Jacobs recounts a complex process of overcoming confusion,
suspicion, and fear as an Anglican priest contending with the native traditionalist
revival. His spiritual journey eventually led him to a new appreciation for the pipe
and the sweat lodge, and for the incomparable beauty of human religious diversity.

One memorable Saturday morning in May of 1959 I "committed my life to Jesus Christ." Thus began a very convoluted spiritual journey. This commitment was preceded by a searching question posed several weeks earlier by my pastor. His question as I lay on a hospital bed was, "Laverne, are you saved?" I knew he was asking about my relationship with God. I also knew I was not satisfied with that relationship. Several weeks later on the side of a road I prayed the "sinner's prayer," guided by my pastor, and began a new relationship with God.

CHRISTIAN ROOTS

The stability and identity I needed as a Native youth growing up in the late fifties and early sixties was provided by that experience. The social and economic conditions of my reserve community caused me tremendous shame. I struggled with all the stereotypes of the lazy, drunken, irresponsible Indian. As a new Christian, I gained a status which I did not enjoy as a Native person. I became a "child of God," an "heir of God and joint heir with Christ," and a "fellow citizen with the saints and members of the household of God" [Romans 8:16, 17; Ephesians 2:19]. Following high school and two years in the work world I entered an Anglican theological college.

I grew to appreciate the devotional life of the Church during my seminary years. I learned about the church fathers, the history, and traditions of the Church. I read the writings of Tillich, Kierkegaard and others. I learned the songs of the Church and embraced its rituals. I studied Greek. This was my formation for the priesthood. I accepted this process willingly and acknowledged western thought and theology as normative and absolute in my preparation for life as a priest and as a Native Christian. These were happy years. The Christian traditions which I had embraced brought meaning and purpose to my life.

RESURGENCE OF TRADITIONAL NATIVE SPIRITUALITY

I was convinced that Native traditions and spirituality were inherently evil and pagan. Such traditions were contradictory to the Christian faith. I was warned about the dangers of syncretism and told I must not compromise my faith as a Christian. Deeply concerned about the centrality of Christ, I resolved that I would not bring dishonour to Christ by seeking after other gods.

In 1975 I returned to my home community to pastor both the Anglican and United congregations. During this period I and members of the faith community struggled with the resurgence of traditional Native Spirituality. Younger members of the reserve in their search for identity were exploring their Native heritage. These young people travelled to powwows throughout North America. They brought back ways and cultural traditions foreign to our community.

YEARS OF STRUGGLE

The years that followed were difficult years marked by religious zeal and conflict. "Born again" members of my parish burned their Native symbols and quit making Native crafts. Christian members of the community boycotted powwows. Followers of the Traditional Ways lobbied to have Native Spirituality taught in the school. Anxious church members launched a counter campaign. Confusion and conflict struck to the core of people's beings. A funeral exacerbated the turmoil. Once a faithful church member, the deceased person left the Church and embraced the Traditional Ways. At death the body was prepared in the Traditional Way with painted face and the use of traditional symbols and rituals. Community members were torn between their desire to support the bereaved family and their fear of Native Spirituality. As the parish priest, I did not know what an appropriate pastoral response should be. I was just as confused and fearful as everyone else.

THE JOURNEY

These years of turmoil and religious conflict were the beginning of a long and painful journey. Early on I attended a conference, enrolling in a workshop by Father John Hascall, a Native Roman Catholic priest. Father Hascall was a Pipe Carrier and spiritual leader in the Midewiwin Lodge. I was deeply disturbed and troubled by his address. In sharing his spiritual journey he seemingly equated Native Spirituality with Christianity. His whole story evoked my worst fears of syncretism.

Within that same period I attended a United Church conference for Native peoples. Two Traditional Elders led sessions on Native Spirituality. The Elders talked about the Pipe and Sweetgrass ceremonies. Provision was made for people to participate in a Sweat Lodge. People chose either to participate in or to observe the Sweetgrass Ceremony. Those actively participating in the ceremony formed an inner circle; those choosing to observe formed an outer circle. All were permitted to talk about the choices they had made. I remained in the outer circle anxiously observing the ceremony. I deliberately chose the outer circle because I did not understand the ceremony and was afraid of compromising my Christian beliefs. There was no way I would join the group in a Sweat Lodge! Engaging in a Sweat was just asking too much of me. I was fearful of aligning myself with the Evil One.

I put these experiences aside determined to devote my energies more fully to the Christian faith. As a part of this new commitment I went to confession and sought forgiveness for delving into pagan rituals. I resolved to refrain from any involvement with Native Spirituality.

This renunciation of Native Spirituality seemed to provoke more confrontation and struggle. Again I sat in the presence of Father John Hascall, the Medicine Priest. On this occasion, I attended a service of the Native community in my home diocese. This service, held in the cathedral, began with Father Hascall praying with the Pipe in the Four Directions. He began the ceremony with a brief explanation saying that certain people would be invited to share the Pipe with him. His assistant called me to come forward. Time stood still. I struggled with the implications of this request: *Was it right for me, as national staff, to share in this ritual? What would such action say to people? Would I be compromising my Christian beliefs? Would it be right to refuse something which was sacred to others and offered to me as a symbol of honour and trust?*

In my turmoil and anxiety I placed the Pipe to my lips and drew upon the sacred substance not knowing what would follow, but trusting and hoping that somehow God was present in this action and praying that I would be protected from that which I did not know or understand. I returned to my seat and watched as the ceremony continued. I looked at the young men, just barely in their teens, who had been invited to be "helpers" to Father John. They were engrossed in the ceremony and service; their faces reflected a deep sense of pride in their Native heritage. As I pondered the whole experience I had the sensation of One saying *"This is you."*

Years later I attended a World Council of Churches assembly in Korea on *Justice, Peace, and the Integrity of Creation.* I was the only First Nations person from Canada in a gathering of several thousand. The process was so European and overwhelming. I felt alienated and alone. I desperately wanted to be back home. In my loneliness, I was approached by four Native Americans who asked me to join them in prayers. I felt relieved to be with my own people. The next morning we gathered on a mound outside the conference hall. As we stood in a circle, one of the men beat a drum and sang a prayer song. Another man prepared the Sacred Pipe for our prayers. Again, I wondered if I should be there. I was torn between my desperate need for support and my fear of Traditional Ways and the possibility of compromising my Christian principles. As the Pipe was handed to me, I asked for protection and prayed to the God that I knew and to Jesus my Brother. During and following this ceremony I felt a certain peace of mind and heart and was assured that I had not compromised my Christian values. In the remaining days of the conference, the daily prayers with the Pipe—the very thing which I feared—sustained me.

A SACRED TIME

Of all Native ceremonies in my ken, the one I feared most was the Sweat Lodge. It is a ceremony I was determined to avoid. In the summer of 1992

I attended a Native gathering sponsored by the Roman Catholic Church. The program included healing circles and the Sweat Lodge. As I read the program I had the ominous feeling that this time I would not be able to run away and that I would participate in a Sweat which filled me with anxiety and fear. I attended the seminar on the healing circle and the Sweat Lodge. I still did not know what to do. After the seminar, a deacon told me of his first experience of praying in a Sweat Lodge, a dramatic and wonderful experience. His glowing account did not allay my fears. It was only at the last moment, comforted by the knowledge that a close friend would be with me, I decided to join in the Sweat. The presence of my friend and the fact that the Elder leading the ceremony was one I trusted enabled me to go forward. Following the example of other men I took a pinch of tobacco and offered it at the Sacred Fire as I entered the Sweat Lodge, crawling on hands and knees behind other participants. When all had entered, the Elder ordered the flap of the lodge closed and began the ceremony. The intensity of the prayers matched the intensity of the heat from the steaming rocks. After several rounds and hours of prayer the ceremony came to a close. As we emerged from the lodge into the coolness of the night, we sat or lay on the ground knit together by the sacred bond of men who had shared a sacred journey. As I lay gazing up into the starlit sky I felt a tremendous sense of restfulness and peace. It was a truly sacred time. There was nothing that was contradictory to the Christian gospel which I embraced.

BOTH NATIVE AND CHRISTIAN

Through these and many other experiences I gained an openness to faith journeys different from mine. I listened to stories of others whose ways are different, but in whose stories I have found the Christ of the Christian gospel. I learned to put aside my fears and step out in faith; and in that step of faith experienced the vastness of God, the Creator. I hear the sounds of many voices, each with a tenor and beauty of its own, but which together sing the praises of God the Creator and Jesus the Son in one great symphony of creation. In the midst of that glorious sound rings the phrase "*This is you—both Native and Christian.*" The meaning of that phrase will be a lifelong dialogue with self. Each new experience and each year will uncover different aspects of that reality like the many facets of a precious gem. This dialogue is a dialogue shared by many First Nations people and which must continue in the midst of a changing world.

· BIBLIOGRAPHY · ▪ ▪ ▪ ▪ ▪ ▪ ▪ ▪ ▪

This selected bibliography of native Christian narrative discourse includes books and articles by native Christian writers (who may or may not currently identify themselves as Christian) published during the past twenty-five years. It also includes a few anthologies of essays or narratives by native Christian leaders that were collected by non-native editors.

Albrite, Joseph, Sr. "What the Moravian Church Means to Us." In *Harmonious to Dwell: The History of the Alaska Moravian Church 1885–1985*. James W. Henkelman and Kurt H. Vitt (Bethel, AK: The Moravian Seminary and Archives, 1985), x.

Anderson, Arthur. "Transcending Traditional Values." *Practice for Ministry in Canada*, September 1990, 17–18.

Anderson, Howard (ed.). *Black Hills III, The Spiritual Formation of Native American Youth: Drawing Strength from Native American Traditions to Shape the Youth Ministry of the Future* (Minneapolis: Native American Theological Association, [1981?]).

——— (ed.). *Recalling, Reliving, Reviewing: Creation Theologies in the Dakota-Lakota, Judeo-Christian, Ojibwe and Winnebago Traditions* (Minneapolis: Native American Theological Association, 1979).

——— (ed.). *Winter Count: Stories of Native American Stewardship* (New York: Office of Stewardship, Episcopal Church Center, [1990?]).

Anderson, Owanah. *Jamestown Commitment: The Episcopal Church and the American Indian* (Cincinnati: Forward Movement, 1988).

Baines, Raymond. "Aliens in Our Own Land." *Engage/Social Action* 1, no. 1 (January 1973), 29–36.

Baldridge, William. "Christian Community in the Next Millennium." *Baptist Freedom*, Fall 1991.

———. "Christian Indians Come of Age: A Time of Tears, A Time of Joy." In *Prairie Evangelicals and Christian Missions: A Study in Cultural Ecology*. Edited by George J. Jennings (Le Mars, IA: George J. Jennings, 1992).

———. "Faith from the American Indian's Point of View: A Meditation." *Minister: A Journal of the American Baptist Ministers Council Speaking to the Practice of Ministry* 8, no. 2 (Winter 1988).

———. "Reclaiming Our Histories." In *New Visions for the Americas: Religious Engagement and Social Transformation*, 23–32. Edited by David Batstone (Minneapolis: Fortress, 1993).

———. "The Quincentenary: 500 Years and Counting." *Minister: A Journal of the American Baptist Ministers Council Speaking to the Practice of Ministry* 12, no. 1 (Fall 1991), 1–2.

———. "Toward a Native American Theology." *American Baptist Quarterly* 8, no. 4 (December 1989), 227–38.

Bear Chief, Clem. "Plucked from the Ashes." *Dialogue* 25 (Winter 1992), 140–49.

Begaye, Russell. "The Story of Indian Southern Baptists." *Baptist History and Heritage* 18, no. 3 (July 1983), 30–39.

Belvin, Frank. "Ministering with American Indians." In *Missions in the Mosaic*, 12–27. Edited by M. Wendell Belew (Atlanta: Home Mission Board, Southern Baptist Convention, 1974).

Bird, John (ed.). *Recovering the Feather: The First Anglican Native Convocation.* ([Toronto, ON?]: Council for Native Ministries, Anglican Church of Canada, 1989).

Brink, Teddy. "Here We Stand . . . " In *Harmonious to Dwell: The History of the Alaska Moravian Church 1885–1985*, x. James W. Henkelman and Kurt H. Vitt (Bethel, AK: The Moravian Seminary and Archives, 1985).

Bushyhead, Ben. "For the Native Community: Help that Empowers." *Engage/Social Action* 15, no. 7 (July/August 1987), 20–26.

Byrd, Sid. "What Happened at Wounded Knee 100 Years Ago." *The Lakota Times*, December 18, 1990, B6 and December 25, 1990, B3.

Campbell, Marllene. "An American Indian Viewpoint." In *Realities and Visions: The Church's Mission Today*, 137–43. Edited by Furman C. Stough and Urban T. Holmes, III (New York: Seabury Press, 1976).

Carlson, Joyce. *Journey from Fisher River: A Celebration of the Spirituality of a People through the Life of Stan McKay* (Toronto: United Church Publishing House, 1994).

————— (ed.). *1992: Aboriginal Reflections on 500 Years* (Winnipeg, MB: Dr. Jessie Saulteaux Resource Centre, [1992?]).

————— (ed.). *The Journey: Stories and Prayers for the Christian Year from People of the First Nations* (Toronto: Anglican Book Centre, 1991).

————— (ed.). *Spirit of Gentleness: Lenten Readings and Prayers* (Toronto: United Church Publishing House [Division of Mission in Canada], 1989).

Charleston, Steven. "American Indian Tradition: Rediscovering an Old Testament." *Areopagus*, Lent 1991, 5–8.

—————. "Columbus from the Native American Perspective: What Have We Learned in 500 Years?" *Word and World* 12, no. 2 (Spring 1992), 106–110.

—————. "Consider the Cargo, Not the Captain." *Sojourners*, October 1991, 25–26.

—————. "Native American Spirituality." In *Jamestown Commitment: The Episcopal Church and the American Indian*, 149–55. Edited by Owanah Anderson (Cincinnati: Forward Movement, 1988).

—————. "Reflections on a Revival: The Native American Alternative." *Theological Education* 20, no. 1 (Autumn 1983), 65–78.

—————. "The Old Testament of Native America." In *Lift Every Voice: Constructing Christian Theologies from the Underside*, 49–61. Edited by Susan Brooks Thistlethwaite and Mary Potter Engle (San Francisco: Harper and Row, 1990).

—————. "Victims of an American Holocaust." *Sojourners* 16, no. 10 (November 1987), 32–33.

Claus, Tom. "A True Indian and a True Christian." *Native Discipleship in the Americas* 4, no. 1 (1993), 8–11, 20–21.

—————. "The Bible and Native Cultures." *Native Discipleship in the Americas* 3, no. 2 (Summer/Fall 1990), 8–9, 18–21, 23.

—————. "The Bible and Peyote." *Native Discipleship in the Americas* 3, no. 1 (Spring 1990), 10–11, 20–26.

Claus, Tom and Dale W. Kietzman (eds.). *Christian Leadership in Indian America.* (Chicago: Moody Press, 1976).

Corbett, Cecil. "An Indian Christmas." *Reformed Liturgy and Music* 22, no. 3 (Summer 1988), 144–45. Reprinted from *Indian Highways* 190 (December 2, 1983).

———. "The Lost Ingredient: Native American Spirituality" (Tempe: Cook Christian Training School, no date).

———. "Theological Institutions before the Altar." *Church and Society* 76, no. 4 (March–April 1986), 64–67.

Corbett, Cecil and Gary Kush. "Cook Christian Training School: new directions for Native American theological education." In *Ministry by the People*, 214–24. Edited by F. Ross Kinsler (Maryknoll, NY: Orbis, 1983).

Cuny, Sr. Genevieve, OSF. "Leadership and Professional Development in Light of the Native American Experience." In *Faith and Culture: A Multicultural Catechetical Resource*, 53–61. Edited by Armantina R. Pelaez (Washington, DC: United States Catholic Conference, 1987).

Cuthand, Adam. "A Native Anglican Indian Speaks." *Canadian Ecumenical News*, December 1981, 3. Reprinted in *Interculture* 15, no. 1 (January–May 1982), 37–9.

Deloria, Vine V., Sr. "The Establishment of Christianity Among the Sioux." In *Sioux Indian Religion: Tradition and Innovation*, 91–111. Edited by Raymond J. DeMallie and Douglas R. Parks (Norman, OK: University of Oklahoma, 1987).

Deloria, Vine, Jr. "A Native American Perspective on Liberation Theology." In *Is Liberation Theology for North America? The Response of First World Churches*, 12–20. Edited by Sergio Torres et al (New York: Theology in the Americas, 1978).

———. "A Native American Perspective on Liberation." *Occasional Bulletin of Missionary Research*, July 1977, 15–17. Reprinted in *Mission Trends No. 4: Liberation Theologies in North America and Europe*, 261–70. Edited by Gerald H. Anderson and Thomas F. Stransky (New York: Paulist Press, 1979).

———. "American Indians and the Moral Community." *Church and Society* 79 (September/October 1988), 27–38.

———. "An Open Letter to the Heads of the Christian Churches in America" (January 28, 1972). Reprinted in *Literature of the American Indian*, abridged edition, 213–20. Edited by Thomas E. Sanders and Walter W. Peek (Beverly Hills: Glencoe, 1976).

———. *Behind the Trail of Broken Treaties: An Indian Declaration of Independence* (New York: Dell, 1974).

———. "Christianity and Indigenous Religion: Friends or Enemies? A Native American Perspective." In *Creation and Culture: The Challenge of Indigenous Spirituality and Culture to Western Creation Thought*, 31–43. Edited by David G. Burke (New York: Lutheran World Ministries, 1987).

———. "Completing the Theological Circle: Civil Religion in America." *Religious Education* 71 (May–June 1976), 278–87.

———. *Custer Died for Your Sins: An Indian Manifesto* (New York: Macmillan, 1969).

———. "Escaping from Bankruptcy: The Future of the Theological Task." *Katallagete* 6 (Summer 1976), 5–9.

———. "GCSP: The Demons at Work." *Historical Magazine of the Protestant Episcopal Church* 48 (March 1979), 83–92.

———. *God Is Red: A Native View of Religion* (Golden, CO: North American, 1992).

————. "Indians and Other Americans: The Cultural Chasm." *Church and Society* 75, no. 3 (January/February 1985), 10–19.

————. "Out of Chaos." *Parabola* 10, no. 2 (1985), 14–22. Reprinted in *I Become Part of It: Sacred Dimensions in Native American Life*. Edited by D. M. Dooling and Paul Jordan-Smith (New York: Parabola, 1989).

————. "Religion and Revolution Among American Indians." *Worldview* 17 (January 1974), 12–15.

————. "Secularism, Civil Religion, and the Religious Freedom of American Indians." *American Indian Culture and Research Journal* 16, no. 2 (1992), 9–20.

————. "The Confusion of History: A Review Essay." *Historical Magazine of the Protestant Episcopal Church* 46 (September 1977), 349–53.

————. *The Indian Affair* (New York: Friendship, 1974).

————. *The Metaphysics of Modern Existence* (San Francisco: Harper and Row, 1979).

————. "The Theological Dimension of the Indian Protest Movement." *The Christian Century* 90 (September 19, 1973), 912–14.

————. "Vision and Community: A Native-American Voice." In *Yearning to Breathe Free: Liberation Theologies in the United States*, 71–79. Edited by Mar Peter-Raoul, Linda Rennie Forcey, and Robert Frederick Hunter, Jr. (Maryknoll, NY: Orbis, 1990).

————. *We Talk, You Listen: New Tribes, New Turf* (New York: Macmillan, 1970).

————. "Why the U.S. Never Fought the Indians." *The Christian Century* 93 (January 7–14, 1976), 9–12.

Dreadfulwater, Andrew. "We'll Have Hats with Feathers in Them . . . But We Won't Be No Indians." *Interculture* 17, no. 4 (October–December 1984), 22–24.

Dudley, Joseph Iron Eye. *Choteau Creek: A Sioux Reminiscence* (Lincoln: University of Nebraska, 1992).

Fassett, Thomas M. "'I and the Earth Are One': Chief Joseph." *Engage/Social Action* 4 (November 1976), 43–46.

————. "Struggle for Survival." *Engage/Social Action*, November 1981, 10–14.

————. "To Learn from Native Peoples." *Christian Social Action*, October 1991, 4–6.

Fontaine, Stan. "The Amerindian Reality: As an Inner Reality." *Kerygma* 15 (1981), 167–85.

Galvan, Michael. "Enculturating the Liturgy in North America." *Liturgy* 5, no. 3 (1986), 41–45.

————. "Native American Catechesis and the Ministry of the Word." In *Faith and Culture: A Multicultural Catechetical Resource*, 15–21. Edited by Armantina R. Pelaez (Washington, DC: United States Catholic Conference, 1987).

————. "No Veneration for Serra." In *The Missions of California: A Legacy of Genocide*, 168–70. Edited by Rupert Costo and Jeannette Henry Costo (San Francisco: Indian Historian Press, 1987).

Hall, Suzanne E. (ed.). *The People: Reflections of Native Peoples on the Catholic Experience in North America* (Washington, DC: National Catholic Educational Association, 1992).

Hampton, Carol. "A Heritage Denied: American Indians Struggle for Racial Justice." *Sojourners*, January 1991, 10–13.

Hart, Lawrence. "Cheyenne Peace Traditions." *Mennonite Life* 36 (June 1981), 4–7.

Hascall, John S. "*The Sacred Circle*: Native American Liturgy." *Liturgy* 7, no. 1 (1988), 35–39.

Helphrey, Juanita J. *Worship Resources* (Minneapolis: Council for American Indian Ministry, United Church of Christ, 1991).

Higgins, Elizabeth. *No Turning Back* (Valley Forge, PA: National Ministries, American Baptist Churches USA, 1985?).

Hobday, Jose. "Dance into Life: The Native American Way." *Cross Currents* 24 (Summer/Fall 1974), 292–95.

———. "Forced Assimilation and the Native American Dance." *Cross Currents* 26 (Summer 1976), 189–94.

———. "Seeking the Moist Heart: Native American Ways for Helping the Spirit." In *Western Spirituality: Historical Roots, Ecumenical Routes*, 317–29. Edited by Matthew Fox, OP (Notre Dame, IN: Fides/Claretian, 1979).

Hofstra, Marilyn M. *Voices: Native American Hymns and Worship Resources* (Nashville: Discipleship Resources, 1992).

Holmes, Arthur, with George McPeek. *The Grieving Indian: An Ojibwe Elder Shares His Discovery of Help and Hope* (Winnipeg, MB: Indian Life, 1991).

Hopkins, Alberta Pualani. "The Challenge of the Future: Creating a Place Called Home." In *The Challenges of the Past, the Challenges of the Future: Essays on Mission in the Light of Five Hundred Years of Evangelization in the Americas*, 73–80. Edited by John L. Kater, Jr. (Berkeley: Church Divinity School of the Pacific, 1994).

Hummelen, Remmelt and Kathleen Hummelen (eds.). *Stories of Survival: Conversations with Native North Americans* (New York: Friendship Press, 1985).

Jackson, Norman W. "The Message Carrier: Legacies of the Missionary Era." *JSAC Grapevine*, January 1989. Reprinted in *News from Indian Country*, March 1989, 29 and April 1989, 26.

Jacobs, Adrian. "The Meeting of the Two Ways." *Indian Life Magazine* 13, no. 3 (June–July 1992), 8–11.

Jacobs, Laverne. "A Challenge to the Church: Include All Native Peoples and Their Cultural Gifts." *Anglican Magazine*, September 15, 1991, 34–35.

———. "Being an Indian in Today's Society." *CCPD: For a Change* (World Council of Churches) 5 (1991).

———. "Let Us Be: Native People's Plea for Self-Determination." *Practice for Ministry in Canada*, November 1991.

———. "Mending the Hoop." *Practice for Ministry in Canada*, September 1993, 15–16.

———. "The Native Church: A Search for an Authentic Spirituality." *Ecumenism* 112 (December 1993), 21–23.

———. "Our System has Failed to Produce a Native Bishop." *Anglican Magazine*, October 1987.

Lee, George P. *Silent Courage, An Indian Story: The Autobiography of George P. Lee, a Navajo* (Salt Lake City: Deseret, 1987).

MacDonald, Mark. *A Strategy for Growth in the Episcopal Church: Joining Multiculturalism with Evangelism* (Bemidji, MN: InterCultural Ministry Development, 1994).

Mammedaty, Kim. "Remember the Sabbath Day." In *And Blessed Is She: Sermons by*

Women, 196–202. Edited by David Albert Farmer and Edwina Hunter (San Francisco: Harper and Row, 1990).

Maracle, John. "The Lost Nations." *Christianity Today*, March 3, 1989, 34–37.

Maracle, Ross. "Shut Out Again." *Practice for Ministry in Canada*, May 1991, 17–18.

Maxey, Rosemary. "A Perspective from the Indigenous Theology Project." *Doing Theology in the United States* 1, no. 1 (Spring/Summer 1985), 33–35.

———. "A Right to Speak." *Doing Theology in the United States* 1, no. 1 (Spring/Summer 1985), 58.

———. "Who Can Sit at the Lord's Table? The Experience of Indigenous Peoples." In *Theology and Identity: Traditions, Movements, and Polity in the United Church of Christ*, 51–63. Edited by Daniel L. Johnson and Charles Hambrick-Stowe (New York: Pilgrim Press, 1990).

McKay, Stanley J. "An Aboriginal Christian Perspective on the Integrity of Creation." *Ecumenism* 100 (December 1990), 15–17.

———. "Native North American Spirituality And Inter-Faith Dialogue." *Ecumenical Trends* 16, no. 6 (June 1987), 108–10.

Meili, Dianne. *Those Who Know: Profiles of Alberta's Native Elders* (Edmonton, AB: NeWest Press, 1991).

Mitchell, Sr. Kateri. "Centered in the Creator: The Native American Experience." *Momentum*, November 1991, 30–31.

———. "Life is a Sacred Circle." *Religion Teacher's Journal*, January 1994, 36–37.

———. "Praying to the Great Spirit." *Religion Teacher's Journal*, September 1992, 20.

———. "Program Development and Native American Catechesis." In *Faith and Culture: A Multicultural Catechetical Resource*, 81–88. Edited by Armantina R. Pelaez (Washington, DC: United States Catholic Conference, 1987).

———. "Questions of Faith and Culture: Native Catechesis." *Caravan,* Winter 1991, 8–9.

Myers, Mike. "Mohawk Nation at War: In Defense of Native Lands." *Theology in the Americas: Documentation Series*, no. 9 (New York: Theology in the Americas, 1979).

———. "The Connectedness of Life." *Doing Theology in the United States*, 1988, 4–11.

———. "The Native Americans and Western Christianity." In *Theology in the Americas: Detroit II Conference Papers*, 85–89. Edited by Cornel West, Caridad Guidote, and Margaret Coakley (Maryknoll, NY: Orbis, 1982).

Nahwooksy, Clydia. "The Threads of Faith." *American Baptist Quarterly* 5, no. 4 (December 1986), 403–7.

Noley, Homer. *A Little Land on Which to Light His Fire* (St. Louis: Christian Board of Publication, 1975).

———. *First White Frost: Native Americans and United Methodism* (Nashville: Abingdon, 1991).

———. "Native Americans in the Church." *Christian Social Action* 5 (April 1992), 25–27.

Nowabbi, Billie. "Roots of Identity." *Doing Theology in the United States* 1, no. 1 (Spring/Summer 1985), 59–60.

———. "They Walked by Faith." *Engage/Social Action*, November 1981, 37–40.

Office of Native American Ministries. *In the Spirit of the Circle* (New York: Episcopal Church Center, 1989).

Parker, Karol. "Returning." *Common Lot* (UCC), Spring 1991, 7–8.

Poor Man, Mercy. "Christian Life Fellowship Church." In *Sioux Indian Religion: Tradition and Innovation*, 149–55. Edited by Raymond J. DeMallie and Douglas R. Parks (Norman, OK: University of Oklahoma, 1987).

"Position Paper of the Native American Project of Theology in the Americas." 1980.

Rollins, Sister Jeanne, O.S.F. "Liberation and the Native American." In *Theology in the Americas*, 202–6. Edited by Sergio Torres and John Eagleson (Maryknoll, NY: Orbis, 1976).

Schultz, Paul N. "Educators as Advocates for Transcultural Inclusiveness." *APCE Advocate*, May 1987, 3–4.

Schultz, Paul and Judith Wellington. *Caring for Creation: A four-session small-group Bible study exploring Christian and Native American perspectives on the stewardship of creation* (Minneapolis: Augsburg Fortress, 1989).

Schultz, Paul and George Tinker. *Rivers of Life: Native Spirituality for Native Churches* (Minneapolis: Augsburg Fortress, 1988).

Scissons, Ralph E. "Are We All Welcome at the Party?" *Church and Society*, January/February 1992, 61–68.

Sehested, Ken (ed.). *The Earth Is the Lord's: Sermons by Kim Mammedaty and Bible Studies by William Baldridge from the 1992 Summer Conference* (Memphis: Baptist Peace Fellowship of North America, 1992).

Slagle, Al Logan. "Tolowa Indian Shakers and the Role of Prophecy at Smith River, California." *American Indian Quarterly* 9, no. 3 (Summer 1985), 353–74.

Sneve, Virginia Driving Hawk. *That They May Have Life: The Episcopal Church in South Dakota, 1859-1976* (New York: Seabury, 1977).

Snow, Chief John. *These Mountains are our Sacred Places: The Story of the Stoney Indians*. (Toronto: Samuel Stevens, 1977).

Snyder, Janice E. "Native American in the Church." *Christian Social Action* 3, no. 1 (January 1990), 23–25.

Solomon, Sister Eva. "Our Lady of Guadalupe: God's Message for the Americas." *Anglican Magazine*, April 15, 1989, 22–24.

———. "Unity and Diversity in Native Spirituality." *Ecumenism* 112 (December 1993), 15–17.

Spider, Emerson, Sr. "The Native American Church of Jesus Christ." In *Sioux Indian Religion: Tradition and Innovation*, 189–209. Edited by Raymond J. DeMallie and Douglas R. Parks (Norman, OK: University of Oklahoma, 1987).

Tekakwitha Conference. "Resolution and Statement by Tekakwitha Conference." In *The Missions of California: A Legacy of Genocide*, 164–65. Edited by Rupert Costo and Jeannette Henry Costo (San Francisco: Indian Historian Press, 1987).

"The Native Clergy Speak." *Anglican Magazine*, October 15, 1990, 9–10.

The Story and Faith Journey of Seventeen Native Catechists: A Consultation in Native Catechesis, November 9–13, 1982 (Great Falls: Tekakwitha Conference National Center, [1983?]).

Tinker, George E. "A Theological Introduction to Cross-Cultural Issues." In *Creation and Culture: The Challenge of Indigenous Spirituality and Culture to Western Creation Thought*, 1–6. Edited by David G. Burke (New York: Lutheran World Ministries, 1987).

———. "American Indians and the Arts of the Land: Spatial Metaphors and

Contemporary Existence." In *Voices from the Third World: 1990* (Sri Lanka: Ecumenical Association of Third World Theologians, 1991), 170–93.

———. "Blessed Are the Poor: A Theology of Solidarity with the Poor in the Two-Thirds World." *Church and Society* 84, no. 4 (March/April 1994), 45–55.

———. "Columbus and Coyote: A Comparison of Culture Heroes in Paradox." *Apuntes* 12 (Summer 1992), 78–88.

———. "Does 'All People' Include Native Peoples?" In *God, Goods, and the Common Good: Eleven Perspectives on Economic Justice in Dialog with the Roman Catholic Bishops' Pastoral Letter*. Edited by Charles P. Lutz (Minneapolis: Augsburg, 1987), 124–36.

———. "For All My Relations: Justice, Peace, and the Integrity of Christmas Trees." *Sojourners* 20, no. 1 (January 1991), 19–21. Revised version of "Gerechtigkeit, Frieden und die Integrität der Weinachtsbäume." Ökumenische Rundschau 38 (April 1989), 169–80.

———. *Missionary Conquest: The Gospel and Native American Cultural Genocide* (Minneapolis: Augsburg Fortress, 1993).

———. "Native Americans and the Land: 'The End of Living, and the Beginning of Survival.'" *Word and World* 6, no. 1 (Winter 1986), 66–75. Reprinted in *Lift Every Voice: Constructing Christian Theologies from the Underside*, 141–51. Edited by Susan Brooks Thistlethwaite and Mary Potter Engle (San Francisco: Harper and Row, 1990).

———. "Spirituality, Native American Personhood, Sovereignty and Solidarity." *The Ecumenical Review* 44 (July 1992), 312–24.

———. "The Full Circle of Liberation: An American Indian Theology of Place." *Sojourners* 21, no. 8 (October 1992), 12–17. Revised version reprinted in *SEDOS* 25 (January 15, 1993), 9–13.

———. "The Integrity of Creation: Restoring Trinitarian Balance." *The Ecumenical Review* 41 (October 1989), 527–36.

———. "Two stories about the 'integrity of creation.'" *One World*, May 1988, 13.

Walters, Elizabeth and Joan Thatcher. *The Trail of Tears—The Indians in America* (Valley Forge, PA: Fund of Renewal [American Baptist Churches in the U.S.A. and Progressive National Baptist Convention, Inc.], 1974).

Wantland, William C. "Our Mother, the Earth." *The Living Church*, July 5, 1992, 10, 12.

Warrior, Robert Allen. "Canaanites, cowboys, and Indians: Deliverance, conquest, and liberation theology today." *Christianity and Crisis*, September 11, 1989, 261–65. Reprinted in *Voices from the Margin: Interpreting the Bible in the Third World*, 287–95. Edited by R. S. Sugirtharajah (Maryknoll, NY: Orbis, 1991).

Weaver, Jace. "A biblical paradigm for native liberation." *Christianity and Crisis*, February 15, 1993, 40.

———. "Native Reformation in Indian Country? Forging a relevant spiritual identity among Indian Christians." *Christianity and Crisis*, February 15, 1993, 39–41.

West, James L. "Indian Spirituality: Another Vision." *American Baptist Quarterly* 5, no. 4 (December 1986), 348–56.

Wilson, Roy I. "God's Revelation: Through All Cultures." *Christian Social Action* 3, no. 1 (January 1990), 8–10.

———. *Medicine Wheels: Ancient Teachings for Modern Times* (New York: Crossroad, 1994).